VANCOUVER & THE CANADIAN ROCKIES

G000066221

SPIRAL
GUIDE

AA Publishing

Contents

Written by Tim Jepson
Revised and updated by Des Hannigan

Revision manages by Bookwork Creative Associates
Series Editor Karen Rigden
Series Designer Catherine Murray

Published by AA Publishing, a trading name of AA Media Limited,
whose registered office is Fanum House, Basing View, Basingstoke,
Hampshire, RG21 4EA. Registered number 06112600.

ISBN: 978-0-7495-6249-6

A CIP catalogue record for this book is available from the
British Library.

© AA Media Limited 2002, 2003, 2006, 2008, 2009
Maps © AA Media Limited 2002, 2003, 2006, 2008, 2009
New edition 2009

Cover design and binding style by permission of AA Publishing
Colour separation by Keenes, Andover
Printed and bound in China by Leo Paper Products

Find out more about AA Publishing and the wide range of travel
publications and services the AA provides by visiting our website at
www.theAA.com/bookshop

A03805
Maps in this title produced from map data supplied by Global
Mapping, Brackley, UK © Global Mapping/TIMB
(except pp160–161, 183, 185 & 206)
Transport map © Communicarta Ltd, UK

The Magazine

A great holiday is more than just lying on a beach or shopping till you drop – to really get the most from your trip you need to know what makes the place tick. The Magazine provides an entertaining overview to some of the social, cultural and natural elements that make up the unique character of this engaging city and region.

THIS IS VANCOUVER
City of Light
and the Long View

Vancouver has long been ranked as one of the world's most vibrant cities and the 21st century is proving the point with such major events as the Winter Olympics boosting the city's status worldwide.

The weather in the streets might not always be the best – it rains in Vancouver…and then it rains some more – but the setting is sublime; the environment is clean and safe; the well-integrated multicultural population embraces diversity with enthusiasm; you can ski pretty much year-round; there's swimming and sunbathing on beaches just minutes from city center downtown; the city's Stanley Park is one of North America's biggest and wildest; and the restaurants are world class.

Vancouver's skyline reflected in the water

Zest for Life

Vancouver gives the lie to Canada's perceived image problem, the notion that this is a country that's worthy but dull, beautiful but boring – nice place, nice people, no fun. With its zest for life, spectacular scenery, excellent nightlife, urban beaches, funky cafés, fashionable bars and wild outdoor activities, Vancouver gloriously rejects the cliché with a flair that rivals West Coast hotspots such as San Francisco and Los Angeles.

Take a walk around Canada Place to see how the city celebrates modern architecture and its magnificent port (► 50). Look up at the mountains – that's where the locals ski in a world that boasts Olympic standard conditions and facilities; then look out to sea – that's where they sail their boats. Or sit in a café on Granville Island (► 56) – that's where they come to shop, stroll and people-watch on the weekend.

Pacific Player

Vancouver's location on the Pacific has resulted in a long history of immigration from China and other Asian countries, and today Vancouver's Chinatown is second in size only to San Francisco's, while about half of the city's 2 million population is of Asian extraction. The Pacific has been a lifeline for British Columbia (BC) since coastal First Nations peoples, such as the Haida, thrived on its maritime bounty. Now, a quarter of the world's population lives on the ocean's rim and the Pacific and its huge markets play an increasing part in Vancouver's social and economic life.

Vancouver Neighborhood Watch

- **Chinatown** One of North America's largest Chinese enclaves. East of downtown and Gastown, with signs everywhere in Chinese and brimming with lively sights and sounds.

- **Downtown** The vital heart of the city, built across a peninsula jutting into Burrard Inlet and centered on Robson and Burrard streets. This is the commercial heart, home to shopping malls, smart hotels, major galleries and towering office blocks like glass pinnacles reflecting each other's facades.

- **Gastown** The redeveloped heart of old Vancouver. Once a skid row, then a prettified tourist trap; now a dynamic mix of shops, bars and restaurants.

- **Granville Island** This one-time semi-industrial wasteland has been converted into a buzzing mix of markets, small businesses, cafés, brewery and specialty stores.

- **Kitsilano** Known affectionately as "Kits," this was the center of alternative Vancouver circa 1960s. Now somewhat smarter, it still retains that earlier laid-back feel, especially on its popular beach.

- **North Shore** A residential area across the water from downtown on the north shore of Burrard Inlet. Includes North Van (North Vancouver), West Van and some of the country's most expensive property.

- **West End** A smart residential district at the west end of the downtown peninsula bounded by high-rise buildings on one side and Stanley Park (➤ 60) on the other.

- **Yaletown** An old warehouse district on the south side of the downtown peninsula that's become one of the city's trendiest locales, full of specialty stores, antiques shops, cafés, restaurants and designer apartments.

Entrance of the Marine Building (left); downtown (middle); Canada Place (right)

Three Great Period Buildings

■ **Marine Building 1930**
355 Burrard Street Vancouver's only surviving art deco masterpiece – and early skyscraper – is enriched with period bas-reliefs and boasts the most beautiful lobby and elevators in the city.

■ **Toronto-Dominion Bank 1920**
580 West Hastings Street This Mediterranean-style building is Vancouver architect Marbury Somervell's finest legacy.

■ **St James Anglican Church 1936**
303 East Cordova Street Historic churches of any vintage are rare in Vancouver, but this Adrian Gilbert Scott creation survives as an elegant tribute to early-20th-century architecture.

GOLD VENEER

Catch the 1981 Daon Building (888 West Hastings Street) in the afternoon sun and the reflected light has an added luster. The reason? Every window is coated with a thin film of gold. Architect Frank Musson made it clear that the quantity of gold used in the process was so minute that it would not be worth anyone smashing the windows and melting the broken shards.

...and Three Great Modern Ones

■ **Vancouver Public Library 1995**
350 West Georgia Street Architect Moshe Safdie's stunning building is no less than a modern-day Roman Colosseum and, with the nearby General Motors Place, provides a focus for the dynamic eastward spread of the city.

■ **Robson Square 1979**
800 Robson Street Leading North American architect Arthur Erickson pulled together a modern plaza and the city's old law courts and government buildings, transforming the latter into the Vancouver Art Gallery.

■ **MacMillan Bloedel Building 1969**
1075 West Georgia Street Arthur Erickson also designed this neo-classical masterpiece for the giant forestry company MacMillan Bloedel.

Creative
VANCOUVER
Something in the air...

There's so much creativity in Vancouver that there really must be something in the air that flows from the mountains and seas that surround this vibrant and stylish city.

Vancouver Rocks!

Vancouver still boasts of homegrown stars like Michael J. Fox as well as famously sexy celebrities such as Pamela Anderson. But the city also nurtures an outstanding rollcall of painters, poets, photographers, writers, rock stars, actors and musicians. High-profile rock star Bryan Adams lived his early years in Vancouver. Top jazz diva Diana Krall was born on Vancouver Island. Singer-songwriter Nelly Furtado comes from Victoria. Vancouver rings the changes from romantic balladeer Sarah McLachlan to the unique sound of folk band the Be Good Tanyas and the raw blast of tattooed punk rocker Bif Naked.

Classical Company

The city boasts some of the finest classical music performances in North America from such outstanding institutions as the Vancouver Symphony Orchestra and the Vancouver Chamber Choir. Making up a triumphant triumvirate of magnificent music is the acclaimed Vancouver Opera company (▶ 80 for information and contact details for all three).

Written on the Streets

In Vancouver you walk in the footsteps of such stellar writers as Douglas Coupland, whose novel *Generation X* defined the zeitgeist of its day, and of Evelyn Lau whose hard-edged semi-autobiographical novel, *Runaway:*

Bryan Adams performing in London (left); singer-songwriter Nelly Furtado (right)

Diary of a Street Kid, painted the darker side of urban Vancouver. The city's writerly tradition is historic. Even Rudyard Kipling called in to the city three times.

Art at the Edge

Vancouver has always had a strong arts culture, not least the work of First Nations artists such as the masterly Bill Reid, a craftsman of First Nations Haida descent. Reid's life and work is immortalized in the downtown Bill Reid Gallery, opened in 2008. A still towering presence in British Columbia art is Emily Carr, whose work can be seen in the Vancouver Art Gallery (► 54). Today Vancouver buzzes with artistic talent. There are hundreds of small private galleries covering every level of art, pottery and sculpture, with the South Granville area and Granville Island being rich browsing grounds while Georgia Street's Buschlen Mowatt Gallery is the top private venue for contemporary art, including the First Nations genre.

RUDYARD'S VANCOUVER YARD

Rudyard Kipling made several visits to Vancouver and liked the city so much that he bought several plots of land, including two on the corner of what are now Fraser and East Eleventh Streets. Kipling owned them for more than 30 years but sold them at an eventual loss.

From **HAIDA** to **HIGH-RISE**

Few cities can claim to have their roots in a mixture of native village and hard-drinking saloon bar. And not many have gone from forest clearing to major metropolis in less than a century. Even fewer take their name from a man who honored the city with his presence for less than a day.

British Columbia – and the patch of land that became Vancouver – were the domain of sophisticated First Nations peoples, such as the Haida, for at least 10,000 years. The first European landing was probably made by Captain Cook in 1778. And one member of Cook's crew was a midshipman by the name of George Vancouver.

George Vancouver

By 1791 young George had become a captain and was employed in mapping parts of the Pacific coast for Britain. He discovered the estuary of the Fraser River just south of Vancouver and sailed around a forested headland and into a magnificent natural inlet, the future site of the great city. Captain George named the place Burrard after one of his crew. He traded with the indigenous Squamish on the headland, now the present-day Stanley Park, then sailed on after spending less than a day in their company. Vancouver's name wasn't given to the nascent city until 1886.

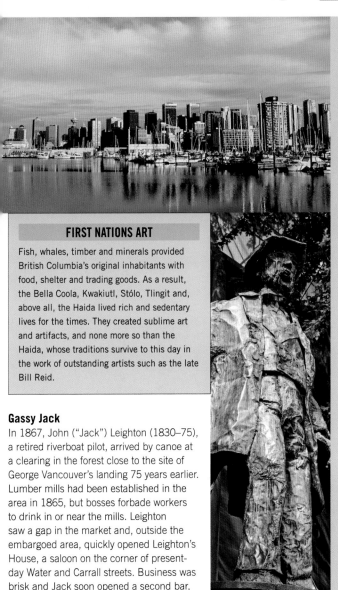

FIRST NATIONS ART

Fish, whales, timber and minerals provided British Columbia's original inhabitants with food, shelter and trading goods. As a result, the Bella Coola, Kwakiutl, Stólo, Tlingit and, above all, the Haida lived rich and sedentary lives for the times. They created sublime art and artifacts, and none more so than the Haida, whose traditions survive to this day in the work of outstanding artists such as the late Bill Reid.

Gassy Jack

In 1867, John ("Jack") Leighton (1830–75), a retired riverboat pilot, arrived by canoe at a clearing in the forest close to the site of George Vancouver's landing 75 years earlier. Lumber mills had been established in the area in 1865, but bosses forbade workers to drink in or near the mills. Leighton saw a gap in the market and, outside the embargoed area, quickly opened Leighton's House, a saloon on the corner of present-day Water and Carrall streets. Business was brisk and Jack soon opened a second bar, where his bragging monologues earned him the nickname "Gassy." In time, a ramshackle settlement, "Gassy's Town," sprang up around the saloons and today a life-size statue of Gassy Jack with whiskey barrel stands in Maple Tree Square, the heart of Gastown.

Hastings Wharf in 1907 (top left); the harbour today (top); Gassy Jack statue (above)

CALL OF THE WILD
The wilderness on your doorstep

Walk the streets of Banff and there's a good chance you'll find yourself face-to-antler with a verge-nibbling elk. Climb aboard many a Vancouver bus and you'll find pine needles on the floor, tramped there by commuters from the forested slopes above the city.

Beware the Bear

Bears are always big news; they fascinate the rest of us and there are plenty of them in Western Canada. Their range extends across most of the Rockies and British Columbia, but you're more likely to spot them by the roadside than on popular trails.

There are two kinds of big bear: grizzly and black. The grizzly is definitely bigger than the rest of us and has a slightly scooped face and a distinctive hump behind its head. The other one is the black bear, which is smaller and nowhere as cuddly as it looks. Both types of bear are fascinating and both are potentially very dangerous. They are not slow and bumbling: They can outrun a racehorse or Olympic sprinter. Another misconception is that bears can't climb trees. They certainly can – so don't put it to the test.

Watching for Whales

In Western Canada the whale matches the bear for the wow factor. There are several companies taking visitors whale-watching even in Vancouver but mainly in Victoria

A grizzly bear (top); tail of a grey whale (left)

A signpost at Takakkaw Falls in Yoho National Park

and Tofino (▶ 98) on Vancouver Island. Here, the offshore waters are on the major migration routes for gray, orca and other whales.

The whales are mostly en route between their breeding and calving grounds in Baja California to the summer feeding grounds in the Bering and Chukchi seas off Siberia, an 8,000km (5,000-mile) journey, the longest migration of any mammal. Most whales are northbound past Vancouver Island between March and April and southbound during late September and early October.

Best Foot Forward

When it comes to the real call of the wild, you should head for the spectacular mountains, forests and remote coasts of Western Canada. In such wild country there are outstanding opportunities for horseback riding and mountain biking as well as watersports such as canoeing and whitewater rafting. There's even fun to be had in mid-air with paragliding or the latest craze, zip-lining, a wild ride down an inclined cable. Yet, the simplest – and cheapest – escape of all is on your own two feet. Be properly equipped for these longer treks, however, and check details with the park authorities before setting off.

Superb Scenery

If all you want is a casual stroll, but in stunning surroundings, you can follow low-level, surfaced walkways of only a kilometer or two at venues such as Johnston Canyon (➤ 134) or crank up the mileage on the uphill trek to the Lake Agnes Teahouse (➤ 185).

For outstanding longer hikes stride on from Lake Agnes, après tea, to the Plain of the Six Glaciers (➤ 137); or head for Yoho National Park (➤ 146) and the superb 20km (12.5-mile) Iceline Trail that follows steep zigzags to the edge of several glaciers above the 256m (840-ft) high Takakkaw Falls; or head along the splendid West Coast Trail in the Pacific Rim National Park on Vancouver Island.

Boardwalk, Pacific Rim National Park (left); a black bear (below); Columbia Icefield (right)

BEAR NECESSITIES

Roadside bear encounters often produce the Rockies' infamous "bear jams," caused when people spot a roadside bear and abandon their cars with cameras and camcorders running. A bear subjected to repeated bear jams may become desensitized to traffic. This can lead to vehicle-bear collisions that are potentially fatal to all. Difficult though it may be, you should resist adding to a bear jam by simply driving slowly by.

THE MAKING OF THE
ROCKIES

The Canadian Rockies have had two makeovers. Once when they formed as the result of geological ructions millions of years ago, and a second time when they were made, in the economic sense, by the coming of the transcontinental Canadian Pacific Railway at the end of the 19th century.

Genesis of the Landscape

The Rockies began with the Canadian Shield, a huge granite mass that covered much of North America around a billion years ago. Throughout millions of years, eroded sediments from the Shield were washed westward across the continent and were deposited in what is now the Pacific Ocean.

During the millennia that followed, these sediments, boosted by the accumulation of lime-rich algae and other sea creatures, grew to a thickness of some 19.5km (12 miles).

All of this colossal weight steadily compressed mud to shale, sand to sandstone and marine detritus to limestone and all survive in the geometric bands of multi-colored rock that you now see in the mountains of Banff and Lake Louise especially.

LADY ON THE LINE

When the Canadian Pacific Railway breached the Rockies in 1886, Lady Agnes MacDonald, wife of the Canadian prime minister, rode the line for 998km (620 miles) on a specially adapted external chair fitted to a cowcatcher on the front of a locomotive. The trip was part of a special symbolic journey to mark the opening of the line. Her most exhilarating moments came as the train careered down the so-called Big Hill, a terrifyingly steep gradient in Yoho National Park. The descent, she remarked, presented "a delightful opportunity for a new sensation." Her husband couldn't match his redoubtable partner; he managed just 40km (25 miles) on the cowcatcher before retreating under cover.

Making Mountains

In those far distant times the future building blocks of the Rockies were still underwater. But enormous collisions between landmasses about 175 million years ago bulldozed the mass of sediments into the vast corrugations of the Rockies' present-day western ranges. Just when the dust began to settle – about 100 million years ago – a second cataclysm raised new mountains that became the Rockies' main eastern ranges.

Wind, rain and glaciers then carved, scoured and eroded at the rate of around 1m (3 feet) every 17,000 years. Most reshaping has taken place during the three main ice ages of the last 240,000 years – a mere moment, geologically speaking, in the Rockies' billion-year history.

Made by Rail

For much of this "mere moment" the Rockies remained almost unsullied wilderness, visited, if at all, by First Nations trappers, fur traders and the occasional European explorer. All this changed dramatically with the coming of the Canadian Pacific Railway (CPR). A bid to start the line began in 1871. Lack of funds and various political scandals delayed work until 1881, but once under way, progress across Ontario and the Prairies was swift. Winnipeg and then Calgary were soon reached.

West of Calgary the line inched toward Banff and the Rockies. When it reached them it transformed the mountains – almost at a stroke – in terms of their accessibility and the way in which they were perceived. A simple event, such as the discovery of hot springs in 1885 by three railways workers, gave birth to the mighty Banff National Park (➤ 133). Soon, the building of grand railway hotels such as the Banff Springs and Chateau Lake Louise began to encourage visitors to the area.

The first trans-Canadian train pulled into Vancouver in 1887. The railway was the making of the city and of many tiny settlements along the way that are now the likes of Calgary and Winnipeg. It was also the making of the once empty prairies – between 1896 and 1913, some 13 million settlers headed west in search of a new life along the line.

The view from The Lookout above Peyto Lake in Alberta

BESTS & FESTS

Although Vancouver is a relatively compact city, here are some suggestions of how to get the best out of your visit.

■ Best City Views
For the best viewpoint in Vancouver, you can't beat the Vancouver Tower. In Victoria the best views are those of the Inner Harbor from the waterfront, and in Calgary from the Calgary Tower (➤ 163).

■ Best Mountain Rides
Cable cars are a shortcut to superb viewpoints. Vancouver has Grouse Mountain and the Rockies have the Banff Gondola (➤ 132), Lake Louise Gondola (➤ 137) and the Jasper Tramway (➤ 142).

■ Best Boat Trips
Ride the SeaBus (➤ 35) to North Vancouver. Don't miss a harbor tour a "bandstand" ferry in Victoria. The Rockies have memorable boat rides: on Lake Minnewanka in Banff and on Maligne Lake in Jasper (➤ 144).

■ Best Off-the-Wall Gigs
Take a tour with Edible British Columbia at Granville Island Public Market (➤ 56). Go skinny dipping at Vancouver's only official "clothes optional" venue at Wreck Beach near the Museum of Anthropology.

■ Best Parks and Gardens
The Butchart Gardens in Victoria (➤ 93), Stanley Park in Vancouver (➤ 60) and Beacon Hill Park in Victoria (➤ 96).

Downtown Calgary

Festival Fever

Brace yourself for festival fever in Vancouver where the buzz reflects a city brimming with self-confidence and creativity at the cutting edge of urban life. Whenever you visit you're likely to find a party in full swing.

Kick off in January with the Chinese New Year Festival & Parade (www.vancouverchinatown.ca) or brighten up February with the Vancouver International Dance Festival (www.vidf.ca). Keep your dancing shoes on in March as Ireland comes to town on St Patrick's Day with Celtic Fest Vancouver (www.celticfestvancouver.com). During May there's the Vancouver International Children's Festival (www.childrensfestival.ca).

Come June and the fabulous Vancouver International Jazz Festival (www.coastaljazz.ca) takes off right into July when the popular Bard on the Beach Shakespeare Festival (www.bardonthebeach.org) starts its three-month run at Vanier Park. Sign off July with Vancouver's Pride Week (www.vancouverpride.ca) and its gloriously flamboyant street parade.

In August the skies light up at night with HSBC Celebration of Light (www.hsbccelebrationoflight.com), an explosive competition between some of the world's biggest and best fireworks displays. There are always film fireworks in September and October with the Vancouver International Film Festival (www.viff.org) while Christmas is celebrated throughout December with various light displays, parades and events all over town. For tickets to events check out www.ticketstonight.ca

MAGAZINES & WEBSITES

For what's on in Vancouver check out:

- *Vancouver Magazine*
  (www.vancouvermagazine.com)
- *Where Vancouver*
  (www.where.ca/Vancouver)
- *Visitor's Choice* (www.visitorschoice.ca)
- *The Georgia Straight* free newspaper
  (www.straight.com)

GREEN PIECE
Environment Matters

Bombs gave birth to the most famous environmental action group of all time – the renowned and sometimes reviled pressure group Greenpeace. The organization was born in Vancouver's English Bay in 1971 when a group of activists set off on board a converted fishing boat to protest against the United States testing nuclear devices in Alaska.

Environmental Protests

The protest boat, the *Phyllis Cormack*, was renamed *Green Peace 1* and the name was later revised into Greenpeace. By 1974 the organization had turned its sights against whaling. The rest is history and Greenpeace now has a worldwide presence wherever perceived threats to the environment are identified.

Canada's commercial and political record on environmentalism is not pristine. Today there is fierce debate over the oil shale industry that has made Calgary, especially, a longstanding boom town, but that raises questions over the industry's perceived threat to sustainability. Government involvement in the granting of logging licenses has long been contentious also.

National Parks

It is probably in the mighty national parks where environmentalism has the most powerful resonance. The sheer scale of such mountain wildernesses as Jasper and Banff makes them seem impregnable; but threats do exist to the parks' often fragile eco systems. We could easily love them to death, such is the growing pressure of tourism. Perhaps the greatest threat is the hidden devastation of global warming and pollution, the inevitable counterpoints to our consumer society and the ironic bedfellows of the delight and admiration we feel for the wilderness. Solutions to these universal threats rest with all of us.

Urban Green

The city goes green as much as the wilderness, and Vancouver is at the leading edge of environmental initiatives while maintaining its image as a hip and sophisticated metropolis. The 2010 Winter Olympics designation has boosted a "Green Vancouver" ethos with a commitment that all new venues for the 2010 Olympics are designed to minimize waste, emissions, energy consumption and water use. Vancouver has more than 200km (124 miles) of cycle lanes and the city is set to introduce a fleet of hydrogen buses to its already environmentally conscious transit system. In 2005 a car-free day was launched in Vancouver that has seen an increasing number of the city's main streets empty of cars each June 15.

**Drift logs in the Pacific Rim National Park (left)
Maligne River, Jasper (right)**

ROOTS ON THE ROOF

In June 2007 Vancouver city planners launched an 'edible landscape' initiative that will require developers to install food-producing garden areas on rooftops and balconies.

THE WORLD
AT YOUR TABLE

Vancouver has one of North America's most ethnically diverse populations. And where a population leads, the recipes and restaurants are never far behind. The city has more than 3,000 restaurants and its inhabitants eat out more than those of any other Canadian city do.

Influences and Ingredients

China is one of the most obvious culinary influences. Cheap restaurants and noodle houses proliferate in Chinatown, with more expensive and refined Chinese restaurants found across the city. Catching up fast are other Asian cuisines, especially Japanese and Vietnamese, closely followed by Thai, Korean and Cambodian. European immigration has also spawned many Italian, Greek and other European influences.

With all of these go the more familiar local staples – fish and seafood are generally outstanding – and the sophisticated fusion cuisine that combines British Columbia's superb natural ingredients such as salmon,

WINE WISE

If you want the true Canadian wine experience a careful check of labels is advised. Blending of domestic product with imported basic wines still takes place in producing some cheaper wines.

For a closer wine experience contact visitor centers in the Okanagan (➤ 110) for details of local vineyards and estates, many of which are open to the public.

Outside dining at Bridges on Granville Island

seafood, game, beef, fresh fruit and vegetables with the culinary styles and ingredients of Italian, Mexican, French and world cuisine generally. Outstanding examples of fusion can be enjoyed at such restaurants as Vancouver's Le Crocodile (➤ 75) and Lumière (➤ 75) or Victoria's Café Brio (➤ 102) and Brasserie L'Ecole (➤ 101).

No Laughing Matter

With western Canada's superb food you might be tempted to try Canadian wine, two words that some years ago would have raised skeptical eyebrows among the world's wine cognoscenti.

Traditionally, beer and whiskey were the thirst quenchers of Canadian life and today domestic beers such as Labatt Blue and Molson Canadian dominate, although regional favorites such as Kokanee lager from British Columbia's Kootenay region are hugely popular, while micro-breweries produce some lip-smacking beverages.

Canadian wine is not yet a world leader and the main producers are in Ontario, but British Columbia's Okanagan region (➤ 110) is building a solid reputation in viniculture with a rack of fruity, deep-tasting vintages. Most Canadian wines are white, although there are increasing varieties of light red wines. Canada's celebrated "ice wine," made from frozen grapes, and noted for the intensity of its flavor and texture, has some world leaders in Okanagan vintages.

OCEANWISE

Vancouver has adopted a sustainable fish industry initiative called Oceanwise (www.oceanwisecanada.com). The scheme is fronted by the Vancouver Aquarium and numbers more than 50 restaurants including West (➤ 76) and Cin Cin (➤ 75). It aims to promote sustainable fishing practices while sourcing the finest products from BC waters.

SNOWSTORMING!

It's always snow time in Western Canada where world-class ski resorts are of such high quality that Calgary hosted the 1988 Winter Olympics while Vancouver now boasts 2010 Winter Olympics status.

Vancouver itself rarely gets snow that lasts, which is something of a bonus a far as street life goes. Yet, within sight of the city are the neighboring winter sports centers of Mount Seymour (www.mountseymour.com), Cypress Mountain (www.cypressmountain.com) and Grouse Mountain (www.grousemountain.com) while a mere two hours north of the city are the world-famous slopes of Whistler and Blackcomb (www.whistlerblackcomb.com).

Powder Option
The Rockies have always been winter wonderlands; not just for all levels but for serious off-piste runs and challenging powder chutes. If your pockets are as deep as snowdrifts, you can always indulge in heli-skiing by reaching exclusive areas by helicopter. But if you want to cut your carbon snowprint – and the potential $600 helicopter flights – try snowcat skiing,

There are plenty of opportunities to ski or snowboard (left and far right); Athabasca Gacier in Jasper National Park (middle left); Whistler (middle right)

ICING ON THE CAKE

Skating is the basis of Canada's favorite spectator sport, ice hockey. Vancouver has nine indoor rinks where you can glide the light fantastic; but for a winter wonderland experience head for Grouse Mountain, where the mountain-top rink has a fairy-tale ambience at night. In the Rockies there are maintained outdoor lake venues at Lake Louise (► 136), Pyramid Lake (► 143) and Emerald Lake (► 148).

---

in which you're whisked away to virgin powder on board a big snowcat. Banff's mainstream ski resorts are Lake Louise, Sunshine Village and Mount Norquay (check them out on www.skibig3.com) while Jasper's best is the long-established Marmot Basin (www.skimarmot.com) just 19km (12 miles) south of Jasper Townsite.

Boarding It
Snowboarding first developed in North America as an inspired mix of surfing and skateboarding transplanted to snow. You might not be up to the "big air" tricks of somersaulting off a launch pad, but there are plenty of opportunities for simple freecarve runs at such mainstream resorts as Cypress Mountain and Lake Louise. And bobsleigh enthusiasts can now enjoy snow tubing at Cypress Mountain and Mount Seymour.

Cross Country
For the experienced, cross-country skiing is a terrific way of enjoying the snowy wilderness. At Cypress, north of Vancouver, there are 19km (12 miles) of cross-country trails and even some backcountry trails are kept clear in winter in the Lake Louise, Jasper and Banff areas.

THE MILD WILD WEST

The Canadian frontier, unlike its U.S. counterpart, was more mild than Wild West. Records show there were just three recorded gunfights in the 19th century – and pretty inept ones at that. Not that it was all plain sailing: The Canadian West still had to be won, and the men who won it were the Mounties. Today, the West is probably wilder than it ever was in the past, at least if you go on the evidence of North America's biggest, baddest rodeo – the Calgary Stampede.

The Canadian West's most potent symbol, the Mounties, was founded in 1873, when it was known as the North West Mounted Police (NWMP). The Mounties' beginnings were shaky – the only uniforms available were a handful of old British army tunics, hence the famous red jackets. The force was hastily formed to counteract an increase in drunken lawlessness that earned the West the nickname "Whoop-up Country."

Stampede!

Come to Calgary in July and you'll see an evocation of the Wild West that really does define Whoop Up! Every year the city lets rip with the Calgary Stampede (www.calgarystampede.com), North America's biggest, richest and most dangerous rodeo.

The total prize money for competitors is around $1 million and the many events are taken extremely seriously, none more so than the famous – and famously dangerous – chuck-wagon races, where another $1 million

The Musical Ride by the Mounties demonstrates their skills on horseback

is up for grabs. Contestants come from all over America and international visitors flock to the event. Local residents let their hair down in no uncertain fashion. Stampede events run the gamut, from bronco-breaking and bull-riding to branding, roping and steer-wrestling.

A highlight of Stampede is the grand parade, a two-hour city march-past of 40 or so floats, 750 horses and 4,000 participants in front of 350,000 onlookers. Even if you don't attend any events, Calgary is still a great place to be during Stampede. Everyone dresses the part – boots, jeans, bolo ties and Stetsons are de rigueur – and entertainment such as dancing, music, fireworks and barbecues is laid on around the city.

Rodeo Roots

The Calgary Stampede was begun in 1912 by rodeo entertainer and entrepreneur Guy Weadick. His first show, The Last and Best Great West Frontier Days, involved 3,000 cowboys, Pancho Villa and his bandits, and "Indians," and attracted around 40,000 people daily, not bad for a city with a then population of around 65,000 (today's daily attendance figures are about 100,000). The event resumed in 1919 after a break caused by World War I and has prospered ever since.

Different events during the Stampede

Finding Your Feet

First Two Hours

British Columbia (BC) and the Canadian Rockies have four principal centers –
Vancouver, Victoria, Calgary, and the Rockies national parks. Transportation
within the cities is provided by bus, light rail, SeaBus or taxi, and airport shuttle
services. Inter-center transportation includes airplane, long-haul buses, ferry,
seaplane and helicopter, or train.

Ground Transportation Fees (excluding tip)
$ under CDN$6   **$$$** CDN$12–$16
$$ CDN$6–$12   **$$$$** over CDN$16

Arriving: Vancouver

■ International flights land at the main terminal of **Vancouver International
Airport (tel: 604/207-7077; www.yvr.ca)**, 13km (8 miles) south of the city
center. There are information and foreign-exchange desks immediately
as you exit customs and immigration. Car rental desks are on Level One
beyond the parking area.

■ The best way into the city is on the **Airporter Bus** (tel: 604/946-
8866 or 1-800/668-3141; www.yvrairporter.com; every 30 minutes
8:20am–9:45pm). It leaves from a bay outside the main door of the
arrivals terminal and makes scheduled drops at major hotels and other
city landmarks ($$$). TransLink bus 424 runs between the airport and
the Airport Bus Station (for downtown connections) every seven minutes
(www.translink.bc.ca).

■ A rapid transit train line, Canada Line (www.canadaline.ca), between
Downtown Vancouver and the suburb of Richmond, is scheduled for
completion in late 2009 as part of Vancouver's 2010 Winter Olympics
infrastructure. It will include a direct link (every six minutes at peak
periods, 25 minutes duration), between the Airport and Waterfront Station
Vancouver from where there are connections with the city SkyTrain.

■ **Taxis** ($$$$) or only slightly more expensive **limousines** leave from
adjoining bays outside the arrivals terminal.

■ Arriving in the city by **bus** or **train** leaves you 2km (1.2 miles) southeast
of the city center at the main rail and bus terminal at VIA Rail Pacific
Central Station, 1150 Station Street (tel: 604/640-3700 or 1-888/842-
7245; www.viarail.ca). From here you can take a taxi to downtown ($$).

■ For **public transportation** links walk 150m (167 yards) from the station
(bear left across the grass as you stand with your back to the station) to
the visible Science World–Main Street **SkyTrain** station (➤ 35) and take
a "Waterfront" train to downtown ($). Tickets dispensed by automated
platform machines (cash only).

■ Vancouver's main downtown area occupies a large peninsula, with Stanley
Park (➤ 60) at its western end and the Gastown district (➤ 68) at its
eastern end. The main east–west street is **Robson Street**, the main north–
south artery is **Granville Street**. The principal downtown area concentrates
in the grid of streets at the intersection of these two thoroughfares, in
particular the area between Robson Street and the waterfront to the north.

City Center Tourist Office

■ The main visitor center is the **Vancouver Touristinfo Centre**, Waterfront
Centre, Suite 210, 200 Burrard Street at the corner of Canada Place

Way, tel: 604/683-2000 or 1-800/663 6000; www.tourismvancouver. com. Open: daily 8:30–6. The center provides **free maps and brochures**. It also offers a reservation service for tours and entertainments, as well as help reserving accommodations, and has an excellent selection of bed-and-breakfast options. The center carries public transportation timetables, and the free *Discover Vancouver on Transit* brochure.

Arriving: Victoria

■ **Victoria International Airport (tel: 250/953-7500; www.victoriaairport.com)** is 19km (12 miles) north of the city center. To reach the center use the **AKAL Airporter** shuttle bus (tel: 250/386-2525 or 1-877-386-2525; www.victoriaairportshuttle.com; $$$$) which covers all flights.

■ Visitors on the integrated bus-ferry connections from Vancouver (► 35) arrive at the city **bus terminal** near the Royal British Columbia Museum (► 90) at 700 Douglas and Belleville streets (tel: 250/382-6161).

■ Victoria is a small city, and **orientation** is easy. The downtown area centers on the waterfront, known as the Inner Harbour, and two parallel north–south streets: Douglas and Government. It's a short walk from the harbor to most hotels and all main sights and landmarks – notably the Empress Hotel (► 86, 100), Parliament Buildings (► 86), and Royal BC Museum. South of downtown stretches a large city park, Beacon Hill Park (► 96).

City Center Tourist Office

■ Victoria's main **Visitor Centre** is on the waterfront close to the Empress Hotel, 812 Wharf Street, tel: 250/953-2033. Accommodations reservations tel: 1-800-663-3883; www.tourismvictoria.com; open: Jun–Aug 8:30–8:30, Sep–May 9–5.

Arriving: Calgary

■ **Calgary International Airport** (tel: 403/735-1200 or 1-877/254-7427; www.calgaryairport.com) lies 9.5km (6 miles) northeast of the city center. There is a small tourist information desk on the first level.

■ The best way into the city is the Airport shuttle bus (tel: 403/291-9617), which runs at least once an hour from 6:30am to 9:30pm ($$). It stops outside eleven downtown hotels. Purchase tickets from the bus ticket desk in Arrivals. Buses depart from the bays immediately outside the terminal.

■ **Calgary Transit Rte 57** (tel: 403/262-1000; www.calgarytransit.com; $) serves the airport, running regularly from the Arrivals level between 5:47am and 12:15am. You need the exact fare. If your destination needs a further bus ride, ask the driver for a transfer.

■ **Taxis** depart from outside Arrivals ($$$$).

■ **Greyhound** buses from BC, the Rockies and Vancouver arrive at the Greyhound Bus Terminal, 877 Greyhound Way SW (tel: 403/260-0877; www.greyhound.ca). The Downtown Shuttle, Rte 31, picks up nearby at the 16th Street intersection, circling main central locations and the **C-Train station** at 7th Avenue SW and 10th Street (► 36). Taxis are moderately priced ($$) to most downtown destinations.

■ For Calgary **transportation** (► 36); Calgary Airport to Banff (► 38).

■ Calgary is a large city with an unfocused downtown area. The key reference points are the Calgary Tower (► 163) and nearby Glenbow Museum (► 164) in the southeast, and the Bow River in the north. Between these lie most of downtown's major malls and buildings, especially on 7th and 8th avenues SW.

■ The city is divided into quadrants (NW, NE, SW and SE), so it's essential to pay attention when reading **addresses**: 1438-4th Avenue SW is a long way from 1438-4th Avenue NE. To read addresses, note that the first digit (or digits) refers to the street number, the last digits (or digit) to the building number. Thus 1438-4th Avenue SW is in the southwest quadrant on 14th Street at number 38 close to the intersection with 4th Avenue.

City Center Tourist Office

■ Calgary's main **tourist office** is in the Calgary Tower, 101 9th Avenue SW, tel: 403/263-8510, 1-800/661-1678; www.tourismcalgary.com or www. discoveralberta.com; open: May–Sep Mon–Sat 8–8; Oct–Apr 8:30–5.

Intercity Connections to the National Parks

■ Buses ($) link to Banff and Lake Louise from Calgary and Calgary Airport.
■ The only public transportation from Banff to Jasper along the Icefields Parkway is operated by Brewster (tel: 1-800/760-6943; www.brewster.ca; open: May to mid-Oct only; $$$$).
■ Greyhound runs several services daily between Vancouver and Calgary ($$$–$$$$) with drop-offs in Yoho and Banff national parks at Field, Lake Louise and Banff town (see above).
■ Greyhound services from Calgary to Vancouver, as the southern BC route via Highway 3, run through Kootenay National Park.

Getting Around

City Transportation and Transfer Fees (in Canadian dollars, excluding tip)		Inter-Center Transfer Fees (in Canadian dollars, excluding tip)	
$ under $5	$$ $5–$10	$ $30–$50	$$ $50–$75
$$$ $10–$20	$$$$ over $20	$$$ $75–$100	$$$$ over $100

Vancouver

Vancouver has an integrated public transportation system that comprises buses, light rail (SkyTrain) and ferry (SeaBus). It is operated by TransLink (tel: 604/953-3333; www.translink.bc.ca). Timetables are available widely: from public libraries, city and municipal halls, tourist offices and TransLink offices and terminals.

Tickets

■ **TransLink tickets** ($) are valid across the transportation system.
■ The tickets are available from **ticket machines** at the SeaBus terminal and on SkyTrain stations, from 7-Eleven stores and all other **stores** displaying a TransLink Faredealer sticker.
■ You can buy tickets **directly from bus drivers**, but you must have the right money – place cash in a box on entering: No change is given.
■ **Flat-rate tickets** ($) apply in Zone 1, a large area covering most of central Vancouver. Tickets cost more for journeys into zones 2 and 3, and for travel on the SeaBus at peak rush-hour periods from Monday to Friday.
■ Tickets are valid for **90 minutes** of travel across the system.
■ **Transfer tickets** are necessary if you plan to use more than one bus during the 90-minute validity of your ticket. Bus drivers on your first journey usually – but not always – present you with a ticket showing the time you boarded the bus. If they don't, then ask for a transfer ticket and retain the ticket to present to drivers or SeaBus and SkyTrain officials on subsequent journeys.
■ **Concession fares** offering a third off regular fares are available for children aged between 5 and 13, and seniors aged 65 or over with proof of age.

Passes

- **Day passes** ($$) are useful if you make three or more journeys a day.
- Passes are **valid** after 9:30am Monday to Friday and all day on Saturday and Sunday.
- They are **available** from the same sources as tickets (➤ 34), though from stores they are sold as **Scratch & Ride** passes – you buy the pass and keep it until you want to use it, when you "scratch off" the day and month, thus validating the pass.

Buses

- Vancouver buses are **clean, quick and efficient**.
- Buy tickets beforehand (see above), or on board by putting the **right money** into the box by the driver.
- **Night buses** run between 2 and 4am on key routes.
- You'll also see blue **West Van** buses, which run from downtown to the suburbs of North and West Vancouver: TransLink tickets are also valid on these services. For information, tel: 604/985-7777.
- The useful **Transit Route Map and Guide** ($) lists all routes and has full details of the system and how it works. It is available from the Touristinfo Centre (➤ 32) and most stores with TransLink stickers. The Touristinfo Centre also provides free timetables and the useful *Metro Vancouver on Transit* pamphlet (free).

SkyTrain

- SkyTrain is a fully automated **light-rail system** that runs 48km (30 miles) above and below ground on the Expo and Millennium lines from the Waterfront station in downtown to the suburb of Surrey to the southeast.
- Most **visitors** are only likely to use the first four stations of the 20-station line – Waterfront, Burrard, Granville and Stadium.
- SkyTrain services run every **two to eight minutes**; a tour takes two hours.
- The rapid transit line, Canada Line (www.canadaline.ca; ➤ 32) will link with SkyTrain connections through the Waterfront Station.

SeaBus

- The **400-seat** SeaBus catamarans operate between the Waterfront SkyTrain station at the foot of Granville Street and Lonsdale Quay across the harbor in North Vancouver.
- The **12-minute** trip across Burrard Inlet to North Vancouver offers sensational views.
- **Departures** are every 15 or 30 minutes depending on the time of day.

Ferries

- Tiny ferries run by private companies (Aquabus and False Creek Ferries) provide quick and enjoyable ways of traveling.
- Services operate between downtown (departures from the foot of Hornby Street) and **Granville Island** (➤ 56), from Granville Island to Vanier Park and its museums, and around False Creek.
- Tickets ($) are bought **on board** the boats.
- For **information** tel: 604/689-5858; www.theaquabus.com or 604/684-7781; www.granvilleislandferries.bc.ca

Lost Property

- **Lost property and found items** on buses, SkyTrain and SeaBus are taken to the TransLink Lost Property office at the SkyTrain Stadium station (tel: 604/682-7887), which is open Mon–Fri 8:30–5. For items left on West Vancouver blue buses, tel: 604/985-7777.

Taxis

■ Vancouver taxis are efficient and moderately priced. Either hail them on the street, or call one of the following: **Black Top** (tel: 604/731-1111), **Vancouver Taxi** (tel: 604/871-1111), **Yellow Cab** (tel: 604/681-1111) or **Maclure's** (tel: 604/683-6666).

Victoria

Most sights in Victoria lie within walking distance of the center, so you're unlikely to need public transportation. The one notable exception is if you wish to visit the Butchart Gardens (► 93). The city's transit system is similar to Vancouver, but note that Vancouver transit tickets are not valid here.

■ **Buses** run on 49 routes in and around the city. They are operated by Victoria Regional Transit and buses run from around 6am to midnight.

■ **Tickets** ($) are issued for two zones and cost a little more than in Vancouver. Tickets can be obtained on board buses (correct money is required as drivers carry no change) or from the Visitor Centre (► 33), 7-Eleven stores or other marked stores.

■ **Day passes** ($$) are available in advance from normal ticket outlets.

■ **Information** on bus services is available by telephone (tel: 250/382-6161; www.bctransit.com); from the *Victoria Rider's Guide* ($) pamphlet carried on buses; from the Visitor Centre; and from the *Explore! Victoria by Bus* brochure, available from the Visitor Centre and many other outlets.

Calgary

Like Victoria, Calgary's main sights are within walking distance of one another. Its **public transportation** system is an integrated network of **buses** and light-rail system known as the **C-Train**. The latter is free along its main downtown stretch along 7th Avenue between 10th Street SW and 3rd Street SE.

■ **Tickets** ($) and **day passes** ($$) are valid on buses and C-Train, and are available from C-Train stations (coin-only machines), stores with a Calgary Transit sticker or on board buses if you have the exact fare.

■ **Transit information**: tel: 403/262-1000; www.calgarytransit.com

Intercity Connections

Vancouver to Victoria

■ Getting to Victoria from Vancouver is easy by **air or ferry**.

■ The most exciting and expensive way is to **fly**, either by helicopter ($$$) or by the floatplanes that take off from and land on water ($$$). These depart from Vancouver's Coal Harbour direct to Victoria's Inner Harbour.

■ **West Coast Air** flies floatplanes from the Tradewinds Marina west of Canada Place, tel: 604/606-6800; reservations 604/606-6888; toll free 1-800-347-2222; www.westcoastair.com

■ **Harbour Air** flies from the same marina to Victoria's Inner Harbour, tel: 1-800/655-0212; www.harbourair.ca

■ **Helijet International Incorporated** flies from the helipad to the east of Canada Place or from the airport, tel: 604/273-4688; toll free 1-800/665-4354; www.helijet.com

■ **Air Canada** flies between the cities' main airports ($$$$), tel: 604/688-5515 or 1-888/247-2262 or 1-800/661-3936; www.aircanada.ca

■ Most independent travelers use the combined **bus-ferry** connection operated by Pacific Coach Lines (tel: 604/662-7575; toll free 1-800/661-1725; www.pacificcoach.com) and BC Ferries (see below). Buy the through ticket ($) from the PCL desk at Vancouver or Victoria bus terminals: In Vancouver tickets are bought from an office in the main rail-bus station building. The inclusive ticket takes you on the bus to the ferry terminals at Tsawwassen (on the Vancouver mainland) or Swartz Bay (Victoria) and onto the ferry with the bus: You then rejoin the same bus for the onward leg after crossing the Georgia Strait, the beautiful island-dotted stretch of sea between the two cities. Buses leave hourly in the summer and every two hours in the winter: Point-to-point journey time is 3 hours 30 minutes; 90 minutes of this is on the ferry.

■ The ferries used by the coaches also carry **cars** and are run by BC Ferries (reservations tel: 250/386-3431 outside North America, or 1-888/223-3779 inside North America; www.bcferries.com). To take a car in peak season ($$$$) you will need to reserve well in advance to guarantee a place and avoid long lines. Tsawwassen is about 40 minutes' drive south of central Vancouver; Swartz Bay is the same distance north of Victoria.

Vancouver to Calgary

■ Visitors flying into Calgary and out of Vancouver, or vice versa, can combine the best of what the region has to offer. Whether you start your trip in Calgary or Vancouver, you have a **variety of options** as to how to cover the ground between the two cities.

■ The quickest option is to **fly** ($$$$) – journey time is one hour. International and long-haul travelers with major carriers can usually make ticketing arrangements that include this internal leg with their inbound and outbound flights. Departures with Air Canada (tel: 604/688-5515; www.aircanada.ca) or smaller regional and charter firms leave roughly hourly between the two cities.

■ Many people **drive**, however, taking in the Rockies and the scenery of BC. The quickest route is along Highway 1, better known as the Trans-Canada Highway (1,055km/655 miles). Alternatively, take the less interesting Highway 3 route, which runs parallel close to the US border. The best option of all is a route incorporating Banff, Jasper, Mount Robson, Highway 5, Kamloops and the Fraser Canyon.

■ **Public transportation** offers similar options. Around six **Greyhound** bus services daily run between Calgary and Vancouver on the Trans-Canada ($$$$). Other Greyhound services ply slower routes on Highway 3.

■ Note that even if you do not reserve a seat, you are alway assured of a place on **Greyhound** buses. If one bus becomes full, another bus is always added to the service.

■ Greyhound services are all **no smoking**. Services make only scheduled stops at Greyhound depots (bus stations). On long-distance services buses stop every few hours for passengers to take meal and snack breaks of around 20 minutes.

■ **Greyhound information**, tel: 403/260-0888 in Calgary, 604/482-8747 in Vancouver or toll free in Canada and the US 1-800-661-8747; www.greyhound.ca.

■ Public **train** connections with VIA Rail (tel: 604/669-3050 or toll free 1-888/VIA-RAIL throughout North America; www.viarail.ca) can be made between Vancouver and Kamloops (8 hours 20 minutes), where there are Greyhound connections to Calgary, or to Jasper (16 hours 30 minutes) for Brewster Transportation bus connections to Banff.

■ **Sleeper accommodations**, recommended for the overnight journey from Vancouver to Jasper, are available as double berths (large seats that become curtained bunks) or private single, double or triple bedrooms (spacious cabins with fold-down beds, table, toilet and closet). Meals are included in the price of sleeper tickets.

- The **Canrailpass** ($549 in 2008) offers unlimited Comfort-class (economy) travel for 12 days within a 30-day period. Extensions of up to three days and upgrades to first class are available.

Calgary to Banff

- Reaching Banff (► 130), the main focus of the Rockies' principal national park, is straightforward from Calgary. The town lies 127km (79 miles) west of Calgary.
- Banff is about 90 minutes' **drive** on the Trans-Canada Highway.
- Visitors arriving at **Calgary International Airport** who are not picking up a rental car can take advantage of several direct **bus shuttle** links from the airport to Banff, removing the need to travel into Calgary. There are several operators, including Brewster (tel: 403/762-6700; toll free 1-877/791-5500; www.brewster.ca). Most operators run two to four services daily: Some services continue to Lake Louise (► 136), 40 minutes beyond Banff.
- Visitors spending time in Calgary should take Greyhound services to Banff and Lake Louise (six daily) from the **city's bus terminal** (► 33).
- Note that there is **no scheduled rail service** between Calgary and Banff. The private Rocky Mountaineer Company (tel: 604/606-7245 or toll free in Canada and the US 1-877/460-3200; www.rockymountaineer.com) runs regular high-priced private services in summer and occasional additional services in winter. Reservations are obligatory.

Long-distance Buses

- Long-distance buses offer a comfortable, safe, reliable and **inexpensive** way of traveling around much of the Rockies and BC.
- The largest operator is **Greyhound** (► 33), whose services include links between Calgary, Banff, Lake Louise, Vancouver and points between.
- **Brewster Transportation** (► 158) runs bus services between Calgary, Banff, Lake Louise and Jasper.
- Most towns have a Greyhound **bus station**, known as a bus depot. Smaller towns may have just an office, often at a filling station or by a central café or restaurant. Buy **tickets** from these offices, not on the bus.
- You can **reserve** and select seats in advance for a small fee for most Greyhound services, but you can always turn up and be sure of finding a seat – if one bus is full, then another is automatically run.
- Visitors intending to travel extensively on the network should consider a **Greyhound Discovery Pass**, valid for unlimited travel for periods of 7, 15, 30 or 60 days. International visitors must purchase the pass online (www.discoverypass.com) at least 21 days in advance; the pass will be mailed to the address billed by your credit card company.

Driving

- Drivers in Canada must be **over 21. Full national driving licenses** from the US, UK and other countries are valid. An International Driving Licence is also valid, but should be accompanied by a national license. **Spot-fines** can be levied for failure to carry your license while driving.
- **Roads** are generally excellent. Fast four-lane roads are known as "expressways"; "highways" (two- or four-lane) link major towns; "secondary highways" are usually undivided roads between smaller towns; "tertiary" roads are minor paved roads; and "gravel" highways are unpaved or bitumen-topped roads often used for logging. They can be very dusty in dry weather and very muddy during rain. All roads are numbered, and most are well signposted. **Distances** are measured in kilometers.

Rules of the Road

- Drive on the **right**. On multilane roads outside built-up areas it is permissible to overtake on the left or right.
- At **crossroads** without traffic lights in built-up areas the first car to arrive has priority; if two cars arrive at the same time the right-hand car has priority.
- It is permissible to **turn right at a red light** if there is no traffic from the left. You must first come to a full stop at the intersection.
- **Flashing yellow lights** are a sign to slow down, and often indicate an accident black spot.
- The use of approved infant seats, for children under 18kg (39.5lb), and front and passenger **seat belts** is compulsory.
- The uniform **speed limit** on expressways is 100kph (62mph); 90kph (56mph) on the Trans-Canada and Yellowhead highways; 80kph (50mph) on most rural roads; and between 40kph (25mph) and 60kph (37mph) in urban areas. Limits are enforced, with spot-fines for violations.
- It is illegal to pass yellow/orange **school buses** (from either direction) which are stationary with their warning lights flashing.
- Driving under the influence of **alcohol** is a serious offense: Alcohol in a car must be carried unopened in the trunk.
- **Parking** is forbidden on sidewalks, near traffic lights, within 5m (16 feet) of a fire hydrant, and within 13m (50 feet) of grade crossings.
- In BC drivers are required to keep **vehicle headlights on** whilst driving, both during the day and at night.

Car Breakdowns

- If you break down, raise the car hood and tie a white cloth to the driver's side to indicate that help is required. Emergency phones are found at the side of most major roads.
- Canada's main recovery agency is the Canadian Automobile Association (CAA), with offices in most major towns and cities. The CAA is integrated with AAA and provides service to its members.

Car Rental

- Cars can be rented on presentation of a **full driving license**, which usually needs to have been valid for at least a year.
- The **best deals** are often those reserved in advance with firms in your home country, or as part of a fly-drive package. When renting in Canada look out for hidden charges, notably federal **Goods and Services Tax** (GST) and **provincial taxes** (▶ 43). A **"drop-off" charge**, often equivalent to a week's rental, is levied if you pick up the car in one town and leave it in another.
- **Collision** or **"Loss Damage Waiver,"** an insurance against accident or damage, is worth considering, but adds to the daily rental rate.
- Check to see whether the rental charge covers **unlimited mileage**, or whether an additional charge cuts in after a **set daily mileage**.
- Many car rental companies now offer **mobile phones** for rent.
- Note that many firms will not rent out cars for use on **gravel roads**.
- All companies require either a large **cash deposit** or a **credit card number** before renting out a vehicle.

Admission Charges

The cost of admission for museums and places of interest mentioned in the text is indicated by the following price categories:

Inexpensive under $5   **Moderate** $5–$10   **Expensive** other $10

Accommodations

Accommodations possibilities in Vancouver, Victoria, Calgary and the Rockies are extremely varied, with a choice of everything from hostels and homey bed and breakfasts to immense luxury hotels. For most travelers, the range of mid-priced motels in or close to all major centers are the best option, but it's worth noting that accommodations across the region in all price categories are busy in summer, so reservations are essential.

Accommodations Prices
Expect to pay per double room:
$ under CDN$100 $$ CDN$101–$200
$$$ CDN$201–$300 $$$$ over CDN$300

Hotels

- Canadian hotels divide into three basic types. The **most basic and cheap** are invariably cheerless hotels found above bars in towns and city centers. Although centrally located, rooms are usually rundown, and may be above a strip joint or a bar with pounding live music.
- At the other extreme are a range of **top-class city and resort hotels**, especially in Vancouver, Banff and Lake Louise, where standards are the equal of any in the United States or Europe.
- **Mid-range chain hotels** are easy to book and mean you know the type of accommodations available in advance. Reliable chains include Best Western, Holiday Inns, Ramada Hotels, Sandman, Travelodge and Westin Hotels although a downtown version of a chain may not be as smart as its out of town or airport area equivalent.

Motels

Motels may be called **travel lodges, motor lodges, inns or resorts**. Whatever their name they all provide **reliable and mid-priced** accommodations, usually on highways outside towns and cities. Standards are generally high, and you can expect a good bed, private bathroom, television and telephone in most rooms. Some also have family rooms, kitchenettes, saunas and swimming pools. Few, however, provide much in the way of food or drink.

Bed and Breakfast

Bed and breakfast (B&B) or **guest house** accommodations are found in towns, cities and rural backwaters across BC and Alberta. Many cities have central reservation agencies, though visitor centers usually carry extensive listings. Rooms do not always have private bathrooms, and the quality of breakfasts varies enormously. Check carefully on a B&B's location and what it offers in the way of food and facilities.

Hostels

Western Canada has hostels affiliated to **Hostelling International** (HI), and there are many more independent establishments. Hostels are usually modern, with cafeterias, credit card reservations and long opening hours. Many offer private rooms as well as single-sex dormitories.

Reservations

- It's vital to reserve accommodations in Vancouver, Victoria, Banff, Lake Louise and Jasper during July and August. At other times of the year, it's a good idea to call a few days in advance to secure a room. To make a reservation simply give a credit card number over the phone, though if you change your mind be sure to cancel in good time – hotels can charge a night's fee against your card.

■ Confirm check-in times, as rooms in some hotels may not be available until mid- or late afternoon. It is best if you inform the desk if you'll be arriving late, as many hotels – especially in busy areas – hold reservations only until 4 or 6pm.

■ AAA and CAA Travel Agencies provide full reservations service for any travel need. These services are available to AAA/CAA members and to the general public, although AAA/CAA members enjoy valuable discounts.

■ Banff and Jasper in the Rockies have reservation agencies (contacted via the visitor information center at each destination – ➤ 131 and 143) that will find accommodations for a small fee. Bed-and-breakfast agencies are common, though most visitor centers help find accommodations free of charge.

■ Note that many hotels advertise toll-free telephone reservation numbers. Often these are only toll-free in Canada or the US. Normal international rates will usually be charged if you call from outside those areas.

Costs

■ European visitors will be pleasantly surprised by the value for money offered by rural hotels and motels, although **room rates** in Vancouver and the Rockies are relatively high. Bed-and-breakfast rates are usually about the same as mid-range hotels.

■ **Prices and accommodations** listings can be obtained in advance from Alberta and BC provincial tourist offices and Canadian travel centers in your home country, though remember that listed prices don't usually include federal and provincial taxes.

■ Room tax in BC is 8 percent, and 4 percent in Alberta. An additional tourism tax is also sometimes levied: 2 percent in BC and 4 percent in Alberta. Federal Goods and **Services Tax** (GST) is levied at 5 percent in both provinces, but a rebate is available over $200.

■ If you're traveling with **children**, inquire about a hotel and motel's "**Family Plan**," where children stay free if they share their parents' room. Most places will also introduce a third single bed into a double room for between $5 and $20.

■ Hotels and motels also offer numerous **off-season or mid-week deals**, or give special **discounts for extended stays**. Vancouver and Victoria hotels aimed primarily at business travelers may offer weekend rates, and most places offer substantial winter reductions.

Diamond Ratings

AAA tourism editors evaluate and rate each lodging establishment based on the overall quality and services. AAA's diamond rating criteria reflect the design and service standards set by the lodging industry, combined with the expectations of our members.

A one (🔷) or two (🔷🔷) diamond rating represents a clean and well-maintained property offering comfortable rooms, with the two diamond property showing enhancements in decor and furnishings. A three (🔷🔷🔷) diamond property shows marked upgrades in physical attributes, services and comfort and may offer additional amenities. A four (🔷🔷🔷🔷) diamond rating signifies a property offering a high level of service and hospitality and a wide variety of amenities and upscale facilities. A five (🔷🔷🔷🔷🔷) diamond rating represents a world-class facility, offering the highest level of luxurious accommodations and personalized guest services.

Food and Drink

Eating in Vancouver, Calgary and Victoria can be a great pleasure, especially in Vancouver, where the multicultural population has fostered a large range of cuisines. Quality is also high in the Rockies and BC, although here the range of eating places is more restricted. Restaurants run the gamut, from small-town diners and fast-food joints to high-class establishments in Vancouver that are the equal of any in the world in terms of cuisine, decor and clientele.

- Prices are generally reasonable, but if your budget's tight there's a **huge choice** of cafés, diners, food malls and fast-food outlets across the region.
- North Americans are generally fairly informal, but the **dress code** for the best restaurants is smart-casual – jacket and tie for men are rarely required.
- **Tipping** is far more prevalent in North America than Europe. All serving staff should be tipped unless service has been poor, even in the cheapest cafés and diners. Tip 15–20 percent of the bill (or check) based on the total cost of the meal before taxes (see below).
- Tip staff in **bars** where drinks are brought to your table.
- **A Goods and Services Tax** (GST) of 5 percent is added to all bills.
- Many eating places don't allow **smoking** at all, even in their outdoor areas.
- **Licensing laws** are strict in much of western Canada. In many bars you must buy food in order to have a drink, and public drinking in parks, beaches and elsewhere is often prohibited.
- The **minimum age for buying alcohol** is 18 in Alberta and 19 in British Columbia.
- Many restaurants start serving **lunch** from noon. Canadians generally eat dinner earlier than most Europeans – from around 6 or 7pm – though the more sophisticated city restaurants usually stay open until 11pm or later. Diners and small-town restaurants often close around 9pm or earlier.

Saving Money

- Some of the best-value food is found in **food halls**, where a variety of small food outlets serve a wide range of sandwiches, snacks and ethnic and fast food. Most are found on the lower or uppermost floors of shopping malls, and virtually all have a large communal eating area.
- **Fixed-price menus** are common at lunch, particularly in Japanese and Chinese restaurants.
- Some city bars have a "Happy Hour" between 5 and 7pm when drinks are cheaper than normal. The practice has drawn criticism, however, and Alberta introduced a law in 2008 banning "Happy Hours" after 8pm.

Diamond Ratings

AAA tourism editors evaluate each restaurant on the overall quality of food, service, decor and ambience – with extra emphasis given to food and service. Ratings range from **one diamond** (♦) indicating a simple, family-oriented establishment to **five diamonds** (♦ ♦♦♦ ♦) indicating an establishment offering superb culinary skills and an ultimate adult dining experience.

Prices
Expect pay for an average meal for two people including drinks:
$ under CDN$50 $$ CDN$50–$100 $$$ over CDN$100

Shopping

Vancouver's excellent downtown shopping is dominated by a department store of long-standing fame – The Bay (► 79) – and by a plethora of malls such as the prestigious Pacific Centre. It also has smaller malls such as the Sinclair Centre (► 79), a converted historic building with a range of more interesting specialty shops and fashion stores, and the Oakridge Centre, where 150 or so stores focus on fashion.

Similar stores can be found in two market-centered enclaves – **Lonsdale Quay** and **Granville Island** – and in hip districts such as Yaletown and the more bohemian Kitsilano district on 4th Avenue between Burrard Street and Alma Street. The main downtown shopping street is **Robson**, once described by fashion designer Gianni Versace, as "one of the 10 streets in the world where you have to have a store." The Gastown district has lots of souvenir shops, but also galleries and shops devoted to Inuit and other aboriginal art and artifacts. Chinatown is full of Asian shops and markets.

Around Vancouver there are also good shopping destinations. **Burnaby**, on the SkyTrain network, is home to BC's biggest shopping mall, **Metropolis at Metrotown**, which has 470 stores, the largest food court in western Canada, and various entertainment and recreational facilities. In **Richmond**, the **Aberdeen Centre** was a trailblazer in Asian retail centers, and has recently broadened its scope – fusion shopping, as it were – and expanded to three times its original size.

Victoria is much smaller than Vancouver, but its main shopping streets – on and around Government Street and Douglas Street – are full of fascinating specialist shops. The city's nearest equivalent to Vancouver's Granville Island is **Market Square** (► 88), a redeveloped Victorian complex of cafés, restaurants, galleries, craft and other small art and design stores. Best buys in the city are food and drink such as chocolates, maple syrup, tea and coffee; books (there are two excellent bookstores), and aboriginal and other craft products and souvenirs. The main mall here is the Mayfair Shopping Centre, with 120 stores and services.

Calgary has its share of malls and department stores, most on and around Stephen Avenue Walk, the pedestrianized heart of downtown. The historic Inglewood neighborhood, on 9th Avenue SE between 10th and 14th streets, is a great place for a stroll, too, with some interesting art galleries, antiques shops, boutiques and eating places, and in Marda Loop, at 33rd Avenue SW and 19th Street SW, there's an eclectic mix of stores. The Chinook Centre, at Macleod Trail and Glenmore Trail SW, is the city's biggest mall.

In the Rockies, only **Banff** has a significant number of stores, notably for outdoor clothes and equipment.

- **Ordinary stores** usually open Monday to Saturday from about 10am to 6pm, often with later opening on Friday and Saturday. **Malls** generally open longer all week from around 7:30am to 9pm.
- Most cities and towns have **24-hour pharmacies and convenience stores** such as Mac's and 7-Eleven.
- **Sunday opening** times across much of Canada have long been restricted by the so-called "blue laws," but these are increasingly being relaxed to allow limited shopping, typically from noon to 5pm.
- Federal **Goods and Services Tax** (GST) at 5 percent is charged on most goods. Beware, as often the tax is not included in the displayed price. Additional **provincial taxes** of 5 to 12 percent may also be levied.

Entertainment

Festivals and Events

■ Among the best festivals are the Calgary Stampede (➤ 29), the Banff Festival of the Arts (➤ 157) and the Victoria International Festival. Vancouver has a massive program of world-class festivals, including jazz, folk and classical music; film, comedy and sports, and the stunning Chinatown Festival.

Art and Culture

■ Vancouver has a rich cultural life, with a wide range of classical and other **music concerts** – including those of the respected Vancouver Symphony Orchestra – and myriad mainstream and alternative **dance and theater** companies. Victoria and Calgary also have a thriving cultural scene.

Nightlife

■ Nightlife in Calgary and Vancouver is what you would expect of major cities, with plenty of **bars**, **clubs** and lively **pubs**. **Comedy clubs** are also popular, as is **live music**, performed in a variety of venues. Victoria is more sedate, though it does have some clubs and several great pubs and bars.

Outdoor Activities

■ Western Canada has some of the greatest opportunities for outdoor activities in the world. **Hiking** possibilities (➤ 126–152) are endless, especially in the Rockies, with superbly kept trails to suit every level of ability. **Mountain bicycling**, **climbing**, **whitewater rafting**, horseback **riding** and **canoeing** are also excellent, as are facilities for more relaxed pastimes such as **golf** and **fishing**. **Sailing** and **boating** are also hugely popular.

■ **Winter sports** are exceptional, especially at Whistler (➤ 71), widely considered one of the world's top three ski resorts and venue for the 2010 Winter Olympics, but also at Banff and Lake Louise in the Rockies. Just about every other winter activity imaginable is available, from **skating** and **tobogganing** to **ice fishing** and **dogsledding**.

Sport

■ **Ice hockey** is virtually Canada's national sport. The Calgary Flames and Vancouver Canucks are both in the main North American National Hockey League. The season runs from October to May. Tickets must generally be bought in advance. Contact visitor centers for details.

Information

■ Canadian visitor centers and provincial tourist offices provide a huge amount of information on every imaginable type of activity and entertainment. Also be sure to check out **weekly entertainment listings** in newspapers and magazines. For information before your trip, simply contact the tourist office or embassy in your home country.

■ During your trip, be certain to call at **visitor centers** (also known as infocentres or similar) which, as well as providing brochures and current information, can often reserve you directly onto tours or sell tickets for shows, concerts and other events. Tickets can also be purchased in cities through central reservation agencies such as **Ticketmaster**.

■ Virtually all centers have staff who can advise on outdoor activities locally, something that is particularly true of national and other park centers, where expert staff can recommend suitable hikes and other activities.

Vancouver

Getting Your Bearings

Sydney would disagree, Rio too, and San Francisco might demur, but it's hard to think of a city more beautiful than Vancouver – or one where it must be such a pleasure to live. Set between ocean and mountain, the city is scenically unrivaled, the waters of the Pacific bounding the downtown core, the peaks of the Coast Mountains rearing majestically in the near distance.

Hedonism among locals is unbridled, and no wonder, for Vancouver's lucky, multicultural residents can ski, sail, sunbathe (Vancouver even has beaches), hike, fish, dive and much more, all within a few minutes of the city center. Wilderness – literally – is just a bus ride away.

Whether or not you take advantage of this natural playground, it's hard to resist Vancouver's summer allure, when the city's café and cultural life – vibrant at the best of times – takes to the streets and parks (Vancouver's infamous rain can put a damper on things the rest of the year).

Outstanding museums, galleries, gardens and shops also abound, but you could simply revel in the cityscapes and still have a great trip – the vibrant port that underpins the city's prosperity, the natural splendor of Stanley Park, the busy market on Granville Island and the grittier corners of Gastown and Chinatown. You can see Vancouver in three days but you'll probably want to stay longer.

| 0 | | 3 km |
| 0 | | 2 miles |

CHANCELLOR BLVD

7 Museum of Anthropology

N.W. MARINE DRIVE

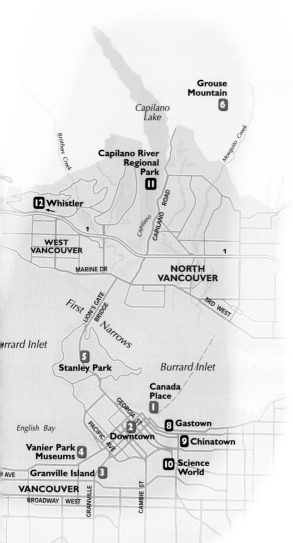

Grouse
Mountain
6

*Capilano
Lake*

Brothers Creek

Mosquito Creek

Capilano River
Regional
Park
11

Capilano

CAPILANO ROAD

12 Whistler

1

WEST
VANCOUVER

MARINE DR

NORTH
VANCOUVER

1

3RD WEST

First

LION'S GATE BRIDGE

Narrows

rrard Inlet

5
Stanley Park

Burrard Inlet

GEORGIA ST

Canada
Place
1

English Bay

PACIFIC AVE

2
Downtown

8 Gastown

9 Chinatown

Vanier Park
Museums **4**

AVE

Granville Island **3**

10 Science
World

VANCOUVER

GRANVILLE ST

CAMBIE ST

BROADWAY WEST

Page 45:
Boats in the marina
at Coal Harbour

Right: John Fluevog Shoes shop
in Gastown

In Three Days

If you're not quite sure where to begin your travels, this itinerary recommends a practical and enjoyable three-day tour of Vancouver, taking in some of the best places to see using the Getting Your Bearings map on the previous page. For more information see the main entries

Day One

Morning
Visit the Vancouver Touristinfo Centre (➤ 32) to book trips, buy passes and tickets, or to pick up brochures and information, then cross Canada Place Way outside the Infocentre to the waterfront and stroll around **❶ Canada Place** (left; ➤ 50–52). Walk to the Harbour Centre and take the elevators for stunning city views from Vancouver Lookout. Explore **❽ Gastown** (➤ 68), breaking for lunch in the Water Street Café (➤ 76) or one of the many other cafés nearby. After lunch you might walk to **❾ Chinatown** (below; ➤ 69), following the well-signed Silk Road Route.

Afternoon
Explore the heart of **❷ downtown** (➤ 53–55) around Hornby, Howe or Burrard streets. Shop or visit the **Vancouver Art Gallery** (➤ 53), with a break for refreshments in the Gallery Café (➤ 77). Walk east on Robson Street to look at the Vancouver Library complex near the corner of Homer Street and Robson Street. Consider an early evening walk to the trendy Yaletown district nearby for a drink or early supper.

Day Two

Morning
Take a bus or ferry to **❸ Granville Island** (➤ 56–57) to explore the city's soul. Catch a ferry to Heritage Harbour and visit one or more of the **❹ Vanier Park museums** (➤ 58–59). Return by ferry to Granville Island for lunch: Buy a picnic from the market stalls or food concessions, or try one of the island's restaurants, such as The Dockside (➤ 75).

Afternoon
Take a bus or taxi to downtown and continue to **5 Stanley Park** (➤ 60–63). Spend the afternoon relaxing, visiting the Vancouver Aquarium and exploring the park on foot, bus or bike.

Evening
Enjoy a refreshment break in one of several cafés around the park, or walk down Denman Street – which has several cafés and bars – for a stroll along English Bay Beach.

Day Three

Morning
Buy a public transportation Day Pass and travel by SkyTrain to Waterfront. Take the SeaBus to Lonsdale Quay in North Vancouver and then – if the weather is fine – catch a bus to the cable-car station at the foot of **6 Grouse Mountain** (above; ➤ 64). Spend most of the morning on Grouse Mountain followed by a possible visit to Capilano Park and suspension bridge. Return to Lonsdale Quay for lunch at the Quay's market, then take the SeaBus to downtown.

Afternoon
Take a bus to the **7 Museum of Anthropology** (right; ➤ 66). Pass a full afternoon viewing the museum's magnificent collection.

▯ Canada Place

Canada Place makes a stunning introduction to Vancouver. Begun in 1986 as the Canadian Pavilion for Expo '86, the long pier offers sensational views of the city's port, the ranks of downtown skyscrapers and the mountains above North Vancouver. Dotted around its panoramic promenades are information boards which offer fascinating insights into the history and background of what you're seeing.

The complex's medley of shops, restaurants, convention center, IMAX Theatre and hotels juts out into the harbor in the manner of a ship, an architectural trick complemented by the distinctive white Teflon roof, designed to resemble the sails of a ship at sea. All you need to do to enjoy the magnificent views is wander the "decks" – the promenades that encircle the building. Allow an hour or so.

Right: One of the decorative sails of Canada Place

Below: Inside Canada Place

First Port of Call

The Canada Place complex lies on the waterfront at the foot of Howe and Burrard streets, on the northern edge of downtown, making it easy to find and easily accessible on your first morning in Vancouver. It's also just a minute's walk from the city's excellent main visitor center, or **Touristinfo Centre** (➤ 32), another good reason for heading here first as you find your feet at the beginning of a visit.

Superb Scenery

From the complex's promenades you can watch the mesmerizing buzz of activity scattered across one of North America's biggest and busiest ports. Helicopters swoop over the water, floatplanes pull themselves heavily into the sky, and boats of all shapes and sizes criss-cross the spectacular mountain-backed harbor. To the west, the waterfront curves to meet **Stanley Park**, downtown's glorious

---

CANADA PLACE: INSIDE INFO

Top tips Tickets are valid all day, so come back to Canada Place in the evening to **enjoy the city lights by night**.
- The Vancouver Lookout in the Harbour Centre is nearly always busy so in peak season consider visiting it before Canada Place to avoid the crowds.

One to miss The **IMAX cinemas** are famous for their huge screens, but only relatively few films have been made to fit them. Check the program to see if there's anything that appeals: Otherwise save this as an option for rainy days.

crown of forest and wilderness (➤ 60). Below you there's likely to be at least one cruise ship moored at the pier – the terminal here handles some 120 cruise ships and around 600,000 passengers annually.

Canada Place juts out into the harbor

As you walk, pause to read the 44 information boards, which deal with everything from the history of the city to the different types of ships and cargoes on the water. The port sprang to life in 1864, when it started exporting fence pickets to Australia. Today it processes some 3,000 ships a year from over 100 different countries, handles over 77 million tons of cargo, and turns over $40 billion of trade every year. The port's Interpretive Centre has some fun, hands-on exhibits.

If the views from Canada Place aren't enough, then walk to the nearby Harbour Centre Building, where in just 60 seconds all-glass SkyLifts carry you 170m (554 feet) to the **Vancouver Lookout**, with a magnificent 360-degree view of the city.

TAKING A BREAK

Either the inexpensive **café** at the tip of Canada Place ($) or the formal restaurants of the Pan Pacific hotel ($$$) nearby.

Canada Place
✚ 199 F4 ✉ Canada Place, #100-999 Canada Place ☎ Information 604/775-7200; www.canadaplace.ca 🕐 24 hours 💲 Free 🍴 Café ($) 🚇 Waterfront 🚌 4, 6, 7, 8 or 50 north on Granville Street

CN IMAX Theatre
✚ 199 F4 ✉ #201-999 Canada Place ☎ 604/682-2384; www.imax.com/vancouver 🕐 Several screenings daily 💲 Expensive 🚇 Waterfront 🚌 4, 6, 7, 8 or 50 north on Granville Street

Vancouver Lookout at Harbour Centre
✚ 199 F4 ✉ Harbour Centre, 555 West Hastings Street ☎ 604/689-0421; www.vancouverlookout.com 🕐 May to mid-Oct daily 8:30am–10:30pm; mid-Oct to Apr 9–9 💲 Expensive 🍴 Food court ($) and restaurant ($$) 🚇 Waterfront 🚌 4, 6, 7, 8, 10, 16, 20 or 50 north to Granville Mall

2 Downtown

Vancouver's downtown core looks much like any other North American city – lots of sleek high-rise buildings, malls, offices and shops – but it has two important differences: The views and the setting. Turn almost any corner and you're greeted with startling panoramas of the sea and mountains, a constant reminder of the spectacular scenery that frames one of the world's most beautiful cities.

Downtown's heart is the grid of streets on and around Robson, Granville and Burrard, though as Vancouver's economy booms, the city's smart center is spreading rapidly – particularly to the east. Robson Street is the key thoroughfare, full of shops and restaurants: On summer evenings this is the place to be, part of a vibrant throng and colorful street life. Granville Street is less smart – at its southern end it's downright seedy – but it also contains some of the city's main cinema complexes. Burrard Street is the smartest of the three streets, and the stretch down to the waterfront and **Canada Place** (► 50) contains some of the city's grandest – and most expensive – hotels, shops and offices.

Cafés and bars in Gastown

Head West or East

West of the downtown core lies the West End, a predominantly residential district. Beyond that again is **Stanley Park** (► 60), an area of near wilderness wonderfully at odds with the concrete, glass and steel of downtown. Heading east you come to **Gastown** (► 68), an only partly successful piece of city rejuvenation, and then a grittier, more down-at-the-heels district that merges into **Chinatown** (► 69).

What to See

On your first downtown venture make for the **Vancouver Art Gallery**, a former city courthouse that has been transformed into a handsomely presented gallery. The venue holds more than 9,000 works including the largest collection of paintings by BC's most acclaimed artist, Emily Carr. Works by Carr are usually on view. Much of the gallery is given over to changing exhibitions of international artists that can be dramatic and challenging. The gallery café has a delightful roof patio.

Plans were announced in early 2008 for a new venue for the gallery in a waterside setting on False Creek's Plaza of Nations.

Downtown is filled with malls and department stores. The most interesting are The Bay store and the Sinclair Centre mall (▶ 79 for more details of these and other downtown stores).

TAKING A BREAK

The **Gallery Café** (▶ 77), with its large outdoor area, is one of downtown's nicest places for lunch or a coffee.

Below: Downtown Vancouver seen from Davie Street

Left: Inside the former courthouse that is now Vancouver Art Gallery

Vancouver Art Gallery
🏳 199 E3 ☒ 750 Hornby Street ☎ 604/662-4700 or 604/662-4719 for 24-hour information; www.vanartgallery.bc.ca 🕐 Art gallery: daily 10-5:30 (also Tue and Thu 5:30-9). Café: Mon-Fri 9-dusk (also Tue and Thu until 9pm), Sat 9:30-6, Sun 10-6 💰 Expensive; by donation Tue 5–9 🍴 Gallery Café 🚇 Burrard or Granville 🚌 3 or 5 and 15 west on Robson Street

---

DOWNTOWN: INSIDE INFO

In more depth To see the best of downtown's **dynamic new buildings**, walk east along Robson Street to the magnificent Vancouver Public Library complex (► 9) – a modern take on Rome's Colosseum.

Hidden gem Follow the **Vancouver city walk** (► 176) to uncover some of downtown's hidden corners. Good targets include Christ Church Cathedral and the Marine Building, two fine pieces of religious and high-rise architecture on Burrard Street. Also, drop into Hotel Vancouver, the city's most historic hotel.

❸ Granville Island

Granville Island is Vancouver's heart and soul, a small redoubt of renovated semi-industrial buildings and waterfront on the southern edge of the downtown peninsula. It contains one of the world's great food markets and a medley of galleries, wharves, walkways, museums, specialty shops, restaurants, artists' studios – even a small brewery.

Transportation

The quickest way to get here is by taxi or a 50 bus from Gastown or bus stops on the west side of the Granville Street Bridge. You'll be dropped underneath the girders of the bridge on the island side, from where you walk back straight onto the largely pedestrianized island. If you have a car, don't dream of driving – parking is all but impossible. Don't walk over the Granville Street Bridge – it's a long, dull hike.

The slower but more enjoyable approach is to walk to the foot of Hornby Street and pick up one of the tiny ferries that ply to the island across False Creek. These same ferries will carry you from the island to **Vanier Park** (➤ 58), the next logical stage of any Vancouver itinerary. Allow at least a couple of hours before moving on.

The high-rises of downtown tower over Granville Island

Regeneration

The island is a triumph of urban regeneration. It was originally reclaimed from swampland in 1917 and used as the site of an iron and shipbuilding factory. By the 1960s it was a derelict wasteland and rubbish dump, and might have stayed that way but for a federally funded project, begun in 1972, that successfully transformed it into an inspired "open-plan" mixture of commercial, residential and light industrial use.

A trip here is rewarding at any time, but especially at weekends, when half of Vancouver descends on the island to buy

🔢 198 C1 ✉ Granville Island Infocentre, 1398 Cartwright Street ☎ 604/666-5784 or 604/666-6655; www.granvilleisland.bc.ca ⏰ Island: 24 hours. Public market: daily 9–7 💲 Free 🍴 Many cafés, bars and restaurants ($–$$$) 🚌 50 ⛴ Aquabus, False Creek Ferry

Granville Island Museums
🔢 198 C1 ✉ 1502 Duranleau Street, Granville Island ☎ 604/683-1939 ⏰ Museums Tue–Sun 10–5:30. Closed Mon 💲 Moderate

A waterside restaurant on Granville Island

food in the glorious covered food market, grab a cappuccino, people-watch, eat brunch outdoors, stroll among the shops and wharves, or sit in the sun watching the numerous street performers. Also worth a brief look are two small museums under one roof: The self-explanatory **Model Trains and Model Ships museum**, and the Granville Island Brewing Company, which has regular moderately priced guided tours and tastings.

The island's also good in the evening, when you can sit and watch the sunset, sip a beer, eat in the restaurants, or take in a revue, play or cabaret at the Arts Club Theatre (➤ 80).

TAKING A BREAK

The popular, laid-back **Backstage Lounge** (➤ 77) has a waterfront view, occasional live music and offers good, inexpensive snacks and meals. Alternatively, try the **Keg Steak House and Bar** on Anderson Street.

GRANVILLE ISLAND: INSIDE INFO

Top tips The island is extremely busy at weekends, so come during the week if you'd prefer to avoid the crowds. Note that many of the shops are shut on Mondays, as is the market during winter.

■ The **Granville Island Infocentre** (tel: 604/666-5784; www.granvilleisland.bc.ca) on Cartwright Street close to the public market, has maps and details of attractions.

■ **Heading back to downtown** you should take a 50 bus from the stop beside the island's single road entrance, not the 51 from the stop on the island opposite the information center.

In more depth You can **rent canoes** from several outlets to paddle around False Creek, or walk east or west on the sea wall along False Creek.

4 Vanier Park Museums

Vanier Park contains three of Vancouver's four major museums, the Vancouver Museum, which recounts the history of the city; the Maritime Museum, which contains a wealth of maritime displays and memorabilia; and the H R MacMillan Space Centre, which is dedicated to the science and exploration of space. All lie close to one another, and all are ideally suited to a visit from Granville Island (➤ 56), which is connected to the park by ferry.

Maritime Museum

Arriving by ferry from Granville Island – by far the best approach to Vanier Park – you disembark at Heritage Harbour, a small quay containing beautiful old boats. These provide the perfect prelude to the nearby Maritime Museum, which is dedicated to Vancouver's strong seafaring traditions. Pride of place among the somewhat dated displays goes to the *St Roch*, a Royal Canadian Mounted Police schooner which in 1944 became the first vessel to make a single-season voyage across the Northwest Passage (a 1,497km/930-mile) traverse between Baffin Island and Alaska's Beaufort Sea). Other highlights – for which you should allow an hour at the most – include many period photographs, models and maritime artifacts, as well as the **Children's Maritime Discovery Centre** and **Pirates' Cove**.

Vancouver Museum

Vancouver's main civic museum suffers by comparison with Victoria's Royal British Columbia Museum (➤ 90), which covers British Columbia's First Nations and other history in a more impressive manner. However, the museum intends to redefine its content and curatorial role toward a greater focus on Vancouver in a modern context. Plans include a possible move to the heart of downtown with the Vancouver Art Gallery building in Hornby Street being considered when it is vacated (➤ 53). Current highlights include re-created Edwardian and Victorian rooms, an old Hudson's Bay Company post, a **Canadian Pacific Railway car** and the immigration section. The last contains an eye-opening mock-up of the conditions endured by those traveling in "steerage," the cheapest way of crossing the Atlantic from Europe.

Ben Franklin, a mini submarine in the Maritime Museum

H R MacMillan Space Centre

Admission to this excellent high-tech space center, observatory and planetarium buys you, among other things, a "virtual" trip to Mars in a full-motion simulator during which you ride close to the sun, tangle with a meteor shower and save a settlement of space colonists. Then you can admire one of the huge motors from **Apollo 17** and wander through the Cosmic Courtyard which is stuffed with interactive displays – have a go at designing a spacecraft or guiding a lunar robot. The **H R MacMillan Planetarium** offers a variety of star and laser shows. Other parts of the center have changing exhibitions and shows.

Studying the exhibits in Vancouver Museum

Maritime Museum

➕ 198 A2 ✉ Vanier Park, 1905 Ogden Avenue ☎ 604/257-8300; www.vancouvermaritimemuseum.com 🕐 Mid-May to early Sep daily 10–5; early Sep to mid-May Tue–Sat 10–5, Sun noon–5 💲 Expensive 🍴 Vending machines 🚌 2 or 22 (Macdonald) from Burrard Street or West Pender Street to Chestnut Street or Cornwall Street

Vancouver Museum

➕ 198 B2 ✉ Vanier Park, 1100 Chestnut Street (150m/160 yards from the Maritime Museum) ☎ 604/736-4431; www.vanmuseum.bc.ca 🕐 Daily 10–5 (also Thu 5–9); closed Mon Sep–Jun and Dec 25 💲 Expensive 🚌 2 or 22 (Macdonald) from Burrard Street or West Pender Street to Cornwall Street

H R MacMillan Space Centre

➕ 198 B2 ✉ Vanier Park, 1100 Chestnut Street ☎ 604/738-7827 (call for evening star and laser show times); www.hrmacmillanspacecentre.com 🕐 Jul to early Sep daily 10–5; early Sep to Jun Tue–Sun 10–5 💲 Expensive. Admission includes complex and one Virtual Voyage, subject to health and minimum height requirement of 1m (3ft). Additional Voyages: moderate 🚌 2 or 22 (Macdonald) from Burrard Street or West Pender Street to Chestnut Street or Cornwall Street

Centre: The fountain outside Vancouver Museum

VANIER PARK MUSEUMS: INSIDE INFO

Top tips By far the best way to visit the Vanier Park museums is on one of the tiny ferries from Granville Island. Some boats go directly to the small landing stage close to the Maritime Museum; others require a change of ferry en route. It's a straightforward procedure – simply ask your ferry operator. Pay your fare on the boat.

■ Choose the Vancouver Museum if you have **time for just one** of the park's three museums. If you're traveling with children, however, the H R MacMillan Space Centre is the best single choice.

5 Stanley Park

Stanley Park is one of the world's great city parks. At more than 350ha (980 acres) – an area greater than the whole of downtown – it rates among North America's largest urban parks, containing not only beaches, formal gardens and a remarkable semiwilderness of forest, but also plenty of hiking and bicycle trails and one of western Canada's leading attractions – the Vancouver Aquarium.

Water surrounds the park on three sides, cradling a heart of virgin forest, tangled woodland glades and a criss-cross of trails. A 10.5km (6.5-mile) road and parallel path and bicycle route run around the perimeter sea wall, offering magnificent views, while on the park's eastern fringe are more manicured gardens and a medley of sights and attractions. These include the aquarium, **Hallelujah Point** (a collection of painted totems, pictured left), the 5,000-bush Rose Gardens, Royal Vancouver Yacht Club and Lost Lagoon, the last a shallow tidal haven for a host of birds.

A typical totem pole in Stanley Park

How you visit Stanley Park – and a visit is essential – will depend on how energetic you're feeling. The best way is to rent a bicycle or rollerblades from one of several outlets at the eastern end of Denman Street and follow the sea wall for all or part of its circuit. Prospect Point offers superlative views, as does Ferguson Point to its west, while the track between the two runs through old-growth forest of western red cedar, hemlock and Douglas fir. Round off a trip on one of the beaches lining the park's western edge – the most convenient is English Bay Beach at the southern end of Denman Street. Near by Second Beach to the north has a saltwater swimming pool.

Vancouver Aquarium

More than a million people a year visit the Vancouver Aquarium, which makes it Canada's most popular visitor attraction west of Toronto's CN Tower. It is the third largest – and one of the best – in North America, with more than 8,000 living creatures representing over 600 different marine species. The prize attractions are the whales and performing dolphins, and though the aquarium has been the target of animal rights campaigners, leading

Above and below: Exhibits in Vancouver Aquarium

environmentalists support its commitment to education and conservation, and plans for a major expansion of the habitats were approved in late 2006.

Displays are themed around several basic habitats: **Arctic Canada**, where you can watch animals of the cold Canadian north such as beluga whales, seals and walruses; the **Pacific Northwest Centre**, filled with beavers, otters and other creatures associated with the waters of British Columbia; the climate-controlled **Graham Amazon Gallery**, where a tropical deluge is unleashed on the hour above sloths, iguanas, piranhas, crocodiles and other rain-forest creatures; and the Tropical Pacific Gallery, which re-creates the coral reefs of Indonesia's Bunaken National Park, complete with angelfish and blacktip reef sharks. Be sure to call ahead for current feeding times for the sharks and sea otters. **Aquaquest – the Marilyn Blusson Learning Centre** is a new facility with exhibits of unique sea creatures, an environmental newsroom

SAVED FOR POSTERITY

Stanley Park was created thanks to the foresight of the city's first council. In the 1860s the area was partly logged, lumbermen being attracted by the vast 800-year-old trees. It was then turned into a military reserve as border tensions rose between Britain and the US. In 1886, within a month of Vancouver's foundation, the city council petitioned for the area to be turned into a permanent park. This took its name from Lord Stanley, Canada's Governor General between 1888 and 1893.

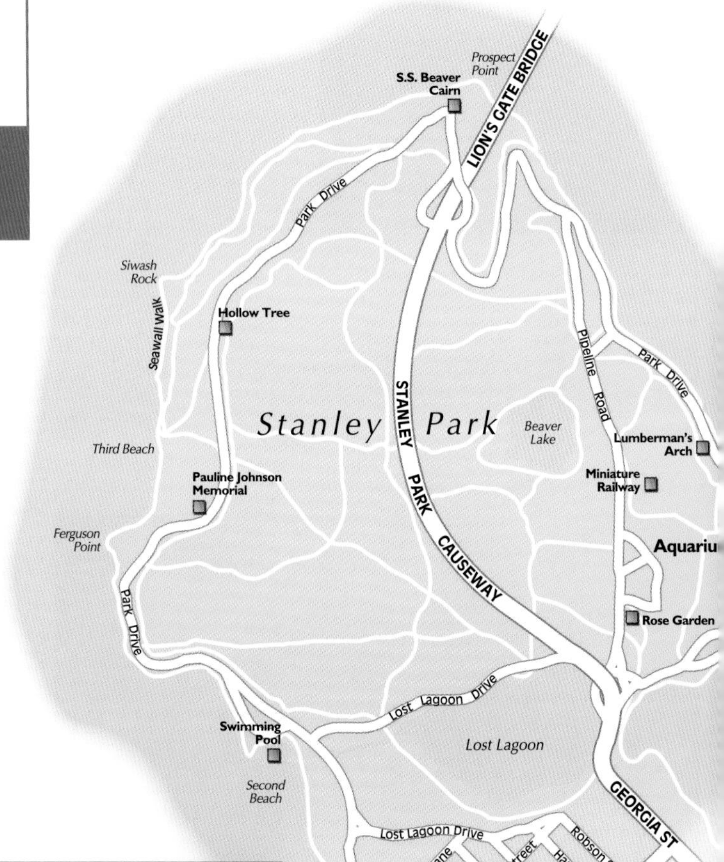

Stanley Park

- Prospect Point
- S.S. Beaver Cairn
- LION'S GATE BRIDGE
- Park Drive
- Siwash Rock
- Seawall walk
- Hollow Tree
- STANLEY PARK CAUSEWAY
- Beaver Lake
- Pipeline Road
- Park Drive
- Lumberman's Arch
- Third Beach
- Pauline Johnson Memorial
- Miniature Railway
- Ferguson Point
- Aquariu
- Park Drive
- Rose Garden
- Lost Lagoon Drive
- Swimming Pool
- Lost Lagoon
- Second Beach
- GEORGIA ST
- Lost Lagoon Drive
- Park Lane
- Robson St
- Chilco Street
- Haro St
- Nelson St
- Beach Avenue
- Comox St
- DENMAN STREET
- English Bay Beach

Brockton Point Lighthouse in Stanley Park

with the latest conservation news, an educational family play area and a viewing gallery where visitors can watch aquarium staff engaged in research projects.

TAKING A BREAK

Cafés along the sea wall, at Prospect Point and Ferguson Point.

Look at that! Vancouver's aquarium is a premier attraction

Stanley Park-Vancouver Parks Board
🖪 198 off C5 ✉ 2099 Beach Avenue ☎ 604/257-8400

Vancouver Aquarium
🖪 198 off C5 ✉ Stanley Park
☎ 604/685-3521 or 659-3474; www.vanaqua.org 🕐 Late Jun to early Sep daily 9:30–7; early Sep to late Jun 9:30–5
💲 Expensive 🍴 Upstream Café ($) and gift shop 🚇 Skytrain: Burrard, then bus 19 🚌 19 on West Pender or Georgia; 135 on West Hastings to Burrard Street, then connect to 19

500 m
500 yds

Wetsuit
Seawall Walk
Park Drive
Brockton Pt
Totem Poles
9 O'Clock Gun
Hallelujah Point
al Vancouver
t Club
Deadman's Island

STANLEY PARK: INSIDE INFO

Top tips Stanley Park is generally safe – one of the biggest dangers is getting lost. Much is so wild that you wouldn't consider being here in the dark, but take commonsense precautions anyway.

■ **Don't walk from downtown** – it's a long and uninteresting trek. Save your energy for walking around the park.

■ If you're not a walker, just **visit the aquarium** and the gardens near Lost Lagoon. You can rent a bicycle at the corner of Denman and West Georgia.

■ In summer, the free **Stanley Park Shuttle** (mid-Jun to late Sep daily 10–6:30) circles the sea wall, connecting all the major attractions. Buses, fueled by propane gas, leave approximately every 12–15 minutes, and the full circuit takes about 45 minutes. The 19 bus from downtown connects with the shuttle.

6 Grouse Mountain

On a first visit to Vancouver there are only two reasons for making the 40-minute journey across the Burrard Inlet from the city's downtown peninsula to North Vancouver: One is the journey itself – views from the SeaBus are impressive – and the second is Grouse Mountain, a high mountain eyrie reached by a cable car, which offers a stupendous panorama of Vancouver and its surroundings.

HIGHLIGHTS

Helijet (tel: 604/270-1484) offers 8-, 15-, 20- and 30-minute **helicopter tours** ($$$$) from the top of Grouse Mountain. **Heli-Picnics** whisk you to a secluded spot, with food from the Observatory Restaurant; a **Fly, Dine and Drive** trip flies you from downtown to dine at the Observatory, with a chauffeured limousine back.

Two Swiss-built cable cars – among North America's largest – run from the cable-car station (290m/950 feet) to the upper station (1,250m/4,100 feet) in about 10 minutes. Once up the mountain, you could spend a few minutes in the interpretive center, where your cable car ticket covers entry to the theater for an impressive video presentation that takes you on an eagle's-eye ride over southern BC. Also here is a restaurant, bistro, snack bars and gift shop, but save these for later (► Inside Info, opposite).

Summer Activities

All manner of activities are laid on in the summer – wilderness it is not. You can join easy guided strolls through the woods

Above: Grouse Mountain cable car

Left: A view of Vancouver from Grouse Mountain

(they run hourly and last around 30 minutes) or sign up for helicopter rides, paragliding, ziplining and guided mountain bike rides. Free attractions include a children's playground and the "Logging Sports," which involve chopping and other lumberjack displays. All activities are in the area near the interpretive center. Just beyond, a smaller **Peak Chairlift** rumbles upward for eight minutes to Grouse Mountain's summit (the ride is included in the cable-car ticket). On a clear day, the **views** are truly extraordinary. Not only can you see most of Vancouver, the Fraser delta and its surroundings, but also the San Juan Islands more than 161km (100 miles) away in Washington State.

🚌 194 C2 ✉ 6400 Nancy Greene Way ☎ 604/984-0661; www.grousemountain.com 🕐 Daily 9am–10pm 💰 Expensive 🍴 Cafés ($) and restaurants ($$) 🚇 SkyTrain to Waterfront, then SeaBus to Lonsdale Quay, then 236 bus from Lonsdale Quay or 232 from Phibbs Exchange

GROUSE MOUNTAIN: INSIDE INFO

Top tips Pick a good day so as to be able to enjoy the views from the summit and set off early to avoid **long lines** at the cable-car station.
■ Consider **reserving a table** at the Observatory Restaurant (tel: 604/998-4402; $$$) for dinner – cable-car rides are free with a reservation – and enjoy the experience of dining in the evening with the lights of Vancouver laid out below.

In more depth Get off the bus on the way back to Lonsdale Quay to explore the Capilano River Regional Park (➤ 70).

⑦ Museum of Anthropology

Vancouver's finest museum is a half-hour bus or taxi ride from downtown, but don't let that deter you, for the Museum of Anthropology is a magnificent modern gallery filled with a striking collection of totem poles and other artifacts created by and associated with BC coastal First Nations peoples.

Architecture

The museum forms part of the huge University of British Columbia campus, well to the west of central Vancouver. The impressive building was designed in 1976 by the distinguished North American architect Arthur Erickson. Its big, bright concrete-and-glass structure was inspired by the post-and-beam wooden dwellings of the region's First Nations peoples, whose art and culture it showcases.

Great Hall

The breathtaking Great Hall houses the world's finest collection of totem poles, most of which belonged to the Haida, Salish, Tsimshian and Kwakiutl, Aboriginal peoples who shared many common cultural and artistic traits. Through the large glass windows you look onto more totem poles framed by the waters of the Georgia Strait. Also here are two longhouses overlooking Point Grey, built according to Haida methods and aligned on the traditional north–south axis.

Masterpeice Gallery

Alongside the Great Hall is the Masterpiece Gallery, which contains beautiful pieces of aboriginal jewelry and ceremonial masks. Nearby are the Visible Storage Galleries, where some 15,000 of the museum's artifacts are contained in pull-out drawers. Also included here are items from other aboriginal cultures in the far north, Africa and Asia.

Right: A totem pole outside the Museum of Anthropology

Statues in the museum

Renewal Project

Starting in September 2008, Vancouver's finest museum has seen extensive renovation and expansion through its Renewal Project, with staged completion by spring and autumn of 2009 and a complete relaunch in January 2010, all inspired by the Winter Olympics. The project includes a new **Major Exhibit Gallery** for touring exhibitions while the greatly improved **Multiversity Galleries** (replacing the Visible Storage Galleries), due for opening in fall 2009, display cases featuring artifacts from the museum's unrivaled collection, including many from India, China and Southeast Asia. There will also be a new South Wing housing a community research suite and a state-of-the-art archeology facility; a redesigned research center; and revitalised public amenities. Funds will also cover the cost of digitisation of 35,000 objects to enhance online research access, a project on view to visitors in the Digitisation Studio.

198 off A1 ✉ 6393 NW Marine Drive
☎ 604/822-5087; 604/822-3825 for recorded information; www.moa.ubc.ca
🕐 Mid-May to early Sep daily 10–5 (also Tue 5–9); early Sep to mid-May Tue–Sun 11–5 (also Tue 5–9) 💷 Moderate 🍴 None
🚌 4, 9, 17, 25, 41, 43, 44, 49, 84, 258, 480

MUSEUM OF ANTHROPOLOGY: INSIDE INFO

Top tips Take a **4 or 10 bus** to the end of the line and on the campus follow the tree-lined East Mall from the bus stop and then turn left into NW Marine Drive. It's about a 15-minute walk.

In more depth While on the UBC campus, turn right out of the museum for a five-minute walk to the small **Nitobe Memorial Garden** (tel: 604/822-6038 or 604/822-9666; open: Mid-Mar to Oct daily 9–5, Nov to mid-Mar Mon–Sat 10–5; inexpensive, combined ticket with UBC Botanical Garden moderate), considered the world's most authentic Japanese garden outside Japan. Beyond it lies the larger university **UBC Botanical Garden** (tel: 604/822-4208 or 604/822-9666; open: mid-Mar to mid-Oct daily 9–5; mid-Oct to mid-Mar 10–3; moderate). This has five separate gardens: Asian, Alpine, Food, Herb and BC Native.

At Your Leisure

8 Gastown

Gastown is a rejuvenated city district five minutes' walk east of **Canada Place** (▶ 50). Full of cafés, bars, converted warehouses and interesting shops, it's a busy and major fixture on the tourist trail: It's also close to the seedier and, at times, downright unpleasant parts of the city en route to **Chinatown** (▶ opposite).

The area contains some of Vancouver's oldest buildings, for it was here that the city was born – the district grew up around a tavern established by "Gassy" Jack Leighton, from whom the quarter's present name derives (▶ 13). Fire ravaged the area in 1886, but the coming of the railroad in 1887 saw a new building boom. By the 1970s, however, Gastown was a sad, seedy and semiderelict Skid Row, but one whose historic buildings and proximity to downtown made it an obvious candidate for renovation.

Today the area is not quite as dynamic a city space as its planners hoped, and certainly less successful than the similar **Granville Island** redevelopment (▶ 56). This said, it's easy to see and well worth a stroll for an hour or so. Look for the plaques identifying 23 historic buildings. Most of what there is to see centers on **Water Street**, which, before Vancouver's port developed, was on the waterfront. Here you'll find a famous

Enjoying the sunshine at tables outside the Luna Café in Gastown

FOR KIDS

There is plenty to amuse children in Vancouver, but there are several attractions aimed specifically at younger visitors. Both the water slides and play areas at **Granville Island Waterpark** (tel: 604/666-5784; www.granvilleislands.com) and the adventure rides and roller coasters at **Playland** (tel: 604/252-3583; www.pne.ca) are popular with children. In Stanley Park the **Miniature Railway** and **Children's Farmyard** (tel: 604/257-8531) add to the fun for youngsters. The train rides feature replicas of historic engines and the farmyard has goats, cows and llamas. A 30-minute drive east of the city center, in Aldergrove, is the **Greater Vancouver Zoo** (604/856-6825; www.gvzoo.com) and in North Vancouver, 10 minutes' drive from downtown, **Maplewood Farm** (604/929-5610; www.maplewoodfarm.bc.ca).

steam-powered clock (1977), whose old paddle-steamer whistle hoots and shrieks every 15 minutes, and a series of specialty shops, galleries, cafés and restaurants, of which the best are the Water Street Café (➤ 76), the Old Spaghetti Factory (➤ 76) and the Inuit Gallery of Canada (➤ 78).

✚ 200 A3
Waterfront
🚇 Skytrain: Waterfront 🚌 3, 4, 6, 7, 8, 50

❾ Chinatown

Chinatown is full of tiny, crowded streets, vibrant markets, and shops full of oriental foods and medicines. It lies east from Gastown, from where the best walking route is south on Cambie, then left on Pender Street. If starting from downtown, you can follow the Silk Road Route from Library Square, a self-guiding walking route marked by colorful banners and street signs. This encircles Chinatown and takes in all the main attractions.

With a population of more than 100,000, this is the third largest Chinatown in North America after San Francisco and New York. It dates to around 1858, when Chinese immigrants flocked here during the Fraser Valley gold rush. Others followed to work on the railroad, gravitating to a district where special clan associations assisted the newcomers.

Discrimination was rife – legal rights and citizenship, for example, were denied to the Chinese until 1947, and during the 1930s white women were forbidden to work in Chinese restaurants because, in the words of the local police chief, "it is almost impossible for them to be so employed without falling victim to some immoral life."

Today Vancouver is far more racially integrated, but Chinatown retains its ethnic integrity: All the signs are in Chinese, all the buildings have a distinct Eastern tinge, and just about every resident is Chinese.

The area is mostly enclosed by Pender, Carrall, Gore and Main streets. Many people make first for the **Sam Kee Building** at the corner of Pender Street and Carrall Street, one of the world's narrowest buildings at 1.8m (6 feet) wide.

Also worth a visit is the **Dr Sun Yat-Sen Garden**, named after the founder of the first Chinese Republic, a regular visitor to Vancouver. The garden was created for Expo '86 with the help of 950 crates of materials from the People's Republic. It was the first authentic Chinese garden created outside China, and one that emulated Suzhou's classical gardens of the Ming dynasty (1368–1644). All the garden's elements, such as hard and soft, big and small, smooth and rough, and flowing and static, carefully balance. At first sight the effect is austere but after a while, the subtleties take effect, and the city outside is subsumed by the garden's peace and tranquillity.

✚ 200 A3
Dr Sun Yat-sen Classical Chinese Garden
✉ 578 Carrall Street near Pender Street
☎ 604/662-3207;
www.vancouverchinesegarden.com
🕐 Mid-May to mid-Jun and Sep daily 10–6; mid-Jun to Aug 9:30–7; Oct 10–4:30; Nov–Apr Tue–Sun 10–4:30 💵 Moderate 🍴 Café ($)
🚇 Skytrain: Stadium-Chinatown 🚌 19 or 22 east on Pender Street

Peaceful Dr Sun Yat-Sen Classical Garden

🔟 Science World

Science World's big silver geodesic dome forms a prominent part of the Vancouver skyline. Built as a pavilion for Expo '86, it now contains science-oriented displays, with plenty of hands-on exhibits guaranteed to appeal to kids. In many ways, the displays don't quite live up to the splendor of the setting and you'll need to make a special journey from downtown to get to the site. This said, if you have children in tow, the laser and 3D shows, the big-screen films in the **Omnimax Theatre**, and the various drum and musical synthesizer displays are all excellent.

➕ 200 A2 ✉ 1455 Québec Street
☎ 604/443-7443; www.scienceworld.ca
🕐 Daily 10–6 🍴 Expensive 🍴 Triple O's by White Spot ($) 🚇 SkyTrain to Science World-Main Street 🚌 3 and 8 north on Granville Mall or 19 on Pender Street

The space-age Science World building

🔟 Capilano River Regional Park

The Capilano Suspension Bridge is among the most visited attractions in the province, with around 750,000 people coming annually to cross the 137m (450 feet) swaying footbridge 70m (230 feet) above the river. Having acquired a taste for the vertiginous thrill, they can move on

FAMOUS VISITORS
Famous names who have braved the Capilano bridge include Marilyn Monroe, Katherine Hepburn, the Rolling Stones, Walter Cronkite and Margaret Thatcher – who so enjoyed the experience that she did it twice.

to the **Treetops Adventure**, crossing seven bridges suspended 30m (100 feet) above the forest floor in the rain forest canopy. The complex also includes a Living Forest exhibit, a First Nations cultural center and Totem Park, and various other diversions. It's very expensive and very touristy, and very busy at peak times, and those who prefer more tranquil surroundings are advised to continue north for the short distance to the free Capilano River Regional Park, off Nancy Greene Way. You can walk and see the river scenery for free, and it also allows you to visit the fascinating **salmon hatchery** there (signed from the entrance), built in 1977 to help spawning salmon and thus restore dwindling stocks.

The best way to include the park in a visit is to see Grouse Mountain

FIRST NATIONS CRAFT
If you are looking for interesting souvenirs to take home, there are some excellent, if somewhat pricey, First Nations craft galleries in the Gastown area of Vancouver. Alternatively, you may find some unusual and authentic pieces sold by licensed street artists in the area.

Farther Afield

12 Whistler

Whistler lies 119km (74 miles) north of Vancouver amid stunning mountain scenery and is known as one of North America's finest ski resorts. So good, in fact, that it has been chosen as the venue for the **2010 Winter Olympic** Games. During the summer, visitors come here to cycle, play golf, or hike, with cable cars and ski lifts giving access to some easy high-level walks. The resort is about 2.5 hours by car or bus from Vancouver, so a day trip is feasible, depending on how much you want to do when you get there. Accommodations are plentiful if you want to stay overnight, but can be expensive. Contact Vancouver's Touristinfo Centre (➤ 32) or the Whistler Infocentre (tel: 604/935-3357) for further information.
➕ 195 D3

and then walk or take a bus down the road (1km/0.5 mile) to the main entrance (there's another entrance at the Cleveland Dam near Grouse Mountain (➤ 64) at the park's northern limit). The Capilano Pacific trail (1.5km/1 mile) runs from the dam to the hatchery, one of several easy forest and river walks in the park. Alternatively, follow riverside trails from the hatchery to Dog's Leg Pool (1km/0.5 miles).

The park is the most accessible of several similar parks in the forests and mountains above North Vancouver: contact the visitor center for details on access, trails and other activities in Lynn Canyon, Mount Seymour, Cypress and Lighthouse parks.
➕ 198 off C5 ✉ 3735 Capilano Road, North Vancouver ☎ Suspension Bridge: 604/985-7474, www.capbridge.com Hatchery: 604/666-1790 ⏰ Suspension Bridge: May–Sep daily 8:30/9–7/8/9; Sep–early Dec daily 9–7/6/5; early Dec–early Jan daily 10–9 (closed Christmas Day); early Jan–Apr daily 9–5/6. Hatchery: Daily from 8am. Closing time varies seasonally ♿ Park: free; Suspension Bridge: expensive; Hatchery: free 🚌 236, 239 or 246 west on Georgia Street

Top: Capilano Suspension Bridge
Right: Whistler is now an all-year resort

Where to... Stay

Prices

Expect to pay per double room
$ under CDN$100 $$ CDN$101–$200 $$$ CDN$201–$300
$$$$ over CDN$300

Vancouver has the range of accommodations you'd expect from a major North American city. The most desirable hotels are close to the waterfront, while mid-range chain hotels are the best all-round choices.

▽▽▽▽ Barclay House $$–$$$

From the first sight of its bright exterior, this heritage-home bed-and-breakfast is simply stunning. Its 1904 character sets off interior furnishings and decor that is luxurious, ultramodern and supremely stylish. Most of the bedrooms have a personal lounge area, and all come with bathrobes, quality toiletries, coffee maker, WiFi, and much more. Continental and hot breakfasts are available.

🛏 198 C5 ⌖ 1351 Barclay Street, V6E 1H6
☎ 604/605-1351; www.barclayhouse.com

▽▽▽▽ The Fairmont Hotel Vancouver $$$–$$$$

The 555-room Canadian Pacific Hotel Vancouver has been a prominent fixture of the city's central downtown area for many years. Although now somewhat overshadowed by newcomers on the waterfront like the Fairmont Waterfront (▶ below), it is the accommodation of choice if you prefer a luxury hotel with a more traditional feel. Modernisation has added 21st-century amenities, such as internet access and spa. Superior Entrée Gold rooms offer still more comfort and services. General facilities include a health club with indoor swimming, whirlpool, sauna and massage.

🛏 199 E3 ⌖ 900 West Georgia Street, V6C 2W6 ☎ 604/684-3131 or 1-800/441-1414; www.fairmont.com/vancouver

▽▽▽▽ The Fairmont Waterfront $$$–$$$$

The 23-story hotel popularly known as "The Waterfront" forms part of the spectacular Canada Place development (▶ 50). About 70 percent of its 489 rooms enjoy views over the port and Burrard Inlet to the mountains above North Vancouver. Rooms are stylishly appointed with blond-wood furnishings and modern Canadian art. Facilities include a health club and outdoor pool, but it's the views and location that make this one of the city's foremost hotels.

🛏 199 E4 ⌖ 900 Canada Place Way, V6C 3L5 ☎ 604/691-1991; toll free 1-800-441-1414; www.fairmont.com/waterfront

▽▽▽▽ Four Seasons $$$–$$$

The 385-room Four Seasons sits at the top of the 200-story Pacific Centre mall at the heart of downtown's shopping and financial districts. Behind its anonymous entrance lies a luxurious interior. Rooms are fairly small, but more spacious deluxe rooms and suites are also available. The health club, swimming pool and fitness center are the best of any hotel in the city. Attention is paid to the tiniest of details – children get milk and cookies at bedtime, and pets have mineral water.

🛏 199 E3 ⌖ 791 West Georgia Street, V6C 2T4 ☎ 604/689-9333; toll free 1-800-268-6282; www.fourseasons.com/vancouver

▽▽▽ Listel Hotel $$–$$$

The Listel lies at the heart of West End Vancouver and is an attractive boutique hotel that has great style in everything from amenities to artwork. The rooms have contemporary coastal artwork and there are various culture-themed package deals. The hotel's O'Doul's Restaurant and Bar offers West Coast cuisine with international flair and with mellow jazz as the music of choice.

✚ 199 D4 ☒ 1300 Robson Street ☎ 604 684.8461; www.thelistelhotel.com

▽▽▽ Sandman Hotel Downtown $$–$$$

Sandman is a good mid-price chain group with hotels across western Canada. Its 216-room Vancouver hotel lies a little to the east of the main downtown area, close to the Vancouver Library and Queen Elizabeth Theatre, but is still within comfortable walking distance of Gastown and the central sights. Rooms are predictable and comfortable in the manner of a chain hotel, but facilities include a sauna and indoor swimming pool.

✚ 199 E3 ☒ 180 West Georgia Street, V6B 4P4 ☎ 604/681-2211; toll free 1-800-726-3626; www.sandman.ca

▽▽▽ Sylvia Hotel $–$$$

The Sylvia has a reputation as a hotel for the hip and bohemian, thanks in part to its restful, laid-back and faintly arty look and atmosphere; to its trendy address – it's right on the beach at English Bay close to Stanley Park and Denman Street; and to its appearance – its an eight-story, ivy-covered mansion in attractive weathered gray stone.

Built in 1912, this is one of the city's oldest buildings, and until World War II was western Canada's tallest structure. The 119 rooms are competitively priced – another reason for its popularity – and decorated in a variety of styles from each of the last four decades of the 20th century. The best are on the upper floors (great views), and there are 18 suites with kitchens suitable for families. The rooms in the 1980s annex are a little smarter, but have less period appeal. The hotel is a fair walk or bus ride to central downtown. To stay here in summer you'll need to make a reservation many weeks in advance.

✚ 198 B5 ☒ 1154 Gilford Street, V6G 2P6 ☎ 604/681-9321; www.sylviahotel.com

▽▽▽ Windsor Guest House $–$$

A fine old home on a quiet street right in the heart of the city, this guest house provides Victorian-style accommodations and friendly service. The house is furnished with dark wood furniture and chintz fabrics, and the lounge has lovely stained-glass windows. In keeping with the Windsor name, rooms are named after members of the British royal family. Some of the bedrooms have private bathrooms, but you may have to share. Breakfast, included in the price, might include Spanish omelet, fresh croissants, fruit and cereals. Dinner is not served, but there are plenty of good restaurants within walking distance. International guests will find that German, Dutch, French and English are among the languages spoken by the staff. Nonsmoking (except for outside decks). The Windsor operates in partnership with the nearby Douglas Guest House, which has similar rates.

✚ 199 off E1 ☒ 325 W 11th Avenue, V5Y 1T3 ☎ 604/872-3060 or 1-888/872-3060; www.dougwin.com

BED-AND-BREAKFAST

Contact a AAA or CAA Travel Agency for all your reservation needs. For information on bed-and-breakfast options check out the website of the Western Canada Bed & Breakfast Innkeepers' Association (tel: 604/255-9199; www.wcbbia.com) or visit www.bbcanada.com, which has links to some 10,000 bed-and-breakfasts.

Where to...
Eat and Drink

Prices

Expect to pay for a three-course meal for two including wine

$ under CDN$50   **$$** CDN$50–$100   **$$$** over CDN$100

Eating in Vancouver can be a rich and multicultural experience. The range of restaurants is enormous, serving a wide variety of ethnic cuisines. Virtually all bars serve food.

✦✦✦ Abigail's Party $–$$

With Kitsilano cool and an interesting fusion of styles – Italian wine bar meets English gastro-pub – Abigail's Party is a relaxing and friendly place. Its kitchen team produces interesting and eclectic dishes, with starters such as scallop and wild mushrooms or goat's cheese pavé, followed by

entrées like duck confit quesadillas, slow-braised lamb shank, Tuscan gnocchi or papaya paella. Weekend brunches include classic and some more unusual choices, which can be washed down with a coffee or a cocktail.

⊞ 198 off A1 **⊠** 1685 Yew Street
☎ 604/739-4677; www.abigailsparty.ca
🕓 Mon–Sat 5:30–2, Sun 5:30–11; Sat–Sun brunch 9–2:30

Aurora Bistro $$$

A strong West Coast ethos distinguishes this multi-award-winning restaurant with its smooth wood scenery and cool interiors.

All ingredients are locally sourced and organic. Starters include such delights as albacore tuna poached in olive oil and bedded on a salad of navy beans, pickled red onions, and smoked tomato vinaigrette, while mains feature such superb dishes as halibut cheek schnitzel and Fraser Valley lamb sirloin. For vegetarians there's a risotto of wild and cultivated mushrooms. The wine list is triumphantly British Columbian and vintages are not cruelly priced.

⊞ 200 off B1 **⊠** 2420 Main Street **☎** 604 873 9944; www.aurorabistro.ca **🕓** Dinner from 5:30pm daily, brunch Sat–Sun 10–2

✦✦✦ Bishop's $$$

Bishop's has topped just about every Vancouver restaurant poll for many years and is where the celebrities dine. Don't let this discourage you, though, as restaurants of this class and caliber ensure that everyone receives a warm and professional welcome. The food is described as "contemporary home cooking,"

which in practice means a modern fusion of a whole range of cuisines – Italian, French nouvelle cuisine, West Coast and Far Eastern. As with Lumière (▶ 75), however, you'll need to travel out here from downtown. You'll need to make a reservation a long time in advance.

⊞ 198 off A1 **⊠** 2183 West 4th Avenue near Yew Street **☎** 604/738-2025; www.bishopsonline.com **🕓** Dinner Mon–Sat 5:30–11, Sun 5:30–10

✦✦✦ C Restaurant $$–$$$

C picks up the prize for Vancouver's best fish and seafood restaurant, although it's a close-run thing with the Fish House in Stanley Park. The restaurant has a waterside setting with great views. Food, by contrast, is intense and imaginative, with a heavy Asian influence – Arctic char or sea bass, for example, might be served with a rich wrap or noodles.

⊞ 199 D3 **⊠** 1600 Howe Street near Pacific Boulevard **☎** 604/681-1164; www.crestaurant.com **🕓** Lunch Mon–Fri, dinner daily

Cardero's $$-$$$

In a great setting, on the inner harbor waterfront just off the Stanley Park Seawall, Cardero's offers an interesting menu of mostly seafood dishes. Starters might include mussels in lemongrass coconut curry sauce, honey molasses back ribs or a fishermen's platter that's perfect for sharing. After that, there are wok dishes, salads, chops and steaks, pasta, pizzas, and the house specialties: cedar-plank salmon, cooked in the wood oven, and baked lobster with lemon drawn butter.

✚ 198 C5 ⊠ 1583 Coal Harbour Quay ☎ 604/669-7666; www.carderos.com ⏰ Mon–Sat 11:30–11, Sun 11:30–10

〜〜〜 CinCin $$$

Steps lead up from Robson Street into a locals' favorite, a tasteful oasis with terracotta tiles, muraled walls, a scattering of statues and an open kitchen with alderwood-fired grill that adds subtle flavors to meat, fish and game. The food is mainly Italian – *cin cin* is Italian for "cheers" – but you can also choose between paella and a variety of other international dishes. The bar is open between meals for antipasti (appetizers) and pizza from the wood-fired oven. Wines are excellent, and all pastries, bread and ice cream are homemade.

✚ 199 D4 ⊠ 1154 Robson Street near Bute Street ☎ 604/688-7338; www.cincin.net ⏰ Dinner daily 5–11

〜〜〜〜 Le Crocodile $$-$$$

Cooking at Le Crocodile looks to hearty French bistro traditions merged with BC-sourced ingredients to produce such dishes as Provençal-style slow-braised lamb shank and fresh fettuccine with grilled tiger prawns and lobster meat, and rich, calorie-laden desserts. Standards are high and the clientele smart.

✚ 199 D3 ⊠ 909 Burrard Street (entrance on Smithe Street) ☎ 604/669-4298; www.lecrocodilerestaurant.com ⏰ Lunch Mon–Fri, dinner Mon–Sat

Dockside Restaurant $$

The popular and bustling Dockside is part of the Granville Island Hotel. There's a wood grill serving up delicious steaks, or you can settle for the finest salmon if you're there for dinner although the Dockside caters for breakfast and lunch as well. There's a waterfront patio, floor to ceiling windows and a big aquarium to entertain.

✚ 198 C2 ⊠ 1253 Johnston Street, Granville Island ☎ 604/685-7070; www. docksidebrewing.com ⏰ Daily 7am–10pm

〜〜〜 Earl's on Top $$-$$$

Wherever you find an Earl's – and there's one in most western Canadian towns – you're guaranteed a good, mid-priced meal in the company of happy locals. The Earl's in Vancouver enjoys a central location on Robson Street, the city's main thoroughfare. Service is brisk, staff are enthusiastic, the atmosphere buzzy but not too buzzy, and the eclectic menu contains ideas borrowed from Italian, North American, Mexican and Far Eastern cuisines.

✚ 199 D4 ⊠ 1185 Robson Street, corner of Bute Street ☎ 604/669-0020; www.earls.ca ⏰ Lunch and dinner daily

〜〜 Lombardo's Ristorante Pizzeria $

Don't be deterred by the mall location. You'll be rewarded with crispy brick-oven pizzas that have been rated the best in Vancouver. There are also pasta dishes, salads and sandwiches. Carry-out is available.

✚ Off map ⊠ 120–1641 Commercial Drive ☎ 604/251-2240; www.lombardos.ca ⏰ Lunch and dinner daily

〜〜〜〜 Lumière $$$

Everything about Lumière makes it a leading Canadian restaurant, from its vivid décor to its often A-list guests and, not least, its subtle merging of modern French cuisine with superb West Coast ingredients. Two set-price, multicourse tasting menus each night make a good way of sampling the balanced and immaculate contemporary French cooking. Portions here are small, however. You'll need to take a taxi, as the restaurant's some way from downtown.

🚹 198 off A1 ⊠ 2551 West Broadway near Trafalgar Street ☎ 604/739-8185; www.lumiere.ca ⏰ Dinner Tue–Sun

The Naam $

Vancouver's longest-serving vegetarian restaurant in Kitsilano has a laid-back ambience that belies the work that goes in to produce a 24-hour service This is retro-Sixties landscape in old wood and farmhouse décor, with art exhibits on the walls and classic folk, jazz and blues as background sound every night. There's an outside patio for summer dining. Breakfast starts at 6am with porridge, huge omelettes, pancakes or crêpes. Lunch and dinner spins between stir fries, nachos enchiladas, burritos, burger platters, wok dishes and curries.

🚹 198 off A1 ⊠ 2724 West 4th Street ☎ 604/738-7151; www.thenaam.com ⏰ 24 hours. Closed Christmas Day

▽▽▽ The Old Spaghetti Factory $

This old converted warehouse in Gastown frequently comes out on top – with White Spot (▲ 77) – in Vancouver newspaper polls to discover the city's best family restaurant. Food is simple and predictable – pastas, salads, steaks, chicken and the like – but well prepared. The atmosphere is informal, and the restaurant's faux Liberty style, with lots of colored glass, plants, mirrors and antique memorabilia, creates a pleasant period ambience. The restaurant's also conveniently located at the heart of Gastown.

🚹 200 A3 ⊠ 53 Water Street ☎ 604/684-1288; www.theoldspaghettifactory.ca ⏰ Lunch and dinner daily

▽▽▽ RainCity Grill $–$$$

You can't pin down this highly popular restaurant's menu or culinary influences – they change almost by the week. Suffice to say you can be sure of interesting food that's affordable in a place that's smart enough for a special occasion but not so smart that you can't join the off-the-street customers who drop by after walking around nearby English Bay. The choice of wine and beer is also good, especially wine by the glass.

🚹 198 B4 ⊠ 1193 Denman Street at Morton Street ☎ 604/685-7337; www.raincitygrill.com ⏰ Lunch and dinner daily, plus brunch Sat–Sun

▽▽▽ Water Street Café $$

Like any area aimed at tourists, Gastown has its share of bland or uninspiring cafés and restaurants. The Water Street Café is a notable exception. Right on the main street near the famous steam clock, it has a pleasant patio eating area for good weather (book ahead to be sure of a place here or by the windows inside) and good tasty bistro-style food. If you come here for lunch rather than dinner, you can sample creative pastas, super-fresh seafood (great oysters), the home-made focaccia and daily specials.

🚹 200 A3 ⊠ 300 Water Street ☎ 604/689-2832 ⏰ Lunch and dinner daily

West $$$

West's décor is chic modern, with leather-paneled walls, mirrors, and subtle lighting complementing the intimate dining experience and the superlative West Coast cuisine. Start with fresh seared Qualicum Bay scallops or a warm salad of Vancouver Island octopus, beetroot, potato and cucumber. Follow with such delectable mains as Fraser Valley veal tenderloin or grilled lobster. You can also choose from three tasting menus, including vegetarian, or settle for a fixed price choice that won't break the bank. The wine list is suitably outstanding.

🚹 199 A1 ⊠ 2881 Granville Street ☎ 604/738-8938; www.westrestaurant.com ⏰ Daily 5:30–11

White Spot $–$$

White Spot restaurants have been around for over 70 years across Vancouver and western Canada. Dishes on offer are basically glorified but high-quality fast food, and offer superb value, variety and reliability. The surroundings are also bright and modern, and enjoy a touch of style and good standards of service – you are seated and served at your table. They're also excellent for families.

🚹 199 E3 ⊠ 580 West Georgia Street
☎ 604/662-3066 🕓 Daily breakfast, lunch and dinner
🚹 199 D4 ⊠ 1616 West Georgia Street
☎ 604/681-8034 🕓 Daily breakfast, lunch and dinner

CAFÉS AND BARS

Arts Club

For something a touch quieter on Granville Island try the Backstage Lounge, part of the Arts Club theater complex. The food's good and there's live music some nights.

🚹 198 C2 ⊠ 1585 Johnson Street, Granville Island ☎ 604/687-1354; www.thebackstagelounge.com 🕓 Daily noon–midnight (also Thu–Fri midnight–2am)

La Bodega

La Bodega is a long-established Spanish bar that looks and feels the part – lots of noise, animation, sangria and fun. It's deservedly popular, so come early for a seat. Tapas – some of the city's best – and other food are available, but most people are here to drink and chat.

🚹 199 D3 ⊠ 1277 Howe Street near Davie Street ☎ 604/684-8815; www.labodegavancouver.com 🕓 Mon–Fri 4:30pm–midnight, Sat 5–midnight, Sun 5–11pm

Bread Garden

The original Bread Garden café formula – healthy food, snacks, coffee, cold drinks, cakes and the like – was so successful that there are now outlets across the city.

🚹 199 D4 ⊠ 812 Bute Street at Robson Street ☎ 604/688-3213; www.breadgarden.com ⊠ 1040 Denman Street ☎ 604/685-2996 🕓 812 Bute branch open 24 hours daily

Caffè Artigiano

The baristas here 'paint' motifs on the final pour of your latte or cappuccino with deceptive skill. Brick laid tables and Italian decor enhance the creative vibe and there's an outside patio. Tasty snacks and cakes are available.

🚹 199 E4 ⊠ 763 Hornby Street (Branches at 1101 West Pender Street, 740 West Hastings Street, 574 Granville Street
☎ 604/694-7737 🕓 Mon–Fri 6:30am–7:30pm, Sat 7–7, Sun 7–6

Gallery Café

The café at the Vancouver Art Gallery is a great central place for coffee, lunch or snacks whether or not you're visiting the gallery.

🚹 199 E3 ⊠ Vancouver Art Gallery, 750 Hornby Street ☎ 604/688-2233; www.gallerycafe.com 🕓 Mon–Sat 9–5:30 (also Thu 5:30–9), Sun 10–5:30

900 West

The big bar, wine bar and restaurant off the main lobby of the central Fairmont Hotel Vancouver is a favorite place to meet for a drink, snack or evening cocktail. Some 50 wines are available by the glass.

🚹 199 E3 ⊠ 900 West Georgia Street ☎ 604/684-3131 🕓 Sun–Thu 11:30am–midnight, Fri, Sat 11:30am–1am

Sylvia

The bar in the Sylvia Hotel (▶ 73) is low key, but that's one of the things that make it popular. Close to the beach, it's a relaxing place for a rendezvous and a quiet drink.

🚹 198 B5 ⊠ Sylvia Hotel, 1154 Gilford Street ☎ 604/681-9321; www.sylviahotel.com 🕓 Daily 11:30am–midnight

Yaletown Brewing Company

A vast pub-restaurant-brewery on a sizable part of the Yaletown district.

🚹 199 D2 ⊠ 1111 Mainland Street ☎ 604/681-2739; www.drinkfreshbeer.com 🕓 Daily 11:30am–midnight (also Thu midnight–1am, Fri, Sat midnight–2am)

Where to... Shop

Vancouver is one of North America's premier shopping destinations. You will find smart department stores and malls, and all the world's great names in fashion and design have shops here. Specialty shops sell crafts and aboriginal artifacts, and there are markets and neighborhood stores where you can buy ethnic foods and general goods.

Chapters

This huge modern bookstore has forced traditional Vancouver bookstores such as Duthie's from the city center – and no wonder, for it's big, bright and browser-friendly with a vast stock and helpful staff. Make this your first stop in the city for all books, maps and guides. It's also open to 11pm daily.

🏠 199 D3 ⬜ 788 Robson Street, corner of Howe 📞 604/682-4066; www.chapters.ca 🚃 5, 17, 20 on Robson

Chintz & Company

This large store just north of trendy Yaletown is crammed with treasures for the home: fabrics, furnishings, accessories, giftware and antique or original beds, wardrobes, tables and other pieces of furniture. It also sells smaller items such as candles, lamps and assorted objets d'art.

🏠 199 D2 ⬜ 950 Homer Street 📞 604/689-2022; www.chintz.com 🚃 2, 15, 17

ABORIGINAL ART

Coastal Peoples Fine Arts Gallery

This was one of the first of several galleries in the emerging Yaletown warehouse district. A light, airy space, it deals in a aboriginal art and artifacts by established and emerging artists. It is particularly recommended for its exquisite gold,

silver and other jewelry.

🏠 199 D2 ⬜ 1024 Mainland Street 📞 604/685-9298; www.coastalpeoples.com 🚃 2, 15, 17

Hill's Native Art

This is the largest of four Hill's galleries, with three floors of First Nations arts and crafts, including a huge range of clothing, Inuit sculptures, jewelry, carvings, blankets, drums and books. Everything in the store has been purchased direct from the artist or artisan. Worldwide shipping is available.

🏠 199 F3 ⬜ 165 Water Street 📞 604/685-4249; www.hillsnativeart.com 🕐 Daily 9–9 🚃 1 or 50 🚉 Waterfront

Inuit Gallery of Canada

This gallery has been a Gastown fixture for years, its exhibits representing some of the best Inuit and other aboriginal art in Canada. Prices are high – justifiably so, given the quality – and even if you can't afford to make a purchase it's

worth coming here just to look.

🏠 200 A3 ⬜ 206 Cambie Street, Gastown 📞 604/688-7323; www.inuit.com 🚃 1 or 50

FOOD MARKETS

Granville Island Public Market

One of North America's finest food markets, this covered hall should not be missed, whether or not you actually want to buy anything from the stunning array of meat, fish, cheese, fruit, wine and specialist food stalls. Much of the food on display can be bought cooked or prepared from the variety of food counters and eaten outdoors overlooking the waters of False Creek.

🏠 198 C2 ⬜ Granville Island 📞 604/666-5784; www.granvilleisland.com 🕐 Daily 9–7 🚃 50, 51

Lonsdale Quay Market

A trip across Burrard Inlet aboard the SeaBus is an essential part of a visit to Vancouver. The ferry docks at Lonsdale Quay just steps from

Where to... 79

this market. Although not quite as impressive as Granville Island's covered food hall, this is still a great place to explore. There are plenty of food counters and outdoor eating with great views across the water. Craft, book and gift stores are on the upper levels.

➕ 200 off C5 ⊠ Lonsdale Quay, 123 Carrie Cates Court, North Vancouver ☎ 604/985-6261; www.lonsdalequay.com ⏰ Sat–Thu 9:30–6:30 (also Fri 6:30–9pm) 🚇 SeaBus from Waterfront

SPECIALTY STORES

Blackberry Books

Vancouver has far bigger bookstores, but none where it is quite such a pleasure to browse as this tiny store on Granville Island. Art, architecture and cooking are specialty areas, but you'll also find a good selection of novels, guides and general titles.

➕ 198 C2 ⊠ 1666 Johnston Street, Unit 3, Net Loft Building, Granville Island ☎ 604/685-4113; www.bbooks.ca 🚇 51

Edible British Columbia

Based in Granville Market and fast-growing in popularity, this unique take on sustainability offers terrific local produce from best wines to preserves, spices and sauces. They also do take-out meals.

➕ 198 C2 ⊠ 565, 1689 Johnston Street ☎ 604/662-3606; www.edible-britishcolumbia.com 🚇 51

Lululemon Athletica

Fashion meets fitness at this temple to stylish tech clothing for yoga, dance and running. And you don't need to be a sports' fanatic to look good in the svelte range that includes tank tops and hoodies, yoga pants, running hats, tote bags and many other accessories that might even make you break into a gentle jog.

➕ 199 D4 ⊠ 1148 Robson Street ☎ 604/681-3118; www.lululemon.com

Murchie's Tea & Coffee

Vancouverites have been coming to Murchie's for their tea and coffee for more than a century. It also sells china, crystal and a selection of teapots and coffeemakers.

➕ 199 E3 ⊠ 825 W Pender Street ☎ 604/669-0783; www.murchies.com 🚇 8

The Bay

The Bay has outlets in most Canadian cities, the chain being a direct descendant of the trading post of the Hudson's Bay Company. Its Vancouver store occupies a period building that looks tired, but the merchandise is of high quality.

➕ 199 E3 ⊠ 674 Granville Street at Georgia Street ☎ 604/681-6211; www.hbc.com 🚇 Granville 🚇 8

Salmon Village

This one-stop salmon outlet offers some delicious wild sockeye smoked salmon and even smoked salmon candy that's been soaked in maple syrup and sprinkled with black pepper. For take-home gifts the best bet is salmon jerky, long-smoked and with a long shelf life.

➕ 199 D4 ⊠ 779 Thurlow Street ☎ 604/988-8785; www.salmonvillage.com 🚇 51

MALLS

Pacific Centre Mall

One of Vancouver's best malls, this three-block affair has more than 200 shops and links underground to the Vancouver Centre mall at 650 West Georgia Street, which has a further 115 stores.

➕ 199 D3 ⊠ 609 Granville Street ☎ 604/688-7236; www.pacificcentre.com 🚇 Granville

Sinclair Centre

This sophisticated mall combines four converted historic buildings – the Post Office (1910), Federal Building (1937), Winch Building and Customs Warehouse (1913). Stores include fashion and accessories. There is a food court.

➕ 199 E4 ⊠ 757 West Hastings Street ☎ 604/488-0617; www.sinclaircentre.com 🚇 Waterfront

Where to...
Be Entertained

Whenever you visit Vancouver you are sure to find a variety of music, dance, theater, opera and movies.

CLASSICAL MUSIC

The Vancouver Symphony Orchestra (tel: 604/876-3434; www.vancouversymphony.ca) generally performs at the Orpheum Theatre (801 Granville Street). The Vancouver Opera (tel: 604/683-0222; www.vanopera.bc.ca) holds its October-to-June season of concerts at the Queen Elizabeth Complex (600 Hamilton Street).

Smaller but well-respected ensembles include the Vancouver Chamber Choir (tel: 604/738-6822; www.vancouverchamberchoir.

com); Early Music Vancouver (tel: 604/732-1610; www.earlymusic. bc.ca); Vancouver Recital Society (tel: 604/602-0363; www.vanrecital. com); and the Vancouver New Music Society (tel: 604/663-0861; www.newmusic.org).

THEATER

Vancouver's largest company is the Playhouse Theatre Company (tel: 604/873-3311; www. vancouverplayhouse.com), which performs at the Queen Elizabeth Complex. Another leading mainstream concern is the Arts Club Theatre (tel: 604/687-1644) on Granville Island, which has a 425-seat main stage and smaller Revue Club Stage. Also popular in summer are

the Bard on the Beach (604/739-0559 or 1-877/739-0559; www. bardonthebeach.org) outdoor shows in Stanley Park (late May to late Sep). Among the many fringe companies, look out for productions at the Firehall Arts Centre (280 East Cordova Street, tel: 604/689-0926).

MOVIE HOUSES

The most central movie houses and multiplex screens are on Burrard and Granville streets near the intersection with Robson Street. For classic, foreign and alternative films, try the Pacific Cinémathèque (1131 Howe Street, tel: 604/688-3456; www.cinematheque.bc.ca), also the headquarters of the Vancouver International Film Festival (late Sep to mid-Oct).

CLUBS & LIVE MUSIC

Vancouver's club, dance and music scene is vibrant, which means the coolest places change regularly.

For mainstream sounds try Plaza Club (881 Granville Street; tel: 604/646-0064; www.plazaclub.net) and for a lively club visit the Roxy (932 Granville Street, tel: 604/331-7999). Fashionable venues are Bar None (1222 Hamilton Street; tel: 604/689-7000; www.dhmbars. ca) and Republic (958 Granville Street; tel: 604/669-3266; www. dhmbars.ca).

INFORMATION AND TICKETS

The main listings magazines are the weekly *Georgia Straight* and monthly *Vancouver Magazine*, both available free from bookstores, libraries, venues and curbside boxes. Alternatively, contact the Arts Hotline (#100–938 Howe Street, tel: 604/684-2787; www. allianceforarts.com) or Ticketmaster (tel: 604/682-8455; www. ticketmaster.ca), which has some 40 city outlets.

Victoria

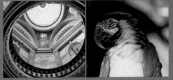

Getting Your Bearings

Victoria has evolved from its longstanding incarnation as a Little England overseas into a vibrant cosmopolitan city. Its role as the capital of British Columbia is belied by its modest size and absence of urban angst, overwhelming skyscrapers or frantic traffic. Life revolves around the natural harbor and between the stately enclave of the Parliament Buildings and the attractive downtown area around Government Street.

To some extent, of course, Victoria still promotes a rather stagy Britishness overlaid with sentimentality. Never has there been a taller, more elegant makeover of Queen Victoria than the statue that stands in front of the Parliament Buildings. Expensive afternoon tea is still a major feature of the Empress Hotel and the Union Jack motif still pops up here and there. But modern Victoria is a unique Canadian city that mixes the best of tradition with up-to-date style and that boasts outstanding attractions.

Foremost among these are the Royal British Columbia Museum, one of Canada's finest museums, and the glorious Butchart Gardens, but the city is equally renowned for its whale-watching, its mellow climate, its fine cafés and restaurants and – best of all – the pedestrian-friendly appeal of its old-fashioned streets and hidden historic corners.

★ Don't Miss

1. Inner Harbour ➤ 86
2. Old Town ➤ 88
3. Royal British Columbia Museum ➤ 90
4. Butchart Gardens ➤ 93

At Your Leisure

5. Pacific Undersea Gardens ➤ 95
6. Miniature World ➤ 95
7. Art Gallery of Greater Victoria ➤ 95
8. Helmcken House ➤ 96
9. Beacon Hill Park ➤ 96
10. Craigdarroch Castle ➤ 97

Farther Afield

11. Pacific Rim National Park ➤ 98

JOHNSON ST BRIDGE

Centennial Square

City Hall

Pandora Avenue

JOHNSON STREET

Maritime Museum

Yates St

STORE Street

WHARF Street

View St

Inner Harbour 1

2 Old Town

GOVERNMENT Street

DOUGLAS Street

Fort St

Art Gallery of Greater Victoria 7

Craigdarroch Castle 10

BLANSHARD STREET

James Bay

Public Library

Humbold Street

5 Pacific Undersea Gardens

6 Miniature World

Belleville Street

Royal British Columbia Museum 3

Crystal Garden

Humbold Street

BC Legislative Buildings

8 Helmcken House

Government Street

Superior St

DOUGLAS STREET

SOUTHGATE ST

0 ___ 300 m
0 ___ 300 yds

Beacon Hill Park 9

Page 81: Detail of a totem pole in Beacon Hill Park

In Two Days

If you're not quite sure where to begin your travels, this itinerary recommends a practical and enjoyable two-day tour of Victoria, taking in some of the best places to see using the Getting Your Bearings map on the previous page. For more information see the main entries.

Day One

Morning
Walk to the ❶ Inner Harbour (➤ 86–87) first and call in at the Visitor Centre first. If you'd like a whale-watching venture, reserve a trip here for this afternoon or tomorrow afternoon. Spend the morning exploring the Inner Harbour and the ❷ Old Town (➤ 88–89), especially the Parliament Buildings (top right), Maritime Museum and Market Square. You could squeeze in the ❸ Royal British Columbia Museum (➤ 90–92) – particularly if you're whale-watching tomorrow – but it's best kept for tomorrow morning or this afternoon if you're not whale-watching.

Lunch
For a light lunch, try the Re-Bar (➤ 103) or a café such as Murchie's Tea & Coffee (➤ 103).

Afternoon
Devote the afternoon either to a whale-watching trip or the Royal British Columbia Museum, and if you choose the latter consider a break from sightseeing with tea in the Empress Hotel (above; ➤ 100) or, if that's too expensive, in the museum's own attractive café.

Evening
Take an early dinner close to the Inner Harbour. Good but busy choices in town are Café Brio (➤ 102) and Pagliacci's (➤ 102). If the weather's good spend time after dinner wandering around the Inner Harbour to take in the sunset, the people-watching opportunities and the street performers.

Day Two

Morning

The morning, when you're fresh, is the best time to enjoy the **3 Royal British Columbia Museum** (➤ 90–92). Outside, you'll see a fine totem pole. If you have time and it is open look around **8 Helmcken House** (➤ 96) just outside the museum in Thunderbird Park and perhaps explore some of the other sights nearby such as the **5 Pacific Undersea Gardens** (➤ 95).

Lunch

Take lunch in the Museum Café, or stroll around the harbor to one of the Old Town's pubs or cafés (➤ 103). Better still, buy a picnic and eat it on the Inner Harbour or in Beacon Hill Park.

Afternoon

You may want to spend the afternoon whale-watching – most trips take around three hours. Alternatively, take a tour, taxi or bus ride to the **4 Butchart Gardens** (left; ➤ 93–94), devote an hour or two strolling in **9 Beacon Hill Park** (➤ 96–97) or visit the city's other more outlying sights such as **10 Craigdarroch Castle** (➤ 97).

WHALE-WATCHING COMPANIES

Cuda Marine (tel: 250/995-2832; www.whalewatchingadventure.com)
Five Star Whale Watching (tel: 250/386-3253; www.5starwhales.com)
Great Pacific (tel: 250/386-2277; www.greatpacificadventures.com)
Ocean Explorations (tel: 250/383-6722; www.oceanexplorations.com)
Orca Spirit (tel: 250/383-8411; www.orcaspirit.com)
Wildcat (tel: 250/384-9998; www.wildcat-adventures.com)

Evening

Return to Vancouver. or enjoy a leisurely dinner in one of Victoria's restaurants before continuing your travels the next day.

⓪ Inner Harbour

The lovely Inner Harbour is the heart of Victoria, a sweeping waterfront that contains several of the city's best-known landmarks – the Empress Hotel, Parliament Buildings and Royal British Columbia Museum – but is equally pleasant just to wander, particularly in the evening, when the gardens and promenades are full of people and street entertainers.

Early Settlement

The harbor area was Victoria's focus from earliest times. The region's original Salish people lived in 10 scattered villages, and it was the site's perfect anchorage as well as its beautiful natural surroundings that persuaded James Douglas, head of the powerful Hudson's Bay Company, to create a new local headquarters for the company here in 1842.

In time a settlement grew up around the company fort. Initially named Fort Camouson, the stockade was later renamed Fort Victoria to honor the British queen. During the 1850s, the settlement and port boomed on the back of the gold rush on the BC mainland. By the time the gold rush faded, Victoria was firmly on the map, and in 1866 was an obvious candidate for the capital of the new Crown Colony of British Columbia. Since then, the tiny provincial capital has barely looked back.

Explore the Area

First stop on any tour of Victoria should be the **Visitor Centre**, which has a wealth of information on the city, its surroundings and Vancouver Island in general. Spend some time exploring the harbor area and Old Town (➤ 88) before seeing the Royal British Columbia Museum (➤ 90).

Above: The Parliament Buildings are illuminated at night

Opposite the Visitor Centre is the massive **Empress Hotel**, opened in 1908 and an unmissable city landmark ever since. There's not a lot to see, but it's worth wandering through some of the lobbies and lounges to soak up their colonial splendor. The Palm Court has a lovely stained-glass dome, and the Crystal Ballroom and Bengal Lounge with its conservatory filled with tropical plants are worth seeking out.

Parliament Buildings

A short walk away on the harbor's southern edge are the Parliament Buildings, BC's provincial legislature, as big and prominent a landmark as the Empress. The two structures were designed by the same man – Francis Rattenbury. Free and absorbing guided tours of the interior are available in summer although, for most people, it's enough just to enjoy the gardens and the exterior. Notice the statue on top of the

dome – George Vancouver – and the two figures guarding
the main door: One is Sir James Douglas, the other Judge Sir
Matthew Baillie Begbie, who acquired the nickname of the
"Hanging Judge" for his severity during the turbulent days of
the gold rush.

TAKING A BREAK

If you want to take tea – one of Victoria's key rituals – you
could try the **Empress Hotel's Tea Lounge**. It's expensive and
touristy, however, and there's a dress code.

➕ 201 B3
Visitor Centre
✉ 812 Wharf Street ☎ 250/953-2033; accommodations reservations toll free
in Canada and the US 1-800-663-3883; www.tourismvictoria.com ⏰ Jun–Aug
8:30–8:30, Sep–May 9–5 🚌 5, 6, 27, 28, 30, 31

Top right:
Inner Harbour

Parliament Buildings
✉ 501 Belleville Street ☎ 250/387-3046 ⏰ Daily 8:30–5. Closed weekends
Oct–Apr. Call for times of guided tours 🎟 Free G5, 27, 28 or 30

THE INNER HARBOUR: INSIDE INFO

Top tips Be sure to visit the waterfront in the evening to watch the sun go
down and enjoy the **street life**.
■ Take a ride in one of the tiny **ferries** that buzz around the harbor.

In more depth The upper promenade wall above the inner harbor features
a series of fascinating plaques, known as the 'Parade of Ships', that detail
famous vessels and maritime events. A handsome statue of the great seaman
James Cook holds center stage. Hugely entertaining buskers perform nightly
on the lower promenade

2 Old Town

Victoria is barely a city at all – which is one of its great charms – but rather an intimate, old-fashioned-looking town with none of the rigid street grids and high-rise buildings of most other North American cities. Its most charming corners lie in the handful of streets behind the Inner Harbour (▶ 86), notably Wharf, Government and Douglas, just a few minutes' stroll away. For details of a walk around the Old Town turn to the Walks section (▶ 179). Alternatively, wander north from the Visitor Centre and harbor on Wharf Street and begin your exploration in Bastion Square, an ensemble of old streets and buildings built close to the site of the northeasternmost bastion of the Hudson's Bay Company's original Fort Victoria.

Maritime Museum

Among the square's many pretty buildings is the former provincial courthouse (1889), site of the city jail and the spot where public hangings took place. These days it plays host to the Maritime Museum, home to a good collection of model boats, period photographs, ships' bells and other maritime memorabilia. On the top floor you can see the old courthouse, reached by a special open elevator: It was commissioned by Chief Justice Davie in 1901, reputedly because he was too portly to manage the stairs.

Market Square

From the museum, walk to Government Street and head north, turning left onto Johnson Street and Market Square. Today the latter is a wonderfully restored period complex filled with cafés, restaurants and interesting little shops, but in 1858 it was the turbulent heart of the old town. You'll notice that the square's central courtyard area is sunk down, the depression marking the site of a former ravine. To its north lay Chinatown, the oldest such enclave in western North America. The whole area was once filled with brothels, stores, saloons and opium

dens, not to mention some 23 factories that turned out around 44 tons of opium a year (the trade, legal until the 20th century, constituted one of BC's lucrative exports).

Chinatown

Today's Chinatown, a couple of blocks north, off Fisgard Street, is considerably smaller and tamer than in times past. Its best street is Fan Tan Alley, full of tiny stores: Don't miss the two stone chimeras by the Gate of Harmonious Interest. They were a gift from Suzhou in China, and legend says they will come to life when an honest politician walks between them.

Above: The Bridgman Building

Middle: A mural in Bastion Square

Government Street

Little to the north of Fisgard Street is really worth the walk, so head south on Government Street or Wharf Street toward the Inner Harbour. Government Street is busier, and is lined with most of Victoria's major stores. Three, at least, are worth making a special point of seeing: Old Morris Tobacconist at 1116 Government, a lovely old cigar and tobacco shop little changed since it was founded in 1892; Murchie's Tea & Coffee almost next door at 1110, source of Victoria's best tea, coffee, cakes and snacks since 1892;

and Munro's Books at 1108, not the biggest but certainly the most civilised bookstore in the city.

TAKING A BREAK

The best place to relax over coffee, if the weather is good, is **Bastion Square** where there are several cafés.

Left: A sculpture by Luis Merino in Market Square

Maritime Museum

🔼 201 B4 ✉ 28 Bastion Square ☎ 250/385-4222; www.mmbc.bc.ca
🕐 Daily 9:30–4:30 💲 Moderate 🍴 Re-Bar or Murchie's (➤ 103) 🚌 5

THE OLD TOWN: INSIDE INFO

Top tip The Old Town has many mock British pubs, but with the exception of the popular Sticky Wicket (➤ 103), most are poor pastiches of the real thing.

❸ Royal British Columbia Museum

This superb museum has been called the best in Canada and one of the top 10 in North America. Its displays embrace the myriad strands of BC's social, cultural and natural history, with emphasis on the province's aboriginal peoples and many natural habitats. It also hosts major touring exhibitions.

Visiting the Museum

You could easily spend a morning or more here, but to do the collection justice – and to escape the tortures of museum fatigue – it may be better to make two separate visits: one to the **Natural History Gallery** and **First Peoples Gallery**; the other to the **Modern History Gallery**. None of the galleries should really be missed.

The Natural History Gallery

The Gallery opens in tremendous style – with a life-size woolly mammoth complete with ominous tusks. Behind it is a skillfully painted landscape evoking the animal's one-time domain, a device that sets the tone for the wonderfully evocative series of dioramas, or re-created landscapes, that follow. In theory, the idea of recreating some of BC's many habitats inside a building sounds nonsensical: In practice the idea is a triumph.

Laid out before you in huge rooms are shorelines, delta landscapes and temperate, coastal, subalpine and boreal forest environments. Each has the animals, trees, vegetation – even the sounds and temperature – appropriate to the individual habitats. Linked with the displays is a welter of audio-visual information explaining the natural nuances of a province that

A replica of part of HMS *Discovery* in the Modern History Gallery

contains Canada's warmest coastline – all 25,599km (15,900 miles) of it – wettest mountains, deepest snowfall and driest interior. Don't skip the film on the life of the beaver.

Other Galleries

The Ocean Station focuses on the surprisingly colorful marine life of British Columbia. The gallery has been designed like a Captain Nemo-style submarine, complete with hatches and controls, from where visitors can peer through portholes at sea creatures and scan the underwater scene with a periscope. A huge hexagonal hatch looks out on a sea-wall diorama populated by all kinds of marine life, and there are lots of hands-on exhibits, from computer games to dry sea stars. The IMAX theater has a companion film, *Deep Sea*, narrated by Johnny Depp and Kate Winslet.

Above: A re-created home brings the past to life

Just as memorable are the exhibits of the **First Peoples Gallery**. Many museums in North America tackle First Peoples, or aboriginal culture, but none as successfully as this one – the displays provide an account of the history and culture of the region's Pacific coastal peoples. The exhibits divide into two sections: One relating to the era before the coming of European settlers, the second to the period after settlement, when aboriginal culture was devastated by disease and land treaties that remain controversial to this day. The thousands of exhibits are dimly lit, and the background colors deliberately muted, creating a reverential and occasionally somber mood that seems somehow appropriate to the material displayed.

The highlights are numerous, but don't miss the short film footage from 1914 entitled In the *Land of the War Canoes* and the reconstructed plankhouse of Chief Kwakwabalasami, in which there's an excellent audiovisual display evoking shamanic, superstitious and other aboriginal beliefs through song, dance and costume. As a complement to this section, spend some time in **Thunderbird Park**, the ground in front of

Right: A detail of one of the totems in Thunderbird Park

A replica
Chinatown
street

Below: Totems
in Thunderbird
Park

the museum. It contains a reproduction tribal "bighouse," or ceremonial hall, and several totems.

The museum's second floor contains most of the **Modern History Gallery**, whose striking and extensive displays explore BC's history after the arrival of European settlers. The gallery is arranged in reverse chronological order.

If the arrangement of displays is somewhat eccentric, however, the displays themselves are superb. Numerous dioramas are used to fine effect, with tableaux that reproduce a full-size Victorian street, Chinatown, an old movie theater, an early fish-canning factory and many more. All aspects of the province are explored, from farming and fishing to logging, mining and the gold rushes of the 19th century. Each theme is illustrated with a wealth of period artifacts, memorabilia and interesting audiovisual displays.

➕ 201 B3 ✉ 675 Belleville Street ☎ 250/356-7226 or 1-888/447-7977; www.royalbcmuseum.bc.ca
🕐 Daily 9–5, Fri, Sat until 10 (IMAX 10–8) 💰 Expensive
🍴 Café ($) 🚌 5, 27, 28, 30, 31

ROYAL BRITISH COLUMBIA MUSEUM: INSIDE INFO

Top tips If time is limited, check whether your visit coincides with one of the 1.5-hour **Highlights** tours of the museum (4 or 5 a month).
■ **Wheelchairs and strollers** are available free of charge from the coat check.
■ **Kids' activity sheets** can be downloaded and printed from the website.

In more depth Guided tours focussing on either the First Peoples Gallery, the Modern History Gallery or the Natural History Gallery are available on certain days.

④ Butchart Gardens

The Butchart Gardens lie about 21km (13 miles) north of central Victoria, and represent the single most impressive gardens in a city that is often called the "City of Gardens." In 2006 they were designated a National Historic Site of Canada, and are unmissable, even if you have only a passing interest in things horticultural.

Wonderful borders in the gardens

The gardens were begun by Jenny Butchart to landscape an exhausted limestone quarry belonging to her husband, Robert Pim Butchart, a mine owner and one of the pioneers of Portland cement in Canada and the US. Jenny's earliest efforts resulted in the Sunken Gardens, opened to the public in 1904. Japanese, Rose and Italian gardens soon followed. Today the site is run by the couple's grandson, covers some 22ha (55 acres), and attracts around 500,000 visitors a year.

The floral display is spectacular – you'll see glorious pictures of the gardens all over Victoria – and embraces around 700 different species and more than a million individual plants, trees and shrubs.

If you come here in the summer months you'll be able to enjoy various other attractions, such as musical entertainment and fireworks displays, designed to enhance the garden's appeal.

TAKING A BREAK

There's a choice of three refreshment places; the inexpensive **Coffee Shop**, the **Blue Poppy** cafeteria and the smart **Dining Room restaurant** in the Butcharts' elegant former home.

➕ 194 C1 ✉ 800 Benvenuto Avenue, Brentwood Bay ☎ 250/652-4422; recorded information 250/652-5256; www.butchartgardens.com 🕐 Daily from 9am; closing time varies seasonally 💰 Expensive 🍽 Coffee Shop ($), Blue Poppy Restaurant ($–$$), Dining Room ($$$) 🚌 75 Central Saanich; Gray Lines shuttle May–Oct (700 Douglas), Pacific Coach Lines mid-Apr to mid-Oct daily 9:30; tickets for both services include admission to gardens

The Butchart Gardens are a brilliant spectacle at any time of the year

BUTCHART GARDENS: INSIDE INFO

Top tips Be warned that **the gardens are busy** – late afternoons are generally the quietest time to visit during summer, except fireworks nights.
■ Most of the plants are labeled, but it's well worth picking up **leaflets** (in 18 different languages) at the visitor center.
■ From mid-June until the end of September thousands of tiny lights illuminate the gardens during **specially extended evening opening times**. During the same period free musical and variety entertainments are held in the evenings from Monday to Saturday, while on Saturday evenings in July and August the gardens are the setting for spectacular fireworks displays.

In more depth At any time of the year, you should pay a visit to the on-site **Seed & Gift Store** which, as well as selling seeds of some of the gardens' plants, has an impressive range of books, gardening implements, cards, calendars, plant catalogs and numerous other gifts.

At Your Leisure

5 Pacific Undersea Gardens

This undersea observatory is one of Victoria's more popular attractions, especially with children. You can see 5,000 different species through the windowed corridors 4.5m (15 feet) below the surface; everything from salmon, sturgeon and starfish to dogfish sharks, wolf eels, red snapper, sea anemones and – star of the show – one of the world's largest captive octopuses. Scuba divers flit almost among the fish, feeding them, while in the adjacent pens you can watch injured seals being treated.

✚ 201 B3 ✉ 490 Belleville Street
☎ 250/382-5717; www.pacificundersea
gardens.com 🕑 Apr–Jun daily 10–6; Jun–Sep 9–8; Sep–Apr 10–5 💲 Moderate 🚌 5, 27, 28, 30, 31

6 Miniature World

Like Pacific Undersea Gardens, this is a children's favorite. In the Empress Hotel complex (➤ 100), its highlights are the world's largest dollhouse – a 50-room affair built in 1880 – and the world's longest model railroad. The latter compresses the 8,000km (5,000 miles) of Canada's transcontinental railway into 34m (37 yards). It took 12,000 working hours to build and cost $100,000. Other exhibits include miniature tableaux of famous battles, Charles Dickens' London, a circus and the Wild West.

✚ 201 B3 ✉ 649 Humboldt Street
☎ 250/385-9731; www.miniatureworld.com
🕑 Jul–Sep daily 8:30am–9pm; May–Jun 9–7; Oct–Apr 9–5 💲 Moderate 🚌 5, 27, 28 or 30 💲 Expensive 🍴 Crystal Tea Garden $ 🚌 5, 27, 28, 30, 31

7 Art Gallery of Greater Victoria

Victoria's public gallery is a delightful venue and one of Canada's finest smaller art museums. It's located about 1.5km (1 mile) inland to the east of the harbor but is an easy walk and there is a nearby bus connection. The gallery is housed in a modern complex attached to a handsome old mansion. There is a large permanent collection of art from Asia, Europe and North America, but the work on display is mainly from Canada and Japan. There is, inevitably, a focus on Emily Carr, the doyen of Canadian women artists and the small, intimate Drury room at the heart of the gallery is devoted to her compelling paintings of the British Columbian wilderness. Typically dark, swirling works, such as *Lone*

Above: Sea anemones at Pacific Undersea Gardens. Below: One of Miniature World's intricate exhibits

Cedar, are matched by such brighter more optimistic works as *Brittany Coast*, 1911, reflecting Carr's time spent in Brittany and Cornwall. There is also a permanent exhibition of Japanese art. Primarily the gallery has a program of changing exhibitions, often of bold, innovative work by modern artists. The adjoining Gyppeswick House has period furnishings and a delightful small garden.

➕ 201 off C3 ✉ 1040 Moss Street ☎ 250/384-4101; www.aggv.bc.ca 🕐 Mid-May to Aug Fri–Wed 10–5, Thu 10–9; Sep to mid-May Tue–Sat 10–5, Thu 10–9, Sun noon–5 💲 Expensive (by donation on first Tue each month) 🚌 11

🔢 Helmcken House

Helmcken House is the oldest home on Vancouver Island. Located in the shadow of the **Royal British Columbia Museum** (➤ 90), it was built in 1852 by Dr John Helmcken, Fort Victoria's doctor, for his bride Cecilia, daughter of Governor James Douglas (who donated an acre of land to the couple). It's worth seeing for its pretty furniture, artifacts and Victorian knick-knacks.

Behind the house is another attractive old building, the white St Anne's Pioneer Schoolhouse, former home to four Québec nuns who came to teach in Victoria in 1858.

➕ 201 B3 ✉ Thunderbird Park, Douglas and Belleville streets ☎ 250/361-0021 🕐 Open on scheduled dates; call for information 🚌 5, 30, 31

Below: Helmcken House, built in 1852, is one of the oldest houses in the region

🔢 Beacon Hill Park

Too many people miss Victoria's magnificent city park, despite the fact that it's only a few minutes' walk up the hill behind the **Royal British Columbia Museum** (➤ 90). Don't make the same mistake. This is one of North America's most appealing parks, not merely because of its pretty mixture of parkland, woods, leafy glades and open meadow, but also because it affords superlative views on its southern flanks across the Juan de Fuca Strait to the Olympic Mountains of Washington State.

The 200-acre (81ha) park dates from a gift of land made by the Hudson's Bay Company to the city back in 1882. Like Vancouver's rambling **Stanley Park** (➤ 60), much of the area still has the feel of virgin forest, with some impressive stands of trees and lots of unkempt and semiwild areas where you can enjoy a real walk and quickly escape the hubbub and crowds of the **Inner Harbour** (➤ 86).

Interspersed with these wilder corners are manicured lawns and flower beds – some 30,000 flowers are planted here annually – plus well-worn paths, ponds and lakes scattered with ducks. Among the many attractions for children are a Children's Farm with sheep, goats and pot-belly pigs, a playground and a wading pool (the last is near the Dallas Road entrance). The park also contains two great symbols of Englishness – a cricket pitch and lawn bowling green – as well as a pitch-and-putt course, the world's

tallest totem pole (carved in 1956) and the Mile Zero marker of the Trans-Canada Highway, the road that begins here and crosses the country from west to east.

The park is safe, but take normal precautions. Women should avoid the area at night if alone.

🏠 201 C2 ✉ Bounded by Dallas Road, Douglas Street, Heywood and Southgate Street ☎ 250/361-0364 🕐 24 hours 💷 Free 🚌 5

⑩ Craigdarroch Castle

Craigdarroch Castle is the pick of several historic buildings on the fringes of Victoria, although "castle" rather overstates what is a large Gothic house, built in fulfilment of a promise made by Robert Dunsmuir to his wife – the prospect of an extravagant home was reputedly the only way he could tempt her away from their native Scotland.

Dunsmuir moved to Canada in 1851 as an employee of the Hudson's Bay Company, but by 1869 had opened his own coal mine and become a business magnate in his own right. The business and political practices of this robber baron were sharp, to say the least, and involved strike-breaking, the hiring of cheap Chinese labor, and, election to the provincial legislature against a candidate backed by his employees. Safety measures in his mines were notoriously lax, and in 1887, 150 men died in an explosion near Nanaimo on Vancouver Island. Strikes were put down with government connivance, and miners ruthlessly evicted from their homes.

Profits from Dunsmuir's enterprises to the tune of $200,000 were sunk into Craigdarroch, which means a "rocky oak place" in Gaelic. No expense was spared: The best marble, granite and sandstone were imported from abroad, and finely worked ceiling panels were crafted for the main hall and staircase. The finished house is an extravagance of stained-glass, paintings, sculptures and precious carpets that extends over four floors and 39 rooms. Dunsmuir, however, never enjoyed its splendor – he died before its completion in 1890. In 1919 Craigdarroch was used as a war veterans' hospital and from 1921 until 1946 was part of McGill University at Montreal.

🏠 201 off C3 ✉ 1050 Joan Crescent, Rockland ☎ 250/592-5323; www.craigdarrochcastle.com 🕐 Summer (usually mid-May to early Sep) daily 9–7; winter (usually early Sep to mid-May) 10–4:30 💷 Expensive 🚌 11 or 14-University from Fort Street, followed by a short walk up hill

Top: The Gothic grandeur of Craigdarroch Castle

FOR KIDS

If you have kids, try taking them to Beacon Hill Children's Farm (tel: 250/381-2532; www.beaconhillpark.ca) or the Victoria Bug Zoo on Courtney Street (tel: 250/384-2847; www.bugzoo.bc.ca).

Farther Afield

⓫ Pacific Rim National Park

Vancouver Island's national park lies 319km (198 miles) from Victoria – you need at least one or two nights here to do it justice – but its mountains, rain forest and wild coastal landscapes, as well as whale-watching opportunities, are the reasons to consider making this excursion from the city. The park stretches for some 130km (81 miles) along part of Vancouver Island's western coast and has three principal components: The Broken Group Islands, an archipelago of tiny islets only really accessible to sailors and kayakers; the West Coast Trail, an increasingly popular but tough long-distance footpath; and Long Beach, a

Five basic boat trips (prices vary) are possible from the village, the closest being **Meares Island** (15 minutes by boat), whose ancient forests have long been the subject of bitter dispute between conservationists and logging companies. The Big Cedar Trail (3km/2 miles) winds through some of oldest and most impressive trees. Other boat and light plane excursions include the islands of Vargas and Flores, Hot Springs Cove – popular for its thermal pools – and the Hesquiat Peninsula. Contact the visitor center for full details of tours and operators.

A walking or driving trip you can organize yourself is down **Long Beach**, 16km (10 miles) of crashing surf and empty sands backed by forest-clad mountains. The water's too cold for swimming, but the area is a favorite among beachcombers and hikers, who can wander virtually at random on the

Above: In Tofino's thermal pools
Right: Drift logs washed up on Long Beach in Pacific Rim National Park

wild beach that stretches between the main centers of **Tofino** to the north and Ucluelet to the south.

By far the most attractive base is Tofino, which is at least a morning's drive or six-hour bus journey from Victoria (Ucluelet is equally convenient but less picturesque). Prettily positioned looking out on the waters of Clayoquot Sound, the former fishing village becomes busy during the summer, its hotels full to bursting with visitors making whale-watching and other boat excursions.

waterfront or follow one or more of eight trails. All are 5km (3 miles) or less in length and are signposted from Highway 4 and the spur to Ucluelet, road links which back the beach for most of its length.

Before doing anything, however, visit the **Wickaninish Interpretive Centre**, also signed off Highway 4, for information on the park and the trails. Some of the best paths take you to Florencia Beach (trails 1, 2, 3 and 5), also known as Wreck Beach, or to South Beach (trail 4), famed for its huge breakers. Also, be sure to walk up Radar Hill (96m/315 feet) close to Tofino, which offers one of the region's best overall panoramas.

Tofino Infocentre

✚ 194 A2 ✉ 121 Third Street (corner of Campbell Street ☎ 250/725-3414; www.tourismtofino.com ⏰ Apr–Sep daily 9–8/9; Oct–Mar Mon–Fri 9–4

National Park Visitor Centre

✚ 194 A2 ✉ Long Beach, off Highway 4 ☎ 250/726-4212; www.pc.gc.ca ⏰ Mid-Mar to mid-Jun daily 10:30–6; mid-Jun to Aug 8–8; Sep to mid-Oct 10–6 🎟 Park fee moderate

IN MORE DEPTH

The best way to visit the **Broken Group Islands** is aboard the MV *Mary Rose*, a freighter that makes more or less daily sailings year-round to Ucluelet or Bamfield (south of the Broken Group Islands). The boat (and a sister ship, MV *Frances Barkley*) leaves from Port Alberni, east of Long Beach, and takes all day to make the round trip. The excursions are very popular, so make reservations (tel: 250/723-8313; www.ladyrosemarine.com).

If you want to walk the 77km (48-mile) **West Coast Trail** you'll need to set aside seven to ten days and plan well in advance. Reservations are available in peak season and can be made up to two months in advance (tel: 250/387-1642 or 1-800/435-5622. Open: Mon–Fri 7am to 9pm from April). Anyone requiring an overnight permit must take part in one of the orientation sessions.

Where to... Stay

Prices

Expect to pay per double room:

$ under CDN$100 $$ CDN$101–$200 $$$ CDN$201–$300

$$$$ over CDN$300

There's really only one choice in Victoria if you're treating yourself – the Empress, frequently ranked as one of the leading hotels in North America. For the more budget-conscious visitor there is also a good range of mid- and lower-priced accommodations.

〰 An Ocean View $$$

A mile from downtown and the waterfront, this modern home has stunning views of the ocean and mountains. The owners have had fun with the decor, with whimsical murals in some of the beautifully furnished rooms. You'll need to reserve the top-floor room for an ocean view – it has a balcony too; otherwise, choose a ground-floor, garden-view room with private patio (and access to the hot tub).

🏠 200 off A4 ✉ 715 Suffolk Street, V9A 3J5 ☎ 250/386-7330 or 1-800/342-9986; www.anoceanview.com

〰〰 Best Western Carlton Plaza $$

Victoria is well provided for when it comes to mid-range and chain hotels. Hotels in the Best Western group are invariably reliable, and the Carlton Plaza is no exception, its 103 modern, air-conditioned and well-equipped rooms providing a comfortable base close to the main sights and shops. Suites are available, as are units with kitchens – useful if you're spending a few days here and want to self-cater. There's another slightly smaller and more expensive Best Western hotel, the Inner Harbour, at 412 Québec Street (tel: 250/384-5122), one block back from the waterfront.

🏠 201 B4 ✉ 642 Johnson Street, V8W 1M6 ☎ 250/388-5513; toll free 1-800-663-7241; www.bestwesterncarltonplaza.com

〰〰〰〰 Empress Hotel $$–$$$$

Absolutely the first choice for a treat, the redoubtable Empress is a Victoria institution. Opened in 1908 by the Canadian Pacific Railway, it embodies the city's sense of tradition and is still the first choice of visiting dignitaries and VIPs. It belongs to the Canadian Pacific chain, owners of the equally celebrated Banff Springs and Château Lake Louise hotels.

The hotel's central position overlooking the Inner Harbour is perfect, but note that it is a big, busy hotel with some 460 rooms. Service is excellent, as are the facilities, notably the health club. The many lounges and dining rooms are splendid, but are also busy – afternoon tea is served to some 80,000 visitors a year.

🏠 201 B3 ✉ 721 Government Street, V8W 1W5 ☎ 250/384-8111; toll free 1-866-540-4429; www.fairmont.com/empress

〰〰〰 Haterleigh Heritage Inn $$–$$$$

The Haterleigh rivals the Empress for price, but otherwise is different in almost every respect. A beautiful 1901 "heritage building" just two blocks from downtown, it has six rooms and is a self-styled "bed-and-breakfast," though of the most upscale variety. The rooms

Where to...
Eat and Drink

Prices
Expect to pay for a three-course meal for two including wine
$ under CDN$50 $$ CDN$50-$100 $$$ over CDN$100

Victoria has a large number of good restaurants. Cuisine is mainly West Coast and Italian with excellent fish and seafood.

RESTAURANTS

▼▼▼ Brasserie L'Ecole
$$-$$$

This modern bistro offers fine French cuisine using the best local produce for dishes at prices that won't break the bank. The décor is persuasively French, all deep reds and browns with dark-stained hardwood floors and with white linen enriching the ambience even more, The slate-topped bar adds to the rustic Gallic style and the mood is intimate and uncrowded with seating for about thirty. You can treat yourself to starters of oysters or Quadra Island mussels followed by delicious mead-braised duck legs, sauerkraut, capers and chestnuts, or such fish dishes as grilled tuna with leek and peppercorn ragout. The wine list is impressive without being overwhelming and there's a terrific selection of beers.

➕ 201 B4 ⊠ 1715 Government Street
☎ 250/475-6260 ⏰ Tue-Sat 5.30-11

---

are spacious and decorated with antiques, and all have private bathrooms. Rates include breakfast, afternoon refreshments and small treats at check-in. Similarly upscale bed-and-breakfasts include the 10-room Beaconsfield (tel: 250/384-4044; www.beaconsfieldinn.com) and Prior House (tel: 250/592-8847; www.prior-house.com).

➕ 201 off A2 ⊠ 243 Kingston Street
☎ 250/384-9995; www.haterleigh.com

RESERVATIONS

AAA and CAA Travel Agencies provide full reservation service for all your travel needs. For a similar service through the Victoria Infocentre call 1-800-663-3883. For further information on **bed-and-breakfast alternatives** contact Western Canada Bed & Breakfast Innkeepers' Association (tel: 604/255-9199; www.wcbbia.com) or visit www.bbcanada.com, with links to 10,000 establishments.

▼▼ James Bay Inn $-$$

This is the third-oldest hotel in Victoria (after the Dominion and the Empress) and is just a few blocks from the Inner Harbour. Rooms are spacious, modern and comfortable, and the "heritage house" annex next door offers four luxury suites with elegant antique furnishing and full kitchens.

➕ 201 A1 ⊠ 270 Government Street, V8V 2L2 ☎ 250/384-7151; www.jamesbayinn.bc.ca

▼▼▼ The Royal Scot Suite Hotel ($$-$$$$)

Set in its own attractive grounds, the Royal Scot offers a good selection of comfortable and well-appointed rooms and suites in a convenient location for Victoria's Inner Harbor and downtown. Facilities include a restaurant, pool, fitness room and a gift shop offering arts and crafts and gourmet foods.

➕ 201 B3 ⊠ 425 Quebec Street
☎ 250/388-5463, 800/663-7515 (toll-free); www.royalscot.com

Café Brio $$$

Tuscan flavor is the signature at this distinctive eatery where a touch of theater has gone into the fittings and decor. Gazpacho starters or crab salad followed by mains of pan-roasted halibut or duck breast are only part of an exciting menu that includes crafted charcuterie. Wines start with reasonably priced whites and reds and soar to such joys as Napa Valley Beringer

🚩 201 off C3 ⊠ 944 Fort Street
🕾 250/383-0009 🕒 Daily from 5:30pm

🎖🎖🎖 Il Terrazzo $-$$$

Il Terrazzo lies in a small alley off another small alley, but makes light of its cramped and hidden location with a spacious interior of bare brick walls, lots of plants and big windows that give an airy, alfresco feeling even though you're indoors. The restaurant is a favorite among visitors and Victorians alike, who flock here safe in the knowledge that they're going to eat good

Italian food in pretty, contemporary surroundings. Dishes range from reasonably priced small pizzas to more expensive main-course classics such as local halibut, pork scaloppine and cumin-scented shank of lamb.

🚩 201 B4 ⊠ 555 Johnson Street, off Waddington Alley 🕾 250/361-0028; www. ilterrazzo.com 🕒 Lunch and dinner daily

🎖🎖🎖 The Mark $$$

Elegant, exclusive and intimate, with dark wood paneling, beautifully set tables and soft lighting, The Mark provides one of the finest dining experiences in Victoria. There's a six-course tasting menu with wine pairings. On the main menu are exquisite starters such as lobster mushroom and rabbit rillettes or a selection of Pacific oysters. Follow this with mains of herb-rubbed rack of lamb or crisp skinned Arctic char and you'll be ready for unfussy desserts such as almond and buckwheat honey parfait or

tiramisu cheesecake, all superbly orchestrated by award-winning chefs. The wine list, needless to say, is outstanding and for those with more eclectic tastes there's even a lengthy list of the finest world teas. Reservations are essential.

🚩 201 B3 ⊠ Hotel Grand Pacific, 463 Belleville Street 🕾 250/380-4487; www.themark.ca 🕒 Daily 5–9:30

🎖🎖 Pagliacci's $$-$$$

Pagliacci's opened back in 1979 when it was impossible to find a cappuccino or Italian food in Victoria. Since then it's been one of the city's favorite restaurants – so popular, in fact, that you can't reserve a table but have to take a chance and wait in line until a table becomes free. The success is partly due to the food – an eccentric Italian, Jewish, West Coast, Brooklyn mixture – and partly to the lively and very genial atmosphere. There's always a buzz of animated conversation, supplemented most nights by live

music. Informal to a fault, this is a place where both adults and children can have fun.

🚩 201 B4 ⊠ 1011 Broad Street
🕾 250/386-1662 🕒 Lunch and dinner daily plus tea, coffee, drinks and cakes 3pm–5pm

Red Fish Blue Fish $

This take-out fish canteen, with some quayside seating, is housed in an "upcycled" steel shipping container. Fish and chips with class, including halibut, albacore tuna, wild salmon and Fanny Bay oysters are on offer and you can watch the harbor chug along as the seaplanes come and go.

🚩 201 B3 ⊠ Broughton Street Pier, Wharf Street 🕾 250/298-6877 🕒 All day

Stage $-$$

A small plate paradise that caters for a growing army of devotees, Stage offers tapas-style dishes on the five themes of fish, meat, charcuterie, vegetables and cheese. There's a cheerful menu that ranges from sausage with onion gravy and mash,

Where to... Shop

Victoria's principal shopping districts are downtown – the area behind the Inner Harbour – and the Old Town core centered on Market Square. The streets containing the main stores and largest number of small specialty shops, intermingled with numerous bland souvenir shops, are Government and Douglas, but interesting shops and stalls can also be found in Market Square itself and small side streets such as Trounce Alley.

The key department store is The Bay (1150 Douglas Street, tel: 250/385-1311), with a huge and varied selection of goods at reasonable prices. For gastronomic treats, head to Murchie's (1110 Government

Murchie's Tea & Coffee

Taking English afternoon tea is something of a ritual among some visitors to Victoria, albeit a rather self-conscious one: The key places to do so are the lounge of the Empress Hotel (▲100) – up to $60 a head, plus taxes – and the outlying Blethering Place at 2250 Oak Bay Avenue. If you would prefer to have tea, coffee, sandwiches and cakes in more ordinary surroundings, come to Murchie's, a central café that's been in business since 1894.

➕ 201 B4 ☒ 1110 Government Street ☎ 250/383-3112 ⓦ Mon–Sat 9–7, Sun 10–7

CAFÉS, PUBS AND BARS

Canoe Brewpub and Restaurant

Located in an 1890s heritage building this popular pub and restaurant offers award-winning hand-crafted beers and a terrific selection of main dishes and bar meals. The loft area is all open beams and planked floor with chandeliers above. There's a lovely terrace area overlooking moorings and you can sit back and enjoy live music on Wednesday and Thursday nights.

➕ 201 B4 ☒ 450 Swift Street ☎ 250/361-1940 ⓦ 11:30 until late

Re-Bar

Re-Bar serves a bewildering range of healthy drinks, as well as excellent organic vegetarian snacks and meals. It's a funky place, great for breakfast and lunch, a beverage break or a shot of exotic juice.

➕ 201 B4 ☒ 50 Bastion Square ☎ 250/361-9223 ⓦ Mon–Wed 8:30–9, Thu–Sat 8:30–10, Sun 8:30–3:30

Sticky Wicket

Victoria is filled with generally poor imitations of British pubs, but the Wicket is by far the best, and certainly most favored by locals. As well as its food and drink, it has a pleasant rooftop patio area and occasional live music. There are rooftop volleyball courts and you can head downstairs for some late night clubbing.

➕ 201 B3 ☒ 919 Douglas Street ☎ 250/383-7137 ⓦ Daily 11:30am–2am

Swan's Brew Pub

Victoria's most popular pub-restaurant is housed in a converted 1913 warehouse. Swan's offers no less than 10 beers from its brewery (such as Pumpkin Ale, and Smooth Sailing Honey Ale), excellent food (including a variety of salads, nachos, fish and chips, shepherd's pie). The complex includes a small hotel and basement nightclub.

➕ 201 B4 ☒ 506 Pandora Avenue, corner of Store Street ☎ 250/361-3310 ⓦ Daily 11am–2am

---

to seafood treats such as mussels and clams and there's a modest, but thoughtful, wine list that won't bankrupt you. Stage is in the Fernwood district east of downtown and is popular with theatergoers from the nearby Belfry Theatre.

➕ 201 off C4 ☒ 1307 Gladstone Avenue, Victoria ☎ 250/388-4222 ⓦ Daily 5pm–midnight

Where to...
Be Entertained

PERFORMING ARTS

Victoria has its own orchestra, the **Victoria Symphony Orchestra** (610–620 View Street, tel: 250/385-6515; www.victoriasymphony.ca, open Mon–Fri 9–4), its own opera company, the **Pacific Opera Victoria** (Suite 500, 1815 Blanchard Street, tel: 250/385-0222; www.pov.bc.ca), and its own musicals and light opera society, the **Victoria Operatic Society** (744 Fairview Road, tel: 250/381-1021; www.vos.bc.ca). All perform mainly at the **McPherson Playhouse** (3 Centennial Square, at Pandora and Government, tel: 250/386-6121 or 1-888/717-6121; www.rmts.bc.ca).

The **Belfry Theatre** (1291 Gladstone Avenue, tel: 250/385-6815; www.belfry.bc.ca) stages around five productions annually (Oct–Apr), and the **Intrepid Theatre Company** (1609 Blanshard Street, tel: 250/383-2663; www.intrepidtheatre.com) organizes two major theatrical festivals: the **Victoria Fringe Festival** (late summer) and the **Shakespeare Festival** (Aug), held near the Inner Harbour.

JAZZ

The best club for live music is **Hermann's** (753 View Street, near Blanshard, tel: 250/388-9166), and there is a major jazz festival: the **Jazzfest International** (tel: 250/388-4423). The Victoria Jazz Society (tel: 250/388-4423; www.jazzvictoria.ca) will have details of other events.

BARS AND CLUBS

Victoria is full of pubs and bars. Try the lively **Irish Times** bar (1200 Government Street, tel: 250/383-7775) with live music that echoes of Irish foot-stomping pubs; the pretty **Swans Pub** (506 Pandora Avenue, tel: 250/361-3310); and **Spinnaker's** (308 Catherine Street, tel: 250/386-2739), Canada's oldest licensed brewpub, and **Bartholomew's** (777 Douglas Street, tel: 250/388-5111). **Lucky Bar** (517 Yates Street; tel:250/382-5825) is a longstanding Victoria favorite with an undiminished take on the best in club music from 90's nostalgia to rock, punk, hip hop, folk and jazz.

INFORMATION AND TICKETS

Head for the **Visitor Centre**, or consult the listings pages of local newspapers and free sheets such as the *Monday Magazine*.

Street, tel: 250/383-3112) for tea and coffee, and **Roger's Chocolates** (913 Government Street, tel: 250/384-7021) for sublime handmade chocolates. For Canadian wine to take home, drop in on **The Wine Barrel** (644 Broughton Street, tel: 250/388-0606).

First Nation crafts can be found at **Cowichan Trading** (1328 Government Street, tel: 250/383-0321), along with a plethora of souvenirs.

Try **Artevo** (616 Fort Street, tel: 250/383-1699) for world collections of paintings, ceramics, glasswork, sculpture and jewelry by numerous fine artists.

A good selection of small boutiques and little specialist stores is found in and around **Market Square**.

The best stock of books and guides on western Canada is held by **Munro's** (1108 Government Street, tel: 250/382-2464). Fort Street is a good place to start looking for antiques and galleries.

British Columbia

Getting Your Bearings

Imagine Canada and the chances are you'll imagine British Columbia. This is the province where the country is seen at its glorious best, where the mountains, forests and lakes are on the grandest scale, where flora, fauna and landscape are at their most diverse, and where the towns and cities – notably Vancouver – are at their most beautiful and cosmopolitan.

No short visit can do justice to the region's immensity – it covers an area larger than the US states of California, Washington and Oregon combined. Aim to explore a couple of its most distinctive corners – the Kootenays for some of the region's loveliest lakes and mountains, Wells Gray for a taste of its wilderness, or the Okanagan for a glimpse of its more pastoral corners.

The distances you'll cover will be considerable, and many of the interior towns, though beautifully located, are of relatively little interest – Nelson in the Kootenays being a notable exception. Neither fact should put you off, for in a region where spectacular scenery is almost universal, it's a pleasure simply to drive from place to place.

Touring by bus, car or RV is easy: The roads are excellent, and most towns and villages have at least one hotel or motel. Your only problem will be resisting the many scenic temptations en route, not to mention the countless opportunities for outdoor activities such as hiking or horseback riding.

The chances are you'll find too much to do and see, but you can always come back – most people do.

Page 105: Balsam Lake, Mount Revelstoke National Park

Left: A lake in Wells Gray Provincial Park

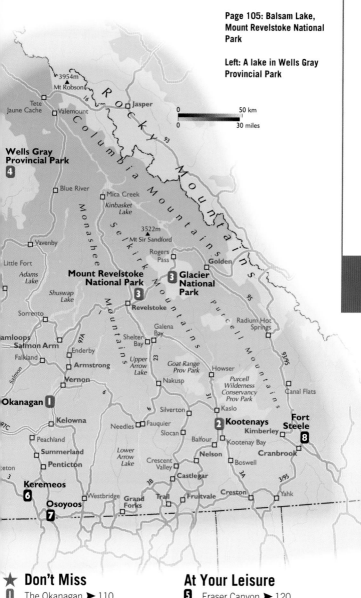

In Five Days

If you're not quite sure where to begin your travels, this itinerary recommends a practical and enjoyable five-day tour of British Colombia, taking in some of the best places to see using the Getting Your Bearings map on the previous page. For more information see the main entries.

Day One

Leave Vancouver at dawn and head east on Highway 1 to Hope and then drive north to Lytton via the **5 Fraser Canyon** (➤ 120). Having ridden the Airtram, you need to decide whether you want to see **4 Wells Gray** (➤ 118–119), an option which would leave you well placed to continue north on Highway 5 – a spectacular mountain drive – to Mount Robson and **Jasper National Park** (➤ 142). If this is the option you prefer, then drive to Kamloops via Cache Creek and north on Highway 5 to Clearwater, the best base for Wells Gray.

Day Two

If you can't make Clearwater on Day 1, overnight at Kamloops and spend the day exploring Wells Gray. If you decide against the park, then on Day 1 drive from Lytton to the **1 Okanagan** (left; ➤ 110–111) via Merritt. On Day 2 spend time exploring the Okanagan, leaving yourself the option of spending Day 3 in the region at the O'Keefe Ranch for recreation.

Day Three

From the Okanagan you have yet more choices. One is to head north to Salmon Arm from Vernon and then east on the Trans-Canada Highway (Highway 1) to see **3 Glacier and Mount Revelstoke National Parks** (➤ 116–117). From here it's a straightforward drive on Highway 1 through Yoho National Park (➤ 146) to Lake Louise and Banff National Park (➤ 133). If you feel the Rockies can wait, then on Day 3 or 4 head east on Highway 6 from Vernon to Needles, Nakusp and New Denver. This is a delightful drive in its own right, and leaves you well placed for exploring **2 The Kootenays** (Kootenay Lake, above; ➤ 112–115).

Day Four

Spend the day driving to or exploring the Kootenays, overnighting in Kaslo or Nelson. Villages not to be missed include Kaslo and New Denver, while some of the most scenic stretches of road are Highway 31A between Kaslo and New Denver, and Highway 3A from Balfour to Creston.

Day Five

Leave the Kootenays via Creston and then follow Highway 95 north toward Cranbrook and the heritage town of **8 Fort Steele** (➤ 121). Continue north on Highway 93–95 to Radium Hot Springs and Kootenay National Park (➤ 112), a far prettier route east than Highway 3 over the Crowsnest Pass to Fort Macleod and southern Alberta.

🄳 The Okanagan

The Okanagan region is the last thing you'd expect of British Columbia. Instead of the province's familiar mountain and forest landscapes, this is an almost Mediterranean region of vine-covered hills, beaches, dulcet lakes, orchards and pastoral river valleys. Vacationers flock here to enjoy its mild climate, wine, water sports and other recreational activities.

Kelowna

The main center is Kelowna, best approached from the west across Lake Okanagan – a much prettier route than Hwy 97, with its strip of malls and fast-food outlets. Once in town, though, things pick up considerably, for the lakefront center is a lovely mixture of parks, gardens, beaches and well-ordered streets lined with cafés, galleries, interesting stores and good restaurants. Rotary Beach and Boyce Gyro Park are the main beaches, together with Bear Creek Provincial Park, just over a kilometer away across the curious floating bridge that spans Lake Okanagan. For good views of the town and surroundings, take the five-minute drive up to Knox Mountain just to the north.

The marina on the west bank of Lake Okanagan in Kelowna

Wine-Growing Region

Another option is to visit some of the region's **vineyards**. There's a signposted Wine Route that starts at Salmon Arm, on Shuswap Lake, and heads south on Highway 97 through Vernon, Kelowna, Peachland, Kaleden and Osoyoos. Most of the 39 wineries on the route are south of Kelowna, so start there if time is limited. The majority sell wines direct, and some offer tours. One of the most interesting is the organic Summerhill Estate, just south of Kelowna, where they use a pyramid to mature the wines. As well as tours and tastings they have a good lakeside restaurant. You can pick up details of the route from visitor centers and stop by at the **British Columbia Wine Centre**, which shares the premises of the **Penticton** visitor center. Penticton, south of Kelowna, takes its name from a Salish phrase meaning "a place to stay forever,"

ORCHARDS
Kelowna and the rest of the Okanagan owe much of their prosperity to **fruit-growing**. Credit for planting the trees goes to Father Charles Pandosy, a member of an Oblate mission founded close to Kelowna in 1859. You can undertake any number of orchard, juice, fruit and food tours – obtain details from visitor centers.

Vineyards swathe much of the Okanagan Valley

a reference to a blessed climate and idyllic surroundings. It is fairly pretty at its center and also has beaches (Skaha and Okanagan are the best), water sports and tours.

Vernon

The same goes for Vernon, north of Kelowna, whose appeal is enhanced by its tree-lined streets and 500 or more listed heritage buildings. It's also close to the region's major point of historical interest, the **O'Keefe Ranch** (12km/7.5 miles to the north), a collection of original pioneer buildings, farming vehicles and equipment, rare animal breeds and associated museum that evoke the flavor of 19th-century frontier life.

✚ 196 A2
Kelowna Visitor Centre
✉ 544 Harvey Avenue ☎ 250/ 861-1515;
toll free in North America 1-800-663-4345;
www.tourismkelowna.com ⏰ May–Jun daily
8–5; Jul–Aug 8–8; Sep–Oct 8–7; Nov–Apr
Mon–Fri 8–5, Sat–Sun 10–4

O'Keefe Ranch
✉ 12km (7.5 miles) north of Vernon, off Hwy
97 ☎ 250/542-7868; www.okeeferanch.ca
⏰ May to mid-Oct daily 9–6 💵 Moderate
🍴 Café

Vernon Visitor Centre
✉ 701 Hwy 97 South ☎ 250/542-1415;
toll free in North America 1-800-665-0795
(accommodations reservations only);
www.vernontourism.com ⏰ Jun–Aug daily
8–6; Sep–May Mon–Fri 9–5

Penticton Visitor Centre
✉ 553 Railway Street ☎ 250/493-4055;
toll free in North America 1-800-663-5052;
www.penticton.org ⏰ Jul–Aug daily 8–8;
May, Jun & Sep Mon–Fri 9–5, Sat–Sun 10–4;
Oct–Apr Mon–Fri 9–5, Sat–Sun 11–4,

THE OKANAGAN: INSIDE INFO

Top tips Don't follow the **busy roads** on the east side of Okanagan Lake: Follow the quieter and prettier roads on the west side, away from the main towns.
■ Come to the Okanagan **off season** if at all possible to sample its undoubted charms – fruit trees in blossom, lakeside villages and vineyard tours – without the crowds.

2 The Kootenays

The Kootenays are a sublime pocket of lakes and mountains in British Columbia's southeast corner, an unspoiled and relatively unvisited enclave of tiny villages, parks, historic sites, forests, ghost towns, spectacular highways and lakeside hamlets set amid some of the province's loveliest landscapes.

NAME ORIGIN
The Kootenays take their name from an aboriginal word meaning "people from beyond the hills," probably a reference to the hunting sorties made by the Kutenai or Kootenai tribes.

Best Approach
Kootenay Country, as it's sometimes called, is loosely based on two major river valleys – the Kootenay and Columbia – their huge respective lakes (Kootenay and the Upper and Lower Arrow lakes) and the three colossal mountain ranges that divide and bound them: the Purcells, Selkirks and Monashees.

What you see of the region depends slightly on your itinerary. From the west the finest approach is on Highway 6 from Vernon to Needles, a majestic drive, while from the Rockies and the east you'll have a more circuitous but almost equally beguiling journey via Fort Steele, Yahk and Creston. Fort Steele (▶ 121) has a well-sited reconstructed pioneer village, while Creston is noted for the Creston Valley Wildlife Management Area (9.5km/6 miles) northwest of the town, a haven for birds and wildlife, including one of the world's largest nesting osprey populations.

Nelson
The biggest and most obvious base in the region is Nelson – "Queen of the Kootenays" – a likeable place with a close-knit community feel, pretty streets, lots of cafés, galleries and bookstores, and more than 350 quaint wooden "heritage" buildings. The town and its surroundings are so picture perfect they've been used as locations for many a film and television production, most famously as the setting for comedian Steve Martin's film *Roxanne*. Brochures detailing walks around the buildings can be obtained from the visitor

center – don't miss the old town Courthouse, designed by Francis Rattenbury, architect of the Empress Hotel and Parliament Buildings in Victoria (➤ 86).

Like most Kootenay settlements, Nelson sprang to life toward the end of the 19th century following the discovery of silver, copper and gold in the hills nearby. Much of the area's mining heritage is recalled in the small **Mining Museum**, best seen in conjunction with the modest Nelson Museum on the edge of town, whose most interesting displays deal with the Doukhobors, a pacifist sect who settled across the region. For more information about the sect, or to see more of the way of life, visit the Doukhobor Village Museum in Castlegar.

Kootenay Lake stretches for more than 160km (100 miles) so there are many spectacular views

Kaslo

While Nelson is an excellent base, with plenty of accommodations, you might well want to stay in one of the region's charming smaller villages. Best of these is urbane little **Kaslo**, a too-good-to-be-true spot on Kootenay Lake, with as picturesque and homey a collection of heritage buildings and gardens as Nelson. As well as the old houses, the village also boasts North America's oldest paddle steamer, or stern-wheeler, the SS Moyie, launched in 1898. This was one of many such vessels that once plied the Kootenays' lakes, with a shallow draft that allowed them, in local parlance, to "float on dew," a necessary prerequisite for loading and unloading minerals and other goods close to the lake shore.

Kaslo is delightful in its own right, but it also has a glorious mountain-ringed setting, with plenty of opportunities for sightseeing by car, walking and other outdoor activities.

The hamlet of Argenta, 35.5km (22 miles) to the north, makes **Trees on** a good target, as does the Kokanee Glacier Provincial Park, **the shore of** a mountain park with marked hiking trails accessed from **Kootenay Lake** several points on highways 6, 31 and 3A.

Lakeside centers

Other pretty centers include **New Denver**, only slightly less picture-perfect than Kaslo, and **Nakusp**, noted for the Nakusp Hot Springs, a well-signposted natural spa with outdoor pools approximately 13km (8 miles) northeast of the village. Both towns have small museums, devoted mainly to the area's mining traditions.

For the most part, however, it's not museums that you'll remember from the Kootenays, but the scenery, and in particular the region's beautiful ensembles of mountain, lake and forest. Much of the landscape can be enjoyed from the road, notably Highway 3A north of Creston, which runs alongside Kootenay Lake to the "world's longest free ferry crossing" (9km/5.5 miles) at Kootenay Bay. En route, as

Glorious colors in Kootenay National Park elsewhere on the region's scenic roads, you'll pass all kinds of tucked-away bed-and-breakfast homes, good alternatives to staying in Nelson or the smaller villages – contact local visitor centers for details. You'll also pass the wonderfully eccentric Glass House, 6.5km (4 miles) south of Boswell on Highway 3A, built in 1955 by a former mortician from 500,000 bottles. Beyond the ferry, 14.5km (9 miles) north of Balfour, you might want to take a soak in the Ainsworth Hot Springs.

➕ 196 C2

Nelson Visitor Infocentre
✉ 225 Hall Street, corner of Lake Street
☎ 250/352-3433 or 1-877/663-5706;
www.discovernelson.com ⏰ Jun–Aug daily
8:30–6; Sep–May Mon–Fri 6:30–5

Kaslo Visitor Infocentre
✉ 324 Front Street
☎ 250/353-2525 ⏰ Daily 9–5

Nakusp Visitor Infocentre
✉ 92 West 6th Avenue
☎ 250/ 265-4234 or 1-800/909-8819;
www.nakusparrowlakes.com ⏰ Daily 10–4

New Denver Visitor Infocentre
✉ Silvery Slocan Museum, 202 6th Avenue
☎ 250/358-2719; www.slocanlake.com
⏰ Early Jul–early Sep daily 9–5

THE KOOTENAYS: INSIDE INFO

Top tips You'll **need a car** to see the Kootenays: Public transportation takes you only to the main centers.

■ **Planning a route** through the Kootenays' twists and turns is difficult. The best of the region's towns and villages are Nelson, Kaslo and Nakusp.

■ The most **scenic drives** are from Vernon to Needles; Creston to Kaslo; and Kaslo or Nakusp to Revelstoke via the ferry crossing at Galena Bay.

■ Don't expect much in the way of **facilities** outside the towns and villages – and note that "villages" marked on maps – such as Balfour, Kootenay Bay, Needles, Crawford Bay and so on – usually amount to little more than a small cluster of houses.

Ones to miss Peripheral Kootenay towns such as Creston, Castlegar, Trail and Rossland are generally less appealing than Kaslo and Nelson.

❸ Glacier and Mount Revelstoke National Parks

The mountain ranges immediately to the west of the Rockies are just as spectacular as the Rockies themselves. Glacier and Mount Revelstoke national parks protect a fragment of these ranges, the Columbia and Selkirk mountains, which offer as seductive a medley of landscapes as their famous neighbors.

Glacier National Park

The national park owes its existence to the Canadian Pacific Railway. Before the railway's arrival the region's terrain was so inhospitable as to be almost deserted. Neither explorers nor aboriginal peoples ventured into its icy interior, which is ringed around with peaks such as Mount Dawson (3,392m/ 11,122 feet), as imposing as the Rockies' peaks to the east.

Some 14 percent of the area has permanent snow cover, with more than 420 glaciers, including at least 68 that have re-formed on previously vanished ice sheets, an unusual phenomenon – most glaciers worldwide are in retreat. The railway was eventually driven through the area in 1885 via Rogers Pass (1,383m/4,534 feet), named after the line's chief engineer, Major Albert Rogers.

Tourists flocked to the pass hotel, but only until 1916, when repeated avalanches forced the railway to use a new tunnel. Visitor numbers dropped away, and recovered only in 1962, when the Trans-Canada Highway (Highway 1) opened over the pass.

Today the road is the best way to see the park – much of the interior is the preserve only of experienced mountaineers. Stop off at the park **visitor center**, half a mile west of Rogers Pass, which has details of shorter walks. Just south of the center you should also stop off to admire the views of the Illecillewaet Neve, one of the park's most visible and impressive glaciers (see right for details of walks).

Mount Revelstoke National Park

This national park lies 16km (10 miles) west of Glacier. A much smaller affair, it was created in 1916,

Right: Looking from Mount Revelstoke to the town of the same name

Below: On the trail of the giant cedar, Mount Revelstoke National Park

WALKS IN GLACIER

There are eight hikes in the park, from a gentle stroll to a challenging full-day mountain hike, all leading out from the Illecillewaet Campground. The shortest are the 1km (0.6-mile) Bear Falls Trail and Meeting of the Waters Trail, and one of the easiest, though longer, is the 1885 Rails Trail (3.8km/2.3 miles each way), following the disused line of the Canadian Pacific Railway. Best of the strenuous hikes are the Great Glacier, Avalanche and Abbott's ridge trails.

largely to protect the floral meadows on Mount Revelstoke. Main access is on the Meadows in the Sky Parkway (25.5km/16 miles), near western entrance and the town of Revelstoke (a good base for both parks, with plenty of accommodations). At the top there are trails through the flowers, notably the paved Meadows in the Sky Trail (half a mile) and longer Miller Lake Trail (6km/3.7 miles one way). Other short trails start from the main Trans-Canada Highway – the best are the Giant Cedars (half a mile) and Skunk Cabbage (1km/0.7 miles) trails, repectively half and 6km (0.3 and 3.7 miles) from the park's eastern gate.

➕ 196 C3
Rogers Pass Visitor Centre
✉ Rogers Pass ☎ 250/837-7500; www.pc.gc.ca/glacier
🕐 Mid-Jun to Aug daily 7:30–8; May to mid-Jun, Sep–Oct daily 8:30–4:30 (closed Tue, Wed in Nov); Dec–Apr daily 7–5

GLACIER AND MOUNT REVELSTOKE: INSIDE INFO

Top tips Park **passes** are required for both Glacier and Revelstoke. Purchase them from park centers – prices are a dollar or two less than for the four Rockies national parks. (Visit www.pc.gc.ca for more on park passes in North America.)

- Glacier marks the border between **Mountain and Pacific time**. Remember to set your watches back an hour traveling west, forward an hour traveling east.
- You can't drive all the way up the Mount Revelstoke road or Meadows in the Sky Parkway – park at Balsam Lake and catch a **shuttle bus** for the 2km (1.3-mile) route to the summit area.
- **Weather** can be poor in Glacier, even in summer, so drive carefully – road conditions can change quickly.
- Interpretation **talks** (currently mid-Jun to Aug, daily at 7pm) at the campground cover subjects that include the wildlife, geology and vegetation of the park; contact the Rogers Pass Visitor Centre (see opposite), for more details.

④ Wells Gray Provincial Park

Wells Gray and its medley of mountains, waterfalls, lakes, mighty rivers and deep forests is one of the finest of British Columbia's parks although it is less visually rugged and mountainous than the Rockies national parks to the east. Some of the best scenic highlights can be seen easily from a road that penetrates the park's lonely heart.

Clearwater

It's debatable whether you'd make a special journey here on a short visit to BC, but if you're traveling from Jasper and **Mount Robson**, then it's easy to spend a night in Clearwater and then spend a day exploring the park. Clearwater's excellent visitor center, on the highway outside the village proper, is the place to pick up details about the park's trails and attractions: It also has details of whitewater rafting and canoeing trips on the Clearwater River and other outdoor activities in the park.

If all you're doing is sightseeing from a car, then just follow the 62.5km (39-mile) Wells Gray Park Road off Highway 5 into the park. All the sights along the road are signposted. The first is Spahats Creek Provincial Park, 8km (5 miles) from Clearwater, where a short trail from the parking area leads to the 61m (200-foot) **Spahats Falls**. The next is the Green Mountain Lookout, accessed via a winding side road just after the main road crosses the Wells Gray Park boundary. At the lookout is a sensational view of some of BC's wildest reaches: So wild that many of the peaks remain unnamed.

Back on the main park road, the next stop is Dawson Falls. Where other waterfalls in the park derive their beauty from high, graceful arcs of water, here the drama is provided by the sheer volume and power of water that cascades over a broad ledge of rock. The falls are 91.5m (300 feet) wide, but just 5m (16 feet) high.

A waterfall of the graceful variety, **Helmcken Falls**, the

Right: At more than twice the height of Niagara, Helmcken Falls impresses in both summer and winter

Below: Ray Farm is mostly ruined now

park's centerpiece, is reached on a signposted access road soon after Dawson Falls. At 137m (450 feet), these falls are two and half

WELLS GRAY PROVINCIAL PARK: INSIDE INFO

Top tips Remember there are virtually **no facilities** in the park, so make sure you have enough fuel in your car for the round trip, and take picnic supplies for the day.
- The park is extremely wild, so even on short walks take various precautions against encountering **bears** (▶ 14) and make sure you have adequate clothing and food.
- Wells Gray is not a national park, so there are **no entrance fees.**

times the height of Niagara, their height complemented by their setting: a broad, dark amphitheater of rock filled with veils of spray and cloaked in the greens and browns of lichens and fractured trees.

From the falls you need to return to the main access road, which then runs in occasional tandem with the Clearwater River. Look out for the short, signposted trail to **Ray Farm**, built by John Ray, the area's first pioneer settler, in 1912. The farm is mostly ruined but the remoteness and surroundings provide a graphic illustration of the rigors of pioneer life.

The park road ends at Clearwater Lake, home to just a campground and a couple of launches. If you have time, walk one of the short marked trails on and around the lakeshore: They're all summarized on an obvious trail board.

➕ 196 B4
Clearwater Visitor Infocentre
✉ 425 E Yellowhead Highway (Highway 5) ☎ 250/674-2646; www.clearwaterbcchamber.com
🕐 Jun–Aug daily 9–7; Sep–May 9–4

At Your Leisure

5 Fraser Canyon

The most interesting route when driving across British Columbia is the Trans-Canada Highway (Highway 1). It runs through semidesert scenery and shadows the Thompson River before turning south at Cache Creek. Between Lytton and Yale it follows the Fraser Canyon, the highlight of the journey, thanks to the scenic splendor of the Fraser River and its impressive gorge. The road climbs, swoops and clings to the side of the canyon, offering views over the river and the mountains above.

River and canyon take their name from Simon Fraser (1776–1862), an explorer and employee of the North West Company, who established the first non-native settlements in western Canada and undertook

Over the abyss: the Airtram at Hell's Gate

prodigious feats of exploration.

Today the road route is straightforward but exhilarating, especially at Hell's Gate (about 9.5km/6 miles north of Yale), where the Fraser's flow is squeezed into a seething mass of whitewater some 38m (124 feet) wide and 61m (200 feet) deep. Here you can ride the **Airtram** cable car toward the canyon bottom, where a suspension bridge crosses the river, and look at displays detailing the Pacific salmon runs up the Fraser.

Yale began life in the 1840s as a Hudson's Bay Company fort known as The Falls. By 1858 it had been renamed Yale, and had become the largest town in North America west of Chicago and north of San Francisco, its population swollen by 20,000 gold prospectors. Today barely 200 people live here, but it's worth a stop for the small museum on its main highway dedicated to its gold-rush heyday.

Some 19.5km (12 miles) south of Yale is the town of Hope. It's a pleasant place to stop, with another modest museum of pioneer memorabilia and opportunities for walking and – unusually – gliding. For details contact the town's visitor center.

Airtram

➕ 195 E2 ✉ 43111 Trans Canada Hwy, Boston Bar, 9.5km (6 miles) north of Yale ☎ 604/867-9277; www.hellsgateairtram.com 🕐 Mid-Apr to mid-May and early Sep to mid-Oct daily 10–4; mid-May to early Sep daily 10–5 💲 Expensive 🍽 Restaurant

Hope Infocentre

➕ 195 D2 ✉ 919 Water Avenue ☎ 604/869-2021; www.hopechamber.bc.ca 🕐 Jul–Aug daily 8–8; Sep–Jun 9–5

Yale Museum

➕ 195 E2 ✉ Douglas Street ☎ 604/863-2324 🕐 Mid-May to Sep daily 9–6 (phone for confirmation)

6 Keremeos

Highway 3 hugs the US border and takes you through some beautiful and varied scenery, beginning with the forests of the Coast Mountains and wild Manning Provincial Park. East of Princeton the scenery remains spectacular, but becomes more pastoral closer to Keremeos, a village beautifully set on a mountain-ringed plain. The local climate here is one of Canada's best, and allows the growing of a wide range of often exotic fruits and vegetables, earning the region the title of "Fruit Stand Capital of Canada."

➕ 195 F1

7 Osoyoos

The desert scenery around Osoyoos is some of the most startling in British Columbia. The Nk'Mip Desert is the historic home of the Osoyoos Indian Band (Nk'Mip), who still own and manage the land. The Osoyoos have created a thriving vacation resort nearby, but are actively conserving this endangered landscape. Self-guiding trails have been marked out, and at the Desert Cultural Centre, visitors can learn about the land and the indigenous people via interactive exhibits, two multimedia theaters and a rattlesnake research program with public viewing areas. There's an indoor habitat housing various desert "critturs," and outside is a sculpture garden and reconstructions of tribal dwellings of the past. The region has Canada's lowest rainfall and an average annual temperature some 10 degrees higher than Nelson.

The town of Osoyoos is also a busy spot when vacationers flock here in summer to enjoy the sunshine and to swim in the warm waters of the lake.

Osoyoos Infocentre
➕ 200 A1 ✉ 9912 Hwy 3
☎ 250/495-5070 or 1-888/676-9667;
www.destinationosoyoos.com

Nk'Mip Desert Cultural Centre
✉ 100 Rancher Creek Road
☎ 250/495-7901 or 1-888/495-8555;
www.nkmipdesert.com 🕐 May–early Oct daily 9:30–4:30; early Oct–Apr Tue–Fri 9.30–4, Sat 11:30–4

The Osoyoos Desert has British Columbia's lowest rainfall

8 Fort Steele Heritage Town

Fort Steele is a partly original, partly reconstructed village put together to resemble the settlement as it might have appeared at the end of the 19th century. The original fort was created around 1884 by Inspector Sam Steele of the North West Mounted Police, who was sent to settle a dispute over land and two wrongfully imprisoned members of the Ktunaxa (or Kutenai) people.

Steele only stayed a year or so, but the settlement later prospered, largely as a result of nearby discoveries of silver, lead and zinc, and on the expectation that the transcontinental Canadian Pacific Railway would pass through the area. In the event, the railway passed through nearby Cranbrook instead. As Cranbrook boomed, Fort Steele declined, only being saved by its restoration as a heritage site in 1961.

Today, the many old buildings are staffed by people in period dress. You have the opportunity to visit an old-time smithy, bakery, general store, printing office and many other "working" enterprises. Among other things, you can also ride a steam engine, board a stagecoach, and watch bread being baked or quilts being made.

➕ 197 D1 ✉ 9851 Hwy 93/95
☎ 250/417-6000 or 250/426-7352;
www.fortsteele.ca 🕐 Jul–Sep 9.30–6.30 (site until 7), May–Oct 9.30–5 (site until 6), Nov–Apr 10–4 💲 Moderate, expensive Jul–early Sep
🍴 Café ($)

Where to... Stay

Prices

Expect to pay per double room:

$ under CDN$100	$$ CDN$101–$200
$$$ CDN$201–$300	$$$$ over CDN$300

Accommodations at all prices, but especially mid-priced motels, are common throughout the Okanagan and larger centers. Elsewhere, villages usually have at least one hotel.

OKANAGAN

🕸🕸 Grapevine Bed and Breakfast $$

This is a peaceful little place, just out of town. The four stylish bedrooms are luxurious and have adjoining bathrooms. The best, on the ground floor, has a wrought-iron bed and a spa tub plus shower. The well-kept gardens include a swimming pool and hot tub.

➕ 196 B2 ⊠ 2621 Longhill Road, V1V 2E5 ☎ 250/860-5580 or 1-800/956-5580; www.grapevineokanagan.com

🕸🕸 Kelowna Lakeshore Inn $–$$

From the front, this might look like any two-story motel, but out back its spacious lawns, with pool, hot tub and picnic tables, border the lake, with views to the hills

beyond. About 60 percent of the rooms have lake views, and all have microwaves, fridges, toasters, kettles, dishes and coffee makers, free local calls and free WiFi.

➕ 196 A2 ⊠ 3756 Lakeshore Road, V1W 3L4 ☎ 1-877/657-5253; www.lakeshoreinn.com

🕸🕸🕸 Lake Okanagan Resort $$–$$$

This beautiful, self-contained lakeside resort hotel lies 17km (10.5 miles) from Kelowna. It is a peaceful place to stay. Facilities include a par 3 golf course, two outdoor pools, tennis courts, marina, beach and horseback riding. Most of the 125 rooms are on the lakeside.

➕ 196 A2 ⊠ 2751 Westside Road, Kelowna, V1Z 3T1 ☎ 250/769-3511; toll free in North America 1-800-663-3273; www.lakeokanagan.com

WELLS GRAY PROVINCIAL PARK

🕸🕸 Dutch Lake Motel $–$$

A great place to stay if you are visiting Wells Gray, this motel is by the side of Dutch Lake. All the rooms have balconies overlooking the lake and some have kitchens. All are climate controlled, and have cable TV and coffee makers. On site, there's a coin laundry, boat rentals, restaurant and RV campground.

➕ 196 B4 ⊠ 333 Roy Road, Clearwater, V0E 1N0 ☎ 250/674-3325 or 1-877/674-3325; www.dutchlakemotel.com

THE KOOTENAYS

🕸🕸 Best Western Baker Street Inn $$–$$$

Downtown Nelson has a sprinkling of old, rather battered and inexpensive hotels, but it's better to spend a little more to stay in the Baker Street Inn, whose 70 rooms offer a more modern and stylish overnight option. Hotels affiliated to the Best Western chain are invariably reliable.

➕ 196 C1 ⊠ 153 Baker Street, Nelson, V1L 4H1 ☎ 250/352-3525; toll free in

North America 1-888-255-3525;
www.bwbakerstreetinn.com

Hillcrest Hotel $$–$$$

It's hard to take your eyes off the spectacular views of snow-capped mountains and the Mount Begbie Glacier from this spot, but the hotel foyer is pretty eye-catching too, with its double-height ceiling and massive wooden pillars. Rooms are spacious, and there are some two-floor suites. The health club has whirlpool, steam room, sauna and exercise equipment.

🚇 196 B3 ☒ 2100 Oak Drive, Revelstoke
V0E 2S0 ☏ 250/837-3322;
www.hillcresthotel.com

William Hunter Cabins
$–$$

What better way to complete a trip to the Kootenays than to spend the night in a real log cabin overlooking the Valhalla Provincial Park? This is no backwoods experience, though. The cabins here are beautiful, with handmade pine furniture, and the queen-size beds have duvets. Each has a fully equipped kitchenette and a living room with sofa-bed and french doors leading onto a deck.

🚇 196 C2 ☒ 303 Lake Avenue, Silverton,
V0G 2B0 ☏ 250/358-2844 or 1-866/741-1238; www.williamhuntercabins.com

GLACIER NATIONAL PARK

Fireweed Hostel $–$$

This pleasant small hostel is modern and comfortable. It's located in the unique little village of Field, a charming complex of wooden houses that lies alongside the Canadian Pacific Railway and is backed by forest-clad mountains. The hostel is ideal if you have outdoor activities in mind and the small dorms can be family booked. There are also a couple of private rooms and a 2-bedroom private suite.

🚇 196 C3 ☒ P.O. Box 37, Field
☏ 250/343-6999, 1-877/343-6999;
www.fireweedhostel.com

Where to...
Eat and Drink

Prices
Expect to pay for a three-course meal for two including wine:
$ under CDN$50 $$ CDN$50–$100 $$$ over CDN$100

Large centers such as Kelowna and Nelson have a variety of restaurants but in more remote regions choice can be limited.

OKANAGAN

Minstrel Café $–$$

This is an artsy place offering superb food and live jazz, blues and world music (Thursday and Saturday evenings). The lunch menu includes salads, wraps and pastas, while dinner adds an international flavor, with tapas to start and entrées such as paella, packed with tiger shrimp, mussels, chicken and chorizo sausage; Pad Thai, and the café's signature dish: slow-braised lamb shank.

🚇 196 A2 ☒ 4638 Lakeshore Road,
Kelowna ☏ 250/764-2301; www.
minstrelcafe.com ⏰ Daily 11:30–late

Ric's Grill $$

Ric's offers a good menu of traditional meat and fish dishes, as well as pastas, stir-fry, burgers and sandwiches.

🚇 196 A2 ☒ 210 Lawrence Avenue,
Kelowna ☏ 250/8691586; www.ricsgrill.com
⏰ Lunch Mon–Fri, dinner Sat–Sun

All Seasons Café
$$-$$$

This elegant restaurant in a heritage home in Nelson provides some of the finest dining in the Kootenays. The chef uses the very best local produce, including a superb sheep's-milk brie, to create truly mouthwatering dishes. Try starters of crispy tiger prawns, then rack of lamb. The wine list has some excellent Canadian vintages.

196 C2 ⊠ 620 Herridge Lane, Nelson V1L 6A7 ☎ 250/352-0101; www.allseasonscafe.com ⓒ Daily from 5pm; Sun brunch 10–2

General Store Restaurant $

Located in the Hume Hotel this cheerful place specialises in terrific breakfasts, all-you-can eat 'italian feasts' and a range of down-to-earth dishes.

196 C2 ⊠ 422 Vernon Street, Nelson ☎ 250/352-5331; toll free in North America 1-877/568-0888 ⓒ All day

Where to... Shop

Few people visit interior BC to shop. This said, Nelson and other Kootenay villages often have good art and craft galleries, while in the Okanagan you can buy interesting wines.

At **Craft Connections** (378 Baker Street, Nelson, tel: 250/352-3006) there's the work of 20 local artists. In Kaslo **Your Art's Desire** (423 Front Street, tel: 250/353-7500) and **Figment's Fine Canadian Crafts** (408 Front Street, tel: 250/353-2566) showcase locally made crafts, including silk scarves and bear bells (used to warn bears of a hiker's imminent arrival). Pick up the widely available British Columbia Wine Institute leaflet describing each Okanagan winery.

Where to... Be Entertained

Kelowna and other Okanagan towns have plenty of bars for the large number of young summer visitors, but in the backwoods part of British Columbia nightlife in the conventional sense is thin on the ground. Here the main forms of entertainment are festivals, of which there are many. Most towns use a historical event or local food specialty as the excuse for several days of celebration, or hold events such as "Logger Competitions."

OKANAGAN

Rose's Waterfront Pub (1352 Water Street, Kelowna, tel: 250/860-1141) is a popular local pub, as is the bar at the **Hotel Eldorado**, where the lakeside verandah is the place for weekend dancing to the sounds of reggae, blues and Caribbean bands.

THE KOOTENAYS

The Kootenays is a hotbed of artistic talent. The **Kaslo Jazz Festival** held on the first weekend in August has live music in a gorgeous setting. Many visitors and locals listen to gigs while on board boats moored on Kootenay Lake. Drop into **Mike's Place Pub** (at the Hume Hotel, 422 Vernon Street, Nelson, tel: 250/352-5331), a classic tavern with a wide selection of locally brewed ales, beer and mixed drinks. The **Royal** (330 Baker Street, Nelson, tel: 250/352-1269) has major music acts.

The Rockies

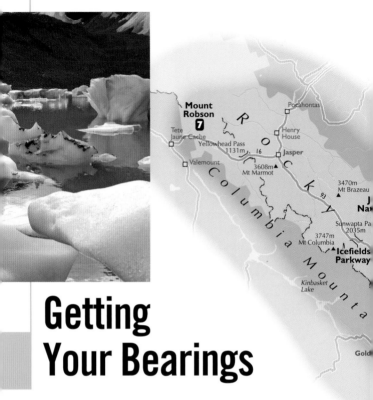

Getting Your Bearings

The Canadian Rockies can hold their own in the most exalted mountain company. A byword for scenic splendor, the great range – one of the world's most majestic – is a mighty patchwork of dramatic peaks, pristine forests, emerald lakes and vast swathes of untrammeled wilderness.

For most visitors, the Rockies mean the four national parks of Banff, Jasper, Yoho and Kootenay, four contiguous parks so magnificent they earned designation as a UNESCO World Heritage Site in 1985. Banff is the most famous, Jasper the biggest; Kootenay and Yoho are much smaller. Scenically, however, there's nothing to choose between the four.

All can be seen easily and quickly from the comfort of a car, but you'd be foolish not to linger occasionally and venture beyond the roads – even if it's just a gentle stroll on one of the parks' many hundreds of well-groomed trails.

It's not only the paths that are good. All facilities for visitors are well developed, at least in the main centers – Banff town, Lake Louise and Jasper – but also extremely busy. Elsewhere, there's next to nothing but wilderness.

Don't get the idea that the hotels and tourist razzmatazz spoil the scenery. Canada treasures the Rockies and the parks, which are consummately run, balancing the needs of tourism and conservation to perfection. A week here would only scratch the surface – but what a surface!

Canoe rental on Pyramid Lake, Jasper
National Park

Page 125: Wild flowers on the
banks of Vermilion River in Kootenay
National Park

Page 126: Jasper National Park

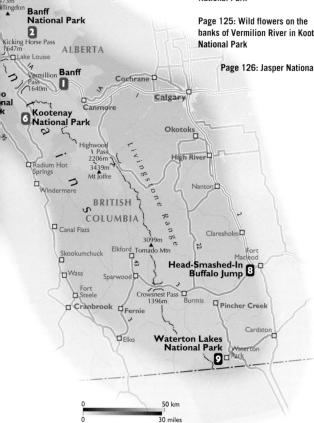

In Eight Days

If you're not quite sure where to begin your travels, this itinerary recommends a practical and enjoyable eight-day tour of the Rockies, taking in some of the best places to see using the Getting Your Bearings map on the previous page. For more information see the main entries

Day One

Morning
Explore **1** Banff (➤ 130–132), visiting the park visitor center, Banff Park Museum and Whyte Museum of the Canadian Rockies. Grab lunch in a café on Banff Avenue (➤ 155).

Afternoon
Continue your exploration of Banff and then either take a half-day walk, ride the Banff Gondola, or take a boat trip on Lake Minnewanka.

Evening
Relax with a stroll along the Bow River to Bow Falls (➤ 131) and then treat yourself to a drink in the Fairmont Banff Springs hotel (➤ 153). Return to town along the river – the road route back, Spray Avenue, is dull.

Day Two

Morning
Drive along the Bow Valley Parkway (➤ 134) to **2** Lake Louise (➤ 136–137), stopping at points of interest en route and perhaps walking all or part of the Johnston Canyon and other short trails. Overnight today and tomorrow at Lake Louise or at the Post Hotel and Spa (➤ 154).

Afternoon
Visit the shores of Lake Louise and then follow the lakeside or Lake Agnes Trail (Lake Agnes right); walk the additional loop if you're feeling strong (➤ 137).

Day Three

Spend the day walking above **2** Moraine Lake (➤ 138–139) – the Consolation and Eiffel Lake–Larch Valley trails are manageable in a day.

Day Four

Travel along the **❸ Icefields Parkway** (➤ 140–141), stopping en route, especially at the Columbia Icefield and Peyto Lake Lookout. Buy a picnic lunch at Saskatchewan River Crossing. Stay two nights in Jasper at the heart of Jasper National Park (right).

Day Five

Morning
Drive along Maligne Lake Road to Maligne Lake (➤ 145) and take a boat trip on the lake.

Afternoon
Either spend more time exploring **❹ Jasper National Park** (➤ 142–145) or head toward **❺ Mount Robson** (below; ➤ 151) for the views and a walk.

Day Six

Enjoy a leisurely drive back along the Icefields Parkway to Lake Louise, exploring the Mistaya Canyon and the Parker Ridge Trail as you go.

Day Seven

Spend the day exploring and walking in **❻ Yoho National Park** (left; ➤ 146–148), returning to Banff or Lake Louise in the evening. Buy lunch at the Truffle Pigs Café (➤ 157) in Field.

Day Eight

Spend the day exploring and walking in **❼ Kootenay National Park** (➤ 149–150), returning to Bannf or Lake Louise later. Buy a picnic in Banff for lunch, as there's next to nothing in the park

⓪ Banff

Some 4.6 million visitors a year flock to Banff National Park, and just about all of them visit Banff, making its 7,500 population swell to around 30,000 during the summer months. Statistics suggest the town is the busiest urban area of any national park in the world. So although the town has a superb setting – mountains ring it on all sides – its busy streets, full hotels and buzzing tour buses are a long way from the quiet and wilderness you might expect of the Rockies.

This said, the town offers plenty of reasons to stop: An excellent visitor center, museums, shops for supplies and souvenirs, and the vast proportion of the park's accommodations and restaurant possibilities. It's also within easy striking distance of walks and drives – peaceful strolls along the Bow River, for example, start from the town center. You could easily spend a day or two here, more if you decided to use it as a base.

The rail station in Banff

Central Banff
Much of what happens in Banff occurs on Banff Avenue, the main street, and near its southern end lies the **Banff Park**

Museum, a lovely old building full of stuffed birds and animals indigenous to the Rockies. Hunting of game animals was banned in Banff in 1913, but predators such as wolves, lynx and eagles were

Exhibits in Banff Park Museum

pursued until the 1930s. Behind the museum is a park running down to the Bow River, and just a few steps away the modern **Whyte Museum of the Canadian Rockies**, with paintings, photographs and temporary exhibitions exploring the Rockies' people and landscapes and the area's emergence as a tourist destination.

Farther Afield

It is worth following the riverside path just over the Bow River bridge and walking through the trees to **Bow Falls**, a powerful waterfall also accessible by a quieter trail on the other side of the river. From the first trail you can walk farther up the Spray River to the south or cut up to the **Fairmont Banff Springs** (► 153), Banff's famous landmark. Tours for nonresidents are available around the 770-room hotel (details in the lobby), but it's enough simply to buy a drink or snack from the café off the main reception area and enjoy the superb views from the terrace.

The **Cave and Basin National Historic Site** is an interpretive center based around the cave and hot springs discovered in 1883. Two easy strolls start from here: The

---

BANFF: INSIDE INFO

Top tips Visit the **Banff Information Centre**, a joint venture between the town's Banff and Lake Louise tourism bureaus for (information on sights and accommodations) and the national park (information on trails and other park activities).

■ It is essential to **reserve accommodations** in Banff well in advance: The information center can help. Alternatively, contact Banff–Lake Louise Central Reservations, which, for a small fee, will find and reserve accommodations (tel: 1-877/542-2633; www.skibanff.com).

■ Banff Transit bus (route 3), from Banff Avenue, will take you to the **Banff Gondola**. Brewster Transportation (tel: 403/762-6700 or 1-877/791-5500; www.brewster.ca) run a guided sightseeing trip too, and the ticket includes the price of the gondola ride.

■ **Rent a bicycle** from one of Banff's many outlets to explore some of the trails and roads close to the town.

■ In high summer the best of the Minnewanka boat trips is the sunset **cruise**.

■ Inquire at the park center about combined tickets to the Cave and Basin Hot Springs, Banff Park Museum and Whyte Museum.

Discovery Trail (15 minutes) and the Marsh Loop Trail (25 minutes), the latter touching the edges of **Vermilion Lakes**, an area rich in flora and fauna despite its proximity to town: Drivers or bicyclists can follow the 4km (2.5-mile) Vermilion Lakes Drive, which is signed off Mount Norquay Road just south of its intersection with the Trans-Canada Highway.

Banff's other major attractions require a car or short taxi ride. The better of the two is the **Banff Gondola** (P131), a cable car 3km (2 miles) south of the town that runs to Canada's highest restaurant, two short trails and stunning views. Easily visited with the cable car are the Banff **Upper Hot Springs**, not far beyond its base, a swimming pool based on hot springs, with waters at a steamy 32°C (90°F).

The Cave and Basin Hot Springs

Farther afield still, a 25km (15.5-mile) round trip, is Lake Minnewanka, a lake-reservoir in a mountainous setting. You can take a 90-minute, 48km (30-mile) boat trip: Contact the Banff Information Centre or Minnewanka Tours (tel: 403/762-3473; www.minnewankaboattours.com) for current sailings.

✚ 197 E3
Banff Information Centre
✉ 224 Banff Avenue ☎ 403/762-8421; 403/762-1550 (park information); www.banfflakelouise.com 🕐 Late Jun–Aug 8–8; Sep; mid-May to late Jun and 1–17 Sep 9–7; Sep 18 to mid-May 9–5 👣 All visitors must buy a national park day pass, either at booths at road entrances or park visitor centers (moderate)

Banff Park Museum
✉ 91 Banff Avenue ☎ 403/762-1558; www.pc.gc.ca/lhn-nhs/ab/banff_e.asp 🕐 Mid-May to Sep daily 10–6; Oct to mid-May, Sat, Sun 1–5. Site tours summer daily 3pm; winter 2:30pm 👣 Inexpensive 🍴 Cafés on Banff Avenue ($–$$)

Whyte Museum of the Canadian Rockies
✉ 111 Bear Street ☎ 403/762-2291; www.whyte.org 🕐 Daily 10–5; archive Mon–Sat 1–5 👣 Moderate 🍴 Cafés on Banff Avenue

Cave and Basin National Historic Site
✉ 311 Cave Avenue ☎ 403/762-1566; www.pc.gc.ca/lhn.nhs/ab/caveandbasin/index_e.asp 🕐 Mid-May to Sep daily 9–6; Oct to mid-May Mon–Fri 11–4, Sat–Sun 9:30–5. Guided tours 11, 2, 4 summer, weekends winter 👣 Inexpensive

Banff Gondola
✉ Mountain Drive, 3km (2 miles) from town center ☎ 403/762-2523; www.banffgondola.com 🕐 Daily 7:30/10am–4/9pm, depending on month 👣 Expensive 🍴 Restaurants ($–$$)

Banff Upper Hot Springs
✉ Mountain Avenue, 5km (3 miles) from town center ☎ 1-800/767-1611 🕐 Late May to mid-Sep daily 9am–11pm; mid-Sep to late May Sun–Thu 10–10, Fri–Sat 10am–11pm 👣 Moderate 🍴 Café and restaurant ($–$$)

② Banff National Park

Banff is the most celebrated of the four major national parks that protect the best of the Canadian Rockies. Within its boundaries lie two renowned mountain resorts – Banff and Lake Louise – two grandiose and scenic highways, a plethora of majestic mountains, innumerable lakes, forests and waterfalls, countless magnificent view points, and numerous opportunities to indulge in summer outdoor activities such as hiking, riding, whitewater rafting, golf and mountain biking.

Lake Louise in the national park

The park is easily seen. Most first-time visitors to the region make for the township of **Banff** (➤ 130), just 90 minutes by road from the center of Calgary, a bustling place that provides everything you're likely to need to explore the rest of the park.

From Banff virtually all visitors make their way to **Lake Louise** (➤ 136), a much smaller center 45 minutes' drive or bus ride to the northwest. Some visitors take the fast and scenic Trans-Canada Highway (or Highway 1) route,

others follow the parallel and still more beautiful
Bow Valley Parkway (► below). Both roads have
numerous spectacular view points and trails, long and
short, that start from roadside trailheads.

Lake Louise

The lake itself divides into two: A staggeringly
beautiful but much visited lake and a small specially
built "village" with a handful of hotels, shops, tour
operators and a visitor center a few minutes' drive
from the lakeshore. This, too, makes a good base for
walks and car touring, but accommodations are in
short supply in peak season and the village is fairly
characterless. Less well-known than Lake Louise,
but in ways even more captivating, is **Moraine Lake**
(► 138) just 13km (8 miles) to the east. Like Lake
Louise it is an excellent base for a wide variety of
half- or full-day circular walks. The single hotel
here, however – Moraine Lake Lodge – needs to be
reserved well in advance.

From Lake Louise the Trans-Canada Highway runs
west into **Yoho National Park** (► 146). Heading
north to Jasper National Park (► 142) is the scenic
Icefields Parkway (► 140), one of the world's great
drives, a 230km (143-mile) odyssey through some of
North America's grandest scenery. Most people simply
follow the highway as a drive – there are only a
handful of hotels, hostels and campgrounds en route
– but you should take time to follow at least one of the many
trails that start from points along the road.

The Parkway leaves you in **Jasper Townsite**, a perfect
base for seeing Jasper National Park, but unfortunately there's
no easy return loop to bring you back to Banff. The obvious
onward route is to head west on Highway 5 past the 3,956m
(12,972-foot) Mount Robson, the Rockies' highest mountain
(► 151), but this commits you to an extended journey to

**Thompson
Mountain with
a meadow in
the foreground**

THE BOW VALLEY PARKWAY

Use Highway 1 to cover the 58km (36 miles) between Banff
and Lake Louise. You won't be disappointed – the scenery is
magnificent. Use the parallel Bow Valley Parkway, however, and
you'll be even happier, for the older road between the two centers
is lined with lots of turnoffs, view points and short trails designed
to make the journey even more memorable. The best view points
(all signed) are at the Merrent turnoff and Backswamp Viewpoint
(8km/5 miles) along the highway heading north. The best short
walk is the highly recommended Johnston Canyon Trail, which
leads over cleverly built catwalks to two sets of waterfalls 1km
(0.6 mile) and 2.5km (1.7 miles) respectively from the roadside
parking area. Alternatively, try the shorter 400m (440-yard)
stroll to **Lizard Lake**. The Muleshoe Picnic Area (21km/13 miles
southeast of Castle Junction) offers good opportunities to spot
birds and other wildlife.

Wells Gray Provincial Park (➤ 118) and the heart of British Columbia. A lot of people simply backtrack along the Icefields Parkway – no great hardship given the stunning scenery.

✚ 197 D3

BIRTH OF A PARK

The Canadian Pacific Railway (CPR) was the making of Banff National Park. Before its arrival at the end of the 19th century the area had been the preserve of First Nations peoples, the odd fur trapper and explorers such as Fraser, Thompson and Mackenzie. On November 8, 1883, three railroad workers, laid off when work on the line stopped for the winter, stumbled across a set of warm, sulfurous springs – the present-day Cave and Basin Hot Springs – while prospecting for gold. They failed in their attempts to lay claim to the springs, and in 1885 the government designated the Hot Springs Reserve a protected area. Two years later the reserve was renamed the Rocky Mountains Park, the world's third national park after the Royal in Australia and Yellowstone in the United States.

The government's early interest in the park was only partly environmental. Far more important was the notion that visitors to the region would consolidate and help pay for the government-backed CPR. The railway's vice president, the hard-dealing William Cornelius Van Horne, famously observed of the Rockies that if "we can't export the scenery we'll import the tourists." To this end he embarked on a series of grand railroad hotels to accommodate the hoped-for influx, the antecedents of Banff's present-day Fairmont Banff Springs (➤ 153), the Château Lake Louise and Yoho's Emerald Lake Lodge.

Lake Louise

No picture can do justice to the matchless beauty of Lake Louise, with its sapphire waters and backdrop of mountains, glaciers and tumbling forests.

The lake is hidden away in the mountains, 5km (3 miles) from Lake Louise Village. Most visitors pass though the village, a modest sprawl of hotels, youth hostel, gas station, visitor center and a small mall, en route for the lake. First impressions of the village may be disappointing, but Lake Louise itself cannot fail to impress. Little detracts from the view, although there's much that should, not least the huge 488-room Château Lake Louise hotel, and the sheer number of visitors – anything up to 10,000 people a day in the height of summer.

The first nonaboriginal to see the lake was an outfitter working for the CPR, Tom Wilson, who was led here by a Stoney aboriginal guide in 1882 (the Stoney had long known of the lake, which they called the "Lake of the Little Fishes"). Wilson called his discovery Emerald Lake but two years later it was renamed Louise, in honor of a daughter of Britain's Queen Victoria, Princess Louise Caroline Alberta, then married to Canada's governor-general.

Beautiful Lake Louise

WHY ARE THE LAKES SO BLUE?
Lake Louise, Moraine Lake and many other lakes in the Rockies owe their intense coloring to superfine particles of glacial silt, or till, known as rock flour. This glacier-ground till absorbs all colors of incoming light except those in the turquoise-blue spectrum – hence the color. The particles are washed into the lakes from melting glaciers in the late spring and summer.

To escape the crowds, take a trail to **Lake Agnes** (➤ 128) or the Plain-of-the-Six-Glaciers. You actually won't have the paths to yourselves – they're the most popular in the Rockies – but, as with the lake, the views are so good you won't mind sharing them.

⊞ 197 D3
Lake Louise Gondola
✉ Off Whitehorn Road,
0.8km (0.5 miles) from Lake Louise Village
☎ 403/522-3555 or 1-800/258-7669;
www.lakelouisegondola.com ⏰ Mid-May to mid-Jun and late Sep 9-4:30; mid-Jun to early Sep 9-5 💲 Expensive

Lake Louise Visitor Centre
✉ Samson Mall ☎ Parks Canada 403/522-3833; www.pc.gc.ca/banff.Banff/Lake Louise Tourism 403/762-8421; www.banfflakelouise.com ⏰ May–late Jun daily 9–5; late Jun to mid-Sep 9–8/7; mid-Sep to Apr 9–4. Closed mid-Oct to Apr 12:30–1

LAKE LOUISE: INSIDE INFO

Top tips Arrive early in the morning, late in the afternoon, or off season to avoid the worst of Lake Louise's **crowds**.
■ Accommodations are more **costly** and more difficult to find here than in Banff.

Hidden gem If you want fantastic views without hiking, take the **Lake Louise Gondola**, a cable car that runs to 2,088m (6,850 feet) on Mount Whitehorn. Signed just east of Lake Louise Village at the ski area.

Moraine Lake

Only a fraction of the number of people who visit Lake Louise visit this lake, just 13km (8 miles) south of Lake Louise on Moraine Lake Road. However, is the equal – many would say the superior – of its more famous neighbor.

The water is a deeper blue, the stupendous snow-dusted Wenckchemna Mountains of the Wenckchemna Valley more spectacular as a backdrop. The name, though, is a misnomer, for the "moraine" that appears to dam the lake at its northern end – a moraine is the debris gouged up or deposited by a glacier – is actually a landslip.

The lake has just one beautifully integrated hotel, café and restaurant, the Moraine Lake Lodge, which offers canoe rental and walks (lake strolls, two-hour, half-day and full-day hikes) that make this one of the best bases in the park if you want to spend two or three days walking (► opposite). The best stroll is along the lakeshore; the best short walk is to Consolation Lake; and the best half- or day-walk is the Moraine Lake–Larch Valley–Sentinel Pass trail, with an additional spur to Eiffel Lake.

Above: Reflections in the still waters of Moraine Lake

Right: Walks range from short to multiday routes

✚ 197 D3

MORAINE LAKE: INSIDE INFO

Top tip Moraine Lake Road is **closed** from mid-October until snow clears (usually mid-May).

WALKING IN THE ROCKIES

Walking in Banff and the other national parks is simple. Banff alone has nearly 1,600km (1,000 miles) of trails, the vast majority of them well kept, well marked and well walked. Standards vary from easy strolls around seashores to multiday backpacking routes. Luckily you don't need to be super-fit and super-equipped to enjoy most of the paths – the vast majority don't require maps, as all popular trails are named, signed and well worn: Simply turn up with boots and bad-weather clothing and start walking. The main problem is knowing which of the many trails to choose. Two or three are mapped on ▶ 182–186, and brief accounts of the best other walks are dotted throughout the text. Staff in visitor centers are trained to advise on hikes, and if you want to tackle more demanding walks there are numerous trail guides. The best known trail guide is the widely available *Canadian Rockies Trail Guide* (Summerthought Books) by Brian Patton and Bart Robinson, which contains most of the major trails in the four national parks.

❸ Icefields Parkway

The Icefields Parkway between Lake Louise and Jasper is one of the world's ultimate drives. For some 230km (143 miles) this magnificent highway runs through scenery of staggering grandeur, passing vast snowcapped peaks, mighty waterfalls, shimmering lakes, immense icefields, flower-scattered meadows and huge swathes of virgin forest.

Break the Drive

Most of the ride is wilderness, with only two points to pick up food and fuel – at Saskatchewan River Crossing and Columbia Icefield (77km/48 miles and 127km/79 miles from Lake Louise, respectively). Campgrounds and youth hostels aside, there are only four hotels en route, all invariably booked months ahead.

Walks and natural attractions are clearly signposted off the road, and even if you intend to drive the road in one go, it's essential to stop to admire some of the waterfalls and viewpoints. There are plenty of half- and full-day trails from points along the road.

Walk Trails

As you leave Lake Louise, the first major highlight is **Hector Lake**, the park's second largest lake. If you want to walk, carry on a few miles to **Bow Lake** (37km/23 miles from Lake Louise), where

Saskatchewan Glacier is part of the Columbia Icefield off the Icefield Parkway

the Bow Lake and Bow Glacier Falls trail (4km/2.7 miles, 55.5m/182-foot ascent) offers the best lake walk of the drive. The road climbs to Bow Summit (2,082m/6,827 feet), the highest point on a Canadian highway, and shortly after passes a sign to **Peyto Lake Lookout**. If you stop nowhere else, stop here, and walk the easy 20-minute trail (91.5m/300-foot descent) to the most breathtaking viewpoint in the Rockies.

Hereafter the road drops, passing the **Mistaya Canyon** – the easy 305m (333-yard) trail here is worth exploring – before arriving at Saskatchewan River Crossing. Some 134km (83 miles) from Lake Louise the road climbs the "Big Hill," a vast curve of highway that offers sensational views. Viewpoints nearby include the Cirrus Mountain Lookout and Bridal Veil Falls, the latter providing access to a rough track (0.8km/0.5 mile) to the **Panther Falls**, the most impressive of

Peyto Lake is a highlight of the Icefields Parkway

the highway's waterfalls. Five kilometers (3 miles) farther on a sign marks the start of the **Parker Ridge Trail** (2.5km/1.5 miles one way, 214m/700-foot ascent) another walk you really shouldn't miss: The ridge offers memorable views.

The Saskatchewan Glacier belongs to the **Columbia Icefield**. The road passes the icefield's fringe a few kilometers after the Sunwapta Pass (2,036m/6,676 feet). Close to the Athabasca glacier lies the Icefield Centre, with food and lodgings, plus an interpretive center. Brewster Transportation offers 90-minute, 5km (3-mile) rides onto the glacier on "Snocoaches," with a chance to walk over part of the ice.

Two more highlights stand out before the slight slackening in scenic intensity that heralds the arrival of Jasper (➤ 142): The **Sunwapta Falls** (55km/34 miles from Jasper), 15 minutes along an easy path from the road, and the **Athabasca Falls** (30km/18.6 miles from Jasper), set just off the Athabasca Parkway, a parallel road that offers an alternative to the Icefields Parkway for the last few miles into Jasper.

➕ 196 C4–C5

ICEFIELDS PARKWAY: INSIDE INFO

Top tips There is a speed limit of 90kpm (55mph) on the Icefields Parkway. Check for further reduced speed limits. There are no services November to March. If you don't have your own vehicle, Brewster Transportation (➤ 158) runs several tours and a **daily scheduled bus service** (summer only) along the Icefields Parkway from Banff and Lake Louise.

■ The **Peyto Lake Lookout** is an absolute must-see on the Icefields Parkway.

■ On no account venture onto the glaciers alone: people die every year from **falling into hidden crevasses**. Sign up for special **guided walks** (3 hours) or walk to the toe of the glacier from the parking area at Sunwapta Lake.

In more depth Beyond the Icefield Centre look out for the sign for the Wilcox Pass Trail (4km/2.5 miles one way, 322m/1,055-foot ascent), widely considered one of the Rockies' best shorter walks.

4 Jasper National Park

In terms of visitor numbers, Jasper ranks second to Banff, but covers an area – 1,067sq km (412 square miles) – greater than the other three Canadian Rockies' parks combined. It's also a wilder and quieter park than Banff, and the atmosphere of its main center, Jasper Townsite, retains far more of the frontier spirit. The landscapes and opportunities for outdoor activities, however, remain as enticing as any in North America.

Where Banff town is all hustle and bustle, **Jasper Townsite**, or Jasper, is quieter and more small-town in feel and appearance. It's also less immediately striking, for here the mountains lie at some distance from the townsite. This makes it more of a base rather than somewhere to spend time for its own sake – the **Jasper Tramway** cable car is the only real local attraction.

   You'll need to join a tour or have a car or bicycle to get the most from the rest of the park, whose main points of interest center on the **Maligne Valley** to the southeast of Jasper, and Miette Hot Springs (a pool complex based around the Rockies' hottest thermal springs). Opportunities for short hikes are more limited than in Banff, but Jasper scores heavily in its many river and **whitewater rafting** possibilities. These include water-based adventures to suit all levels of adrenaline rush, from rides down raging torrents to gentle river trips. Jasper also makes a perfect base for visiting Mount Robson (▶ 151), the Rockies' highest peak, 16km (10 miles) west of the Jasper National Park boundary

Above: Patricia Lake

Below: A national park sign outside the information center

Maligne Tours boathouse on Maligne Lake

off the Yellowhead Highway (Highway 16).

Jasper Townsite

Jasper takes its name from Jasper Hawes, an employee of the North West Company, which established a trading post in the district after it was opened up by explorers such as David Thompson at the beginning of the 19th century. The town's present-day origins, however, date back to the first years of the 20th century, when the Grand Trunk Pacific Railway sought to emulate the success of the Canadian Pacific Railway by building a rail route across Canada. Like the CPR it hoped to use the scenery as a bait for travelers, and in 1908 the Jasper Forest Park was duly established, followed in 1911 by a tent city on Jasper's present site (known as Fitzhugh after the company's vice president). The name Jasper was formally adopted soon after, when the site was officially surveyed. Jasper National Park was established in 1930.

Today the town gathers around two main thoroughfares, **Connaught Drive** and **Patricia Street**, the former home to the railway station and bus terminal, the excellent park visitor center (46m/50 yards) east of the station), the Chamber of Commerce and town information center, and most of the shops, hotels and restaurants. Maligne Tours, the town's main tour operator (➤ 158), is also on Connaught Drive about 136m (150 yards) south of the station.

The only real in-town attraction is the **Yellowhead Museum and Archives**, whose modest displays relate to the history of Jasper and the surrounding area. The best short

---

JASPER NATIONAL PARK: INSIDE INFO

Top tips Visit the park **information center** for full details of all park activities.
■ If you're without transportation, **shuttle buses** run to the Jasper Tramway in summer from Jasper's major hotels.
■ Maligne Tours runs a **shuttle bus to Maligne Lake** from Jasper if you don't have a car. The service is coordinated with cruise departures.

In more depth With a car or bike you might visit **Patricia and Pyramid lakes**, around 5km (3 miles) northwest of Jasper. Both have picnic areas, easy trails and opportunities for boating, canoeing, riding and water sports. Lakes Edith and Annette (6km/3.7 miles northeast) are a little quieter, and offer trails and pleasant grassy and sandy areas on which to stretch out.

Maligne Falls
and Canyon

walk to take is the Old Fort Loop east of town: Details from
the park visitor center.

Out of town, be sure to take a ride on the **Jasper Tramway**,
a cable car 6.5km (4 miles) south of Jasper on Whistler
Mountain Road (off the Icefields Parkway). It's busy in
summer, so expect to wait unless you arrive early, but the wait
is worth it for the views from the 2,300m (7,540-foot) upper
station, where there's a restaurant, interpretive center and a
trail that continues up Whistler Mountain (2,495m/8,151
feet) for even more majestic panoramas.

Maligne Valley

The Maligne Valley is Jasper's most popular excursion.
Maligne Lake Road runs east from Jasper for around 48km
(30 miles) along virtually its entire length, passing two
worthwhile stops en route – Maligne Canyon and Medicine
Lake. It then culminates in magnificent style at Maligne Lake,
the largest – and by general consent – most beautiful lake in
the Rockies. Most people drive or take a tour along the road
and then join one of the fantastic 90-minute boat trips on the

lake. These rides are extremely popular, however, so be sure to reserve in advance through Maligne Tours (► 158).

First stop in the valley is **Maligne Canyon**, 11km (7 miles) from Jasper, a gorge carved by the Maligne River. An easy trail loops down part of the canyon from the parking area (allow 25 minutes), with interpretive boards explaining the canyon's origins along the way. The Maligne area takes its name from the French for "wicked," an epithet applied by a French Jesuit missionary, Father de Smet, to a crossing he made of the Maligne River in 1846.

After 32km (20 miles) Maligne Lake Road reaches **Medicine Lake**, best known for its strange fluctuations in level, the result of water entering and draining from lakebed sink holes – there is no natural surface outlet. The mechanics of the huge underground complex of springs and channels riddling the limestone bedrock are not yet fully understood. Few people linger at Medicine Lake, however, but head for **Maligne Lake**, a sublime ensemble of water, forest and mountain. You'll find parking areas, a warden station, restaurant and a quay, together with the easy Lake Trail (3km/2 miles) along part of the eastern shore.

Above: A black bear near Patricia Lake, and couple canoeing on the lake (above right)

➕ **196 C5**

Parks Canada Information Centre
✉ 500 Connaught Drive, Jasper ☎ 780/852-6176 or 780/852-6177 for trail office; www.pc.gc.ca/jasper 🕐 Apr to mid-Jun and Oct daily 9–5; mid-Jun to early Sep 8:30–7; early Sep–Sep 30 9–6; Nov–Mar 9–4
💲 Park permit moderate

Jasper Chamber of Commerce
✉ 632 Connaught Drive ☎ 780/852-3858; www.jaspercanadianrockies.com
🕐 Mon–Fri 9–5

Yellowhead Museum and Archives
✉ 400 Pyramid Lake Road ☎ 780/852-3013 🕐 May–Sep 10–5; Oct–Apr Thu–Sun 10–5 💲 Inexpensive

Jasper Tramway
✉ Whistler Mountain Road ☎ 780/852-3093 or 1-866/850-8726; www.jaspertramway.com 🕐 Mid-Apr to mid-May and late Aug–early Oct daily 10–5; mid-May to late Jun 9:30–6:30; late Jun–late Aug 9–8
💲 Expensive

5 Yoho National Park

Yoho takes its name from a Cree aboriginal word meaning "awe" or "wonder," a fitting memorial to the sheer majesty of the landscapes in a region many consider to be the finest in the Rockies. Glorious trails provide some of the country's best hiking, although roads also provide a spectacular window onto some of the park's most remarkable scenery.

Canadian Pacific Railway

Yoho is neatly bisected by the Trans-Canada Highway, which runs in tandem with the old Canadian Pacific Railway roughly east to west along the valley of the Kicking Horse River. Just off the highway at the heart of the park lies **Field**, the park's only village and site of the visitor center. Close by are two side roads that provide access to some of the best trails: One along the Yoho Valley, the other to Emerald Lake.

Shorter trails strike off from points along the Trans-Canada, which is also dotted with limited accommodations options. A third region, around **Lake O'Hara**, contains some stupendous paths and a beautiful lodge hotel, but road access and numbers are strictly limited (▶ 148).

Field

As with Banff, Yoho owes its creation largely to the Canadian Pacific Railway. The company built its first hotel at Field in 1886, prompting the creation of a small reserve a few months later. In 1911 the area was extended and became Canada's second national park. The railway is still one of the park's sights, most notable for its famous **Spiral Tunnels**, 7km (4.3 miles) east of Field. The figure-eight tunnels allow you to watch the front of trains emerging from one part of the mountains before the rear has entered at the tunnel entrance.

Field today still looks much as it must have done in the 19th century: A simple frontier village dwarfed by the looming bulks of Mount Stephen and Mount Dennis. The slopes of the latter contain the celebrated **Burgess Shales**, layers of sedimentary rock that contain the fossils of some 120 different types of soft-bodied creatures more than 515 million years old. The site is one of only three found to contain such creatures, whose soft-bodied structure made them ill-suited to the fossilization process. Access to the beds, a UNESCO World Heritage Site, is restricted, but the shales can be seen on guided walks: Contact the visitor center for details.

Trans-Canada Highway

Far easier to see are the sights along the two side roads off the Trans-Canada Highway. The first of these, coming from Lake Louise, is a narrow road with hairpin bends (unsuitable for RVs) that runs north up the **Yoho Valley** about 3km (2 miles) east of Field. About 14.5km (9 miles) from the Trans-Canada are the **Takakkaw Falls**, whose 256m (838-foot)

**Right:
Emerald Lake**

Takakkaw Falls

drop makes them some of the highest road-accessible falls in North America. The parking area is the start of many of the trails: The most popular short walks are Point Lace Falls (3km/2 miles one way, minimal ascent) and Laughing Falls (3.5km/2.3 miles one way, 60m/200-foot ascent). The best day walk is the Twin Falls Trail (8km/5 miles one way, 300m/1,000-foot ascent), which stronger walkers can link with the Whaleback Trail (20km/12.5 miles total round trip) for one of the Rockies' most highly rated walks.

The second road off the Trans-Canada runs 8km (5 miles) north from 2km (1.2 miles) west of Field to beautiful **Emerald Lake**, site of the Emerald Lake Lodge, Yoho's hotel equivalent of the Château Lake Louise and Banff Springs. Buy snacks or meals at the bar or restaurant, sustenance for walks such as the easy paths from the parking area to Hamilton Falls (1.6km/1-mile round trip) and the nature trail around the lake (5km/3 miles). More demanding walks run to Emerald Basin (4.3km/2.7 miles one way, 252m/825-foot ascent) and Hamilton Lake (5.5km/3.4 miles one way, 856m/2,805-foot ascent).

Park Visitor Centre
✚ 197 D3 ✉ Highway 1, 1.6km (1 mile) east of Field ☎ 250/343-6783; www.pc.gc.ca/yoho 🕐 Jan–Apr and mid-Sep to Dec daily 9–4; May–late Jun and early to mid-Sep 9–5; late Jun–early Sep 9–7 💰 Moderate

---

YOHO NATIONAL PARK: INSIDE INFO

Top tips Yoho can be seen as a day trip by car from Lake Louise (the park is 50km/31 miles across).
■ **Accommodations** are costlier and more difficult to find here than in Banff.

In more depth The fragile ecosystems around **Lake O'Hara**, a scenically stunning area south of the Trans-Canada, mean that all car, bicycle and motorcycle access along the access road is prohibited. The only access to the Lake O'Hara Lodge hotel, the campground and extensive trail network is by a special thrice-daily bus service. Places must be booked (tel: 250/343-6433).

6 Kootenay National Park

It's not the scenery's fault that Kootenay is the least visited of the four Rockies national parks – its grandiose mountain landscapes are as mesmerizing as any in Canada. They're also some of the easiest to see, as all you need to do to revel in the park's ranks of snow-dusted peaks and tumbling forests is to follow a single highway.

A trail follows part of the Marble Canyon

The fact that Kootenay is undervisited – the term is relative, as 3 million people annually come here – is that more visitors prefer to follow the main Trans-Canada Highway through Yoho National Park. In doing so they're missing the Rockies' most easily visited park, a narrow strip of land either side of the Kootenay or Banff–Windermere Parkway (Highway 93).

The park has its origins in a road built in 1910 to link the prairies with the west coast ports. Money ran out with 21.5km (13.5 miles) built and British Columbia had to cede 5 miles (8km) either side of the road to the Canadian government for cash to complete the project. In 1920, 1,406sq km (543 square miles) of land were designated a national park.

Take a Hike

As with the other parks, you could see Kootenay easily from the comfort of a car, but you'll be rewarded if you stop at one or two selected spots for a couple of short hikes. The first halt coming from Lake Louise is the **Vermilion Pass**, where the Fireweed Trail (1km/0.5 mile) runs through an area of forest destroyed by fire in 1968 but which is already regenerating. Around 3km (2 miles) south is the **Stanley Glacier Trail** (5km/3 miles, 366m/1,200-foot ascent), which has good views of the eponymous glacier.

A far easier interpretive trail (1km/0.5 mile) follows part of the beautiful **Marble Canyon**, a 196m-deep (122-foot) gorge, a walk that can be combined with a trail leading south to the **Paint Pots** (also accessible from the highway 2km/1.2 miles south). The Paint Pots are a series of pools where waters and mud are stained by iron-laden water bubbling up from mineral springs. Aboriginal peoples from Alberta and British Columbia came to the spot – which they considered sacred

– to gather the colored clays which they baked and ground to make ocher. This was added to animal fat or fish oil to be used in rock, tepee and body painting.

Vermilion River

The tiny settlement at Vermilion Crossing has a store, fuel, lodgings, summer visitor center and fine views of Mount Verendyre. One other viewpoint, the **Kootenay Valley Viewpoint**, stands out on the road to the south before it exits the park near Radium Hot Springs. To its south, near the red-rocked Sinclair Pass, you'll see the trail sign for the Kindersley Pass Trail (9.5km/6 miles), the best of the longer day hikes.

Park Visitor Centre
✚ 197 D3 ✉ 7556 Main Street East, Radium Hot Springs ☎ 250/347-9505, off season: 250/343-6783; www.pc.gc.ca/kootenay 🕐 Mid-May to mid-Jun and early Sep to mid-Sep daily 9–5; mid-Jun to early Sep 9–7; mid-Sep to mid-Oct 9–4

KOOTENAY NATIONAL PARK: INSIDE INFO

In more depth Kootenay takes its name from the region's Kootenai or Ktunaxa First Nations peoples, whose name means "people from beyond the hills." It was these peoples who discovered the hot springs at the southern tip of Kootenay Park, now open to 300,000 bathers a year as part of the **Hot Springs Pools** (May to mid-Oct daily 9am–11pm; mid-Oct to May noon–9/10pm; moderate), 1.6km (1 mile) north of Radium Hot Springs village. The springs were bought for $160 in 1890 by Roland Stuart, who sold them to the Canadian government a few years later for inclusion in the park for $40,000. The almost odorless waters emerge from the earth at 44.5°C (112°F) and are mildly radioactive. The radioactivity is harmless – about the same as a luminous watch.

Top tips The best way to see the park is as a **day trip** from Banff, or as part of a loop that takes in Kootenay before heading north from Radium Hot Springs on Highway 95 and picking up the Trans-Canada at Golden to return to Banff or Lake Louise through Yoho National Park.
■ The Hot Springs Pool is busy, with up to 3,000 bathers daily in high summer, so aim to visit off-peak or late in the evening to **avoid the crowds**.

One to miss Radium Hot Springs has a wide selection of accommodations, but it's not a pretty place, so aim to **stay in Banff** or elsewhere as a base for Kootenay.

At Your Leisure

7 Mount Robson

Mount Robson (3,956m/ 12,972 feet) is the highest peak in the Rockies. It's also one of the most impressive, thanks partly to its relative isolation – which emphasizes its height – and to its colossal south face, a sheer rise of some 3,120m (10,230 feet). The source of its name is disputed, but to First Nations peoples it was known as the "Mountain of the Spiral Road" after its distinctive rock strata, which resemble a winding path.

The mountain and its surroundings are protected by Mount Robson Provincial Park, an extension of Jasper National Park in all but name. Most visitors content themselves with a view of the mountain from the visitor center on Highway 16 (88.5km/55 miles from Jasper). The alternative is to walk all or part of the Berg Lake Trail (22.4km/14 miles one way) to the lake at the foot of the peak. Campgrounds en route make this the Rockies' most popular backpacking trail, but day hikers can simply follow the first third of the trail to Kinney Lake (7km/4 miles one way). Note that there are few facilities locally except for the visitor center.

➕ 196 C5 ✉ Mount Robson Travel Infocentre, Hwy 5 ☎ 250/566-4846 🕐 Visitor Centre: May to mid-Jun, Sep daily 8–5; mid-Jun to Sep 8–8, Oct 1– Oct 7 8–4; closed Oct 8–Apr 30

Mount Robson Park is home to the Rockies' highest peak

8 Head-Smashed-In Buffalo Jump

Strictly speaking, this extraordinary heritage site is not in the Rockies, but if you're heading to or from Waterton Lakes National Park, then it definitely warrants a detour. Similar buffalo jumps were common across North America, and were the result of thousands of years' hunting experience on the part of indigenous peoples. Buffalo would be corralled and then stampeded over a cliff, where the dead animals would be stripped for food, hide and bone. The site supposedly takes its evocative name from a young hunter foolish enough to watch the spectacle from below, just as the buffalo were hurtling toward him. Today it is a Unesco World Heritage Site and consists of an impressive interpretive center and the protected 10m-deep (33 foot) bed of ash and bones that accumulated over some 10,000 years of annual jumps.

A buffalo leading a protected life in a paddock in Waterton Lakes National Park – it won't be forced over the Buffalo Jump

🔢 197 F1 ✉ Porcupine Hills, Hwy. 785, 18km (11 miles) from Fort Macleod ☎ 403/553-2731; www.head-smashed-in.com 🕐 Mid-May to mid-Sep daily 9–6; mid-Sep to mid-May 10–5 🎫 Moderate 🍴 Café ($) 🚌 Regular Greyhound bus connections from Calgary to Fort Macleod

9 Waterton Lakes National Park

Waterton Lakes National Park protects 523sq km (202 square miles) of the Canadian Rockies in southwest Alberta close to the US border. Its size – less than an eighth the size of Banff National Park – and peripheral position mean that it's usually ignored by most visitors unless they're entering Alberta by road from Montana and other US border states. Otherwise the best approach is to divert here from Calgary, before seeing Banff National Park.

Size apart, the park's scenery is the equal of the more famous national parks to the north, and offers good day and half-day hikes from the only center, Waterton Townsite. One of the most popular excursions is to walk across the US border on the Waterton Lakeshore Trail (13km/8 miles) to Goat Haunt in Glacier National Park, the larger US sister park of Waterton Lakes National Park. Together they form the Waterton-Glacier International Peace Park, which joined the Unesco World Heritage Sites list in 1995. From here you can catch one of the regular pleasure boats on the lake back to Waterton Townsite. Consult the park visitor center for details of other walks. Also be sure to drive the park's two specially built scenic roads, both accessed from close to Waterton Townsite.

🔢 197 F1 ✉ Entrance Road, Waterton Townsite ☎ 403/859-2224; www.pc.gc.ca/waterton 🕐 Park: year round; visitor center: Jun–Aug daily 8am–9pm; May and Sep to mid-Oct 9–5

Where to...
Stay

Prices

Expect to pay per double room:

$ under CDN$100 $$ CDN$101–$200

$$$ CDN$201–$300 $$$$ over CDN$300

Banff, Jasper and Lake Louise have a large number of hotels, motels and B&B options, but it is vital to have advance reservations. Elsewhere you pass through wilderness, so plan carefully.

BANFF

▼▼▼ Banff Aspen Lodge $$–$$$

Good value, spectacular mountain views and easy access to downtown combine to make this attractive lodge popular with visitors. Most of the rooms have a balcony or patio where you can enjoy those views, and the hotel has an outdoor hot tub, steam room and sauna, laundry facilities and internet access terminal. A continental breakfast is included.

🖪 197 E3 ⊠ 401 Banff Avenue, T1L 1A9
☎ 403/762-4401, reservations:
1-800/661-0227; www.banffaspenlodge.com

▼▼▼ Buffaloberry Bed and Breakfast $$$

This beautiful house blends modern styling with the utmost comfort. The four bedrooms are spacious and individually styled, and come with private bathrooms, underfloor heating, air replacement system, internet access, TV/DVD and an internal sound system. Guests can relax in the Greatroom, with its wood-burning fireplace and patio overlooking Mount Norquay Ski Area. A deliciously satisfying breakfast is included.

➕ 197 E3 ⊠ 417 Marten Street, T1L 1G5
☎ 403/762-3750; www.buffaloberry.com

▼▼▼ Fairmont Banff Springs $$$–$$$$

Such is the Fairmont Banff Springs' fame that it is sometimes easy to overlook its size. The hotel is on a large scale, and with 770 rooms, intimate it is not. Also, not all rooms have dramatic mountain views. What you're paying for here is the experience of staying in a slice of history and one of North America's most famous hotels – which is not necessarily the same as saying one of its best hotels. Be sure to find out just where your room is located. Note, too, that the hotel is some way from the center of town. This said, the hotel's amenities are second to none. All rooms are well appointed – mini bars, ironing board, phones, television and coffee makers – and guests have access to golf, tennis courts, horseback riding, exercise room and facilities

RESERVATIONS

AAA and CAA Travel Agencies provide a full reservation service for all your travel needs. Contact **local visitor centers** in Banff, Lake Louise and Jasper for help with accommodations (➤ 32–34) or try **Banff–Lake Louise Central Reservations** (tel: 403/277-7669; www.skibanff.com) who will charge a small fee. For bed-and-breakfast options visit www.albertabedandbreakfast.com, www.canadianbandbguide.com or www.bbalberta.com.

in the superlative spa, rated one of the best in North America.

197 E3 PO Box 960, Spray Avenue, T0L 0C0 403/762-2211; toll free in North America 1-800-441-1414; www.fairmont.com

Rimrock Resort $$-$$$$

This stunning modern hotel is the best place to stay in Banff if you want to treat yourself. It lies about 2.5km (1.5 miles) out of town off the road to the Banff Gondola (free shuttle buses run to and from central Banff) and enjoys some sensational views. The main lobby is an architectural tour de force, with huge windows and colossal chimneypiece, while the 351 spacious, air-conditioned rooms are smartly appointed. Facilities include indoor swimming pool, 24-hour room service, two restaurants, saunas, masseuse, weight room and squash court.

197 E3 300 Mountain Avenue, T0L 0C0 403/762-3356; toll free in North America 1-800-661-1587; www.rimrockresort.com

LAKE LOUISE

Lake Louise Inn $$-$$$$

Renovated in 2008, this is the most reasonably priced place to stay in the Lake Louise area. Located in the village, it offers variously priced rooms in a spacious five-building complex, including 27 rooms with air-conditioning and 55 with kitchenettes. Rooms are pleasant and comfortable without being memorable. Facilities include an indoor swimming pool.

197 D3 210 Village Road, Lake Louise Village, T0L 1E0 403/522-3791; toll free 1-800-661-9237; www.lakelouiseinn.com

Post Hotel and Spa $$$-$$$$

The luxurious Post provides an alternative to the legendary Chateau Lake Louise, with prices that don't cause such a sharp intake of breath. It has a huge range of accommodations, from spacious rooms and suites to cabins and an eight-bed house. All have a whirlpool tub in the bathroom, and some have fireplaces, seating areas, balcony or patio. The quieter rooms overlook the garden and forest, but everyone gets a view of the mountains. The luxurious spa includes an indoor pool, fitness equipment and treatments, and the restaurant is acclaimed (▶ 156).

197 D3 200 Pipestone Road, T0L 1E0 403/522-3989 or 1-800/661-1586; www.posthotel.com

JASPER

Alpine Village $$-$$$$

These classic cabins are in a delightful location about 2km (1 mile) south of Jasper overlooking the Athabasca River and with views of Mount Edith Cavell. Just about everything is in traditional pinewood construction and the interiors are very comfortable and stylish. Accommodations range from one-room cabins to two-bedroom cabins.

196 C5 93A Highway South, Jasper 780/852-3058, 1-800/709-1827 (reservations); www.alpinevillagejasper.com

Fairmont Jasper Park Lodge $$$-$$$$

This Canadian Pacific hotel is Jasper's equivalent of the Banff Springs and Chateau Lake Louise. Five kilometers (3 miles) out of town on Lac Beauvert in beautiful countryside, it operates as a virtually self-contained resort village, with 442 rooms (either rustic or modern in style), golf course, tennis courts, boating, horseback riding, six restaurants, heated outdoor swimming pool, fishing and exercise room.

196 C5 1 Old Lodge Road, T0E 1E0 780/852-3301; or toll free in North America 1-800-441-1414; www.fairmont.com

Jasper House Bungalows $-$$

This complex is right in Jasper National Park, with walking trails leading from the cabin door, and great hiking opportunities nearby. There are four types of cedar cabin,

Where to...
Eat and Drink

Prices

Expect to pay for a three-course meal for two including wine

$ under CDN$50 $$ CDN$50-$100 $$$ over CDN$100

In Banff and Jasper there are a large number of restaurants, many of which are sophisticated and excellent quality. There are also plenty of informal places, cafés and snack bars. Cuisine is predominantly North American.

BANFF

Le Beaujolais $$$

Dining rooms in Banff's top hotels such as the Rimrock and Banff Springs are outstanding, but this is the best individual restaurant. The elegant interior is wood paneled, the tables are covered in crisp white linen, and the food is thoroughly French. Eat à la carte, or from one of the set-price menus and select a wine from the 600 on the menu. Jacket and tie are optional for men, but this is somewhere to make an effort, and you'll need a reservation.

197 E3 212 Banff Avenue, corner of Buffalo Street 403/762-2712; www.lebeaujolaisbanff.com Daily from 6pm

Juniper Bistro and Lounge $$-$$$

Known also as Muk-a-muk (the Chinook word for feast), this bistro is part of the Juniper Hotel. It offers a good selection of West Coast cuisine with lunch specialities such as bison stew and a "taste of the Rockies" platter comprising elk pastrami, bison whiskey sausage, candied salmon, artichokes, olives, chutney and pickle. Dinner dishes include tomato soup with organic gin and a tasty seafood hot pot of sea scallops, wild salmon, halibut, prawns and mussels in a light tomato fennel broth.

197 E3 1 Juniper Way (Mount Norquay Road) 403/763.6205

Maple Leaf Grille $$-$$$

Canadian cuisine? Yes, there is such a thing, and this is a good place to sample it. Enjoy the best Canadian ingredients in such perfectly balanced dishes as back county bison tenderloin with double-smoked bacon, Quebec blue cheese and a red wine reduction, or Brome Lake duck with vanilla bean risotto and ginger braised rhubarb sauce. The lunch menu might include a wild

spaced out amid trees on the banks of the Athabasca River. Sleeping either two or four people, they all have bathrooms, and some have a separate bedroom and a kitchenette in the living area. The Executive Suites, accommodating two people, also have a fireplace and a balcony overlooking the river. Unlike many cottage accommodations, there's a dining room serving breakfast and dinner – either of which can be delivered to your bungalow.

196 C5 On Icefield Parkway 3.5km (2 miles) S of Jasper 780/852-4535; www.jasperhouse.com

BED-AND-BREAKFAST

Jasper has a large number of bed-and-breakfast rooms that make good overnight options given the high prices and unremarkable nature of most of the town's hotels. Try the Chamber of Commerce and information center for details (▶ 143).

game platter (venison, bison, duck), bison stroganoff, or Salt Spring Island mussels steamed in sake, coconut and ginger sauce, plus superior sandwiches, salads and pizzas. Brunches offer some exciting choices too.

➕ 197 E3 ✉ 137 Banff Avenue ☎ Toll-free 1-888/255-6488; www.banffmapleleaf.com ⏱ Daily 11–3, 5–late

Saltlik Restaurant $$–$$$

This striking, modern restaurant serves classic Albertan food – especially steak prepared in a contemporary fashion. Tasty seafood dishes are also available. The adjoining bar is a good place for a drink, light meal or bar snack when the dining room is closed.

➕ 197 E3 ✉ 221 Bear Street ☎ 1-888/458-32333; www.saltliksteakhouse. ca ⏱ Bar daily from 11:30am. Dining room 5pm–11:30pm

Silver Dragon $–$$

The Silver Dragon, which also

has a thriving branch in Calgary's Chinatown, serves great value Cantonese and Peking cuisine. In daylight hours ask for a table by the front window, for spectacular mountain views while you enjoy your Peking duck, hot ginger-fried beef or fresh shellfish from the tank. In summer, you can enjoy patio dining, and year round there's a take-out service.

➕ 197 E3 ✉ 211 Banff Avenue, 3rd Floor ☎ 403/762-3939; www.silverdragonrestaurants.com ⏱ Daily 11:30–10:30

LAKE LOUISE

Laggan's Mountain Bakery and Deli $

If you just want a quick bite to eat, Laggan's is a friendly place with a great range of soups, sandwiches, bagels and salads, and some irresistible pastries to fill that last little corner. They offer a selection of coffees too. For anyone planning a picnic, the deli is the perfect place

to pick up a ready-made feast.

➕ 197 D3 ✉ Samson Mall, Lake Louise ☎ 403/522-2017 ⏱ Daily 6am–7pm

Lake Louise Station $–$$$

A novelty, but a successful one: This restaurant occupies the beautifully restored 1909 Lake Louise train station, the village's oldest building, but also has tables in vintage railroad dining carriages. Dining is casual in the station, a little smarter in the carriages. Food is mostly West Coast – herb-crusted salmon, burgers, Caesar salad, steaks, buffalo and the like. There's also a lounge bar and in good weather you can enjoy a barbecue in the station garden.

➕ 197 D3 ✉ 200 Sentinel Road ☎ 403/522-2600; www.lakelouisestation. com ⏱ Daily 12–4:30, 5–9

Post Hotel $$$

This is one of the best restaurants in the Rockies, its cuisine a sophisticated fusion of European, Canadian, California and Asian

cooking – alongside Albertan beef, foie gras and English pea sauce, you might find fresh scallops on jicama root, and red pepper and mango pineapple salsa with cilantro oil and jasmine rice. Fine food is complemented by 850 wine selections from a cellar with more than 20,000 bottles.

➕ 197 D3 ✉ 200 Pipestone Road ☎ 403/522-3989; www.posthotel.com ⏱ Daily 11:30–2, 5–9.30

JASPER

Andy's Bistro $$$

This place is quite a find – it's a European-style bistro owned and run by Swiss-born chef Andy Allenbach. The exciting menus include both classic and innovative recipes. Starters might include bacon-wrapped pepper salmon, or frog's legs Provencal. Main courses may offer venison tenderloin with blueberries, tortilla crusted salmon, pan-fried veal, Atlantic salmon with fresh asparagus, strawberries and Martini Bianco, and bison steak with horseradish and green peppercorn sauce. The menu does change regularly, however, and is available on their website. Everything is cooked to order, so allow plenty of time.

➕ 196 C5 ✉ 606 Patricia Street ☎ 780/852-4559; www.andysbistro.com ⏰ Dinner daily from 5pm

Bear's Paw Bakery $

This welcoming café and bakery is very popular, both for its snacks, soups, coffee or cakes, and for its sandwiches and other take-out items. The varied homemade food is healthy and well prepared. Also good is the similar Coco's Café at 608 Patricia Street.

➕ 196 C5 ✉ 4 Cedar Avenue ☎ 780/852-3233; www.bearspawbakery.com ⏰ Daily 6–6 (later in summer)

Villa Caruso $$–$$$

A long-time carnivores' favorite, Villa Caruso serves beef, seafood and other dishes

are finished in a wood-fired oven, and steaks are cooked in dramatic, sizzling fashion in an open kitchen over a flame grill.

➕ 196 C5 ✉ 2nd Floor, 640 Connaught Drive ☎ 780/852-3920 ⏰ Daily 3pm–11pm

YOHO

Truffle Pigs Bistro $$–$$$

Eating-out opportunities in and around Yoho National Park are limited, so it's not competition that has set the standard for this popular place. At Truffle Pigs you can eat breakfast, lunch and dinner and is part of the Kicking Horse Lodge at the tiny village of Field. The Truffle is known for its local and regional sourcing and organic preferences. They will cater for special diets where possible. General supplies for self-caterers are also available

➕ 197 D3 ✉ Trans Canada Highway, Field ☎ 250/343-6303; www.trufflepigs. com ⏰ Late May–Sep daily 8:30am–10pm; Oct–Apr Mon,Thu 4–9, Fri–Sun 11:30–9

Where to...
Be Entertained

ARTS

The focus of most music, theater, dance and other cultural activities in Banff is the Banff Centre, St Julien Road (tel: 403/762-6100; www.banffcentre.ca). As well as hosting performances, exhibitions and other events, it is the power behind the prestigious annual summertime Banff Festival of the Arts.

NIGHTLIFE

Banff has plenty of restaurants, pubs and bars that stay open late, and in places like the Elk and Oarsman, 119 Banff Avenue (tel: 403/762-4616) and Rose and Crown, 202 Banff Avenue (tel:

403/762-2121), there's sometimes live music and dancing (usually Thu–Sat). You can also catch a movie at the Lux Cinema, 229 Bear Street (tel: 403/ 762-8595). Outside Banff, nightlife is scarce. In Lake Louise your best bets are hotel bars and lounges, in particular those of the Post Hotel, 200 Pipestone Road (tel: 403/522-3989) and Lake Louise Inn, 210 Village Road (tel: 403/522-3791). The same is true in Jasper, although the Athabasca Hotel, 510 Patricia Street (tel: 780/852-3386) has dancing and live music most nights.

SHOPPING

The Rockies are not a natural place to shop, mainly because outside

Banff Townsite there are very few shops. In Banff, however, you'll find an enormous number of outdoor clothing and equipment stores. Most line Banff Avenue, or streets nearby. One of the bigger stores is **Mountain Magic Sportswear** (225 Bear Street, tel: 403/762-2591; www. mountainmagic.com). For books, head to the **Banff Book & Art Den** (94 Banff Avenue, tel: 403/762-3919; www.banffbooks.com).

Lake Louise village also has several stores, mostly in the small, central **Samson Mall** (a group of shops rather than an indoor mall). The best outdoor store is **Wilson Mountain Sports** (tel: 1-866/929-3636; www.lakelouisewilsons.com), which as well as selling clothes and equipment, also rents out and repairs bicycles, tents and other mountain equipment.

In Jasper, visit **On-Line Sports & Tackle** (600 Patricia Street, tel: 780/852-3630) for all outdoor equipment sales and rental.

TOURS

One of the largest and longest-established tour operators in **Banff National Park** is **Brewster Transportation** (tel: 1-877/791-5500; www.brewster.ca), which runs tour buses and excursions to the Columbia Icefields from Banff, Lake Louise and Jasper. In Jasper the major operator is **Maligne Tours** (tel: 780/852-3370 or 1-866/625-4463; www.malignelake. com), which offers trips to Maligne Lake, boat rides, whitewater rafting, horseback riding, guided walking trips and fishing trips. In Banff, **Lake Minnewanka Boat Tours** (tel: 403/762-3473; www.lakeminnewankaboattours. com) offers trips on pretty Lake Minnewanka.

ACTIVITIES

Banff and the other Rockies national parks offer numerous outdoor activities, and an equally large number of tour operators and outfitters. One of the easiest activities to organise for yourself is **mountain-bicycling** – there are plenty of outlets in Banff and Jasper with hourly, daily and weekly rental rates for a wide variety of bicycles.

Horseback riding is also easy to arrange. Rides can last from an hour to a couple of weeks, and can be set up through companies such as **Holiday on Horseback** in Banff (tel: 403/762-4551; www. horseback.com), **Emerald Lake Lodge** in Yoho (tel: 250/343-6321) or **Skyline Trail Rides** in Jasper (tel: 780/852-4215 or 1-888-852-7787; www.skylinetrail.com).

Many companies offer **white-water rafting** – everything from a gentle glide down the Bow River in Banff to the raging white-knuckle rides in the Kicking Horse Canyon. Try **Wild Water Adventures** in Lake Louise (tel: 403/522-2211; www.wildwater.com), or – in Jasper, which has a good choice of trips for all levels of experience – **Jasper Raft Tours** (tel: 780/852-2665; www.jasperrafttours. com) and **Whitewater Rafting** (tel: 1-800/557-7238; www. whitewaterraftingjasper.com).

You can play **golf** at the Banff Springs Golf Course and the Jasper Park Lodge. Both venues rent equipment. **Fishing** and rental of equipment can be arranged in most of the parks: In Banff contact **Alpine Anglers** (tel: 403/762-8223; www.alpineanglers.com). Both Jasper and Banff also have municipal **swimming pools**.

INFORMATION

For full and current information on outfitters, tour operators and outdoor activites contact the excellent visitor and park centers in Banff, Lake Louise, Jasper, Field (for Yoho National Park) and Radium Hot Springs (for Kootenay). See individual entries for contact details.

Calgary

★ **Don't Miss**
1. Calgary Tower ➤ 163
2. Glenbow Museum ➤ 164

At Your Leisure
3. Eau Claire Market ➤ 168
4. Fort Calgary Historic Park ➤ 168
5. Calgary Zoo ➤ 169

Farther Afield
6. Royal Tyrrell Museum of Palaeontology ➤ 170

Getting Your Bearings

Calgary rises from the rippling grasslands of prime Albertan prairie in a glittering phalanx of towers and skyscrapers, its majestic city center one of the most modern in North America. Raised from almost nothing at the end of the 19th century, the city has largely prospered since the 1970s on the back of a burgeoning oil and gas industry, proceeds from which helped forge downtown's modern cathedrals of steel and glass.

Before the oil and gas, Calgary was a cattle town – beef is still an important commodity – and before that a hunting ground for the Blackfoot, Sarcee and Stoney peoples. Today the cowboy heritage is celebrated in the famous Calgary Stampede (➤ 29–30), while the art and culture of the Blackfoot and others are honored in the magnificent Glenbow Museum, Calgary's premier attraction. The Glenbow alone would make Calgary worth a visit, something it's as well to remember when planning a trip, for too many people treat Calgary as simply a convenient entry point for the Rockies – it's just 90 minutes or so by car from the city airport to the mountain-shaded streets of Banff.

Resist the Rockies' siren call – if you can – and give one of Canada's most immediately likable and laid-back cities the couple of days it richly deserves.

Page 159:
Calgary
skyline

Top left:
The city and
Saddledome
seen from
Crescent Drive

In a Day

If you're not quite sure where to begin your travels, this itinerary recommends a practical and enjoyable tour of Calgary, taking in some of the best places to see using the Getting Your Bearings map on the previous page. For more information see the main entries.

9:00am
Visit the Calgary visitor information center in the **❶ Calgary Tower** complex (► 163) and then ride to the top of the tower for sweeping views across the city.

10:00am
Cross 9th Avenue SE to the **❷ Glenbow Museum** (► 164–167), where you could easily spend the best part of the morning – there's a café for refreshments.

Lunch
Walk north through downtown to the **❸ Eau Claire Market** (► 168), where there's a huge range of food concessions, cafés and restaurants for lunch. Alternatively, buy a picnic from the market stalls and – if the weather's fine – eat it in nearby **Prince's Island** (► 168).

2:00pm
Wander around Prince's Island Park and then walk back to the center of downtown and explore the stores and the malls on 8th Avenue SW (► 174). Make a special point of seeing the Devonian Gardens, a huge indoor garden on the upper floors of Toronto Dominion Square.

3:30pm
Catch the C-Train eastbound on 7th Avenue SW to City Hall. From here walk four blocks east to **❹ Fort Calgary Historic Park** (above; ► 168–169). Alternatively, take a taxi or C-Train to **❺ Calgary Zoo** (► 169).

Calgary Tower

The Calgary Tower is one of the city's most distinctive landmarks, despite the fact that, since it was built, it has been crowded and overshadowed by the construction of newer and taller structures. However, the tower still provides a wonderful view of the city and beyond – on a clear day you can see as far as the Rockies.

When it was completed in 1968, the Calgary Tower was a symbol of the city's new oil-funded dynamism and commercial vigor. At 191m (627 feet) it was also one of the city's tallest structures. These days, the downtown focus has shifted slightly, and as a result the area in which the tower stands has been a touch sidelined. Newer skyscrapers, not least the nearby Petro-Canada Building, completed in 1985, also mean that it now no longer dominates the Calgary skyline quite so magnificently.

Don't be put off: The views from the **observation gallery** are still highly worthwhile, extending beyond the city's broad low-rise suburbs to the rippling prairies and mountain peaks beyond. In 2005, a new view was added, with the construction of a section of **glass floor** in the Observation Deck. Now those who have the nerve can feel suspended in mid-air as they look down at the ground 160m (525 feet) below.

TAKING A BREAK

Try the revolving Sky 360 restaurant (tel: 403/508-5822) at the top of the tower.

202 D1 ✉ 101 9th Avenue SW
☎ 403/266-7171; www.calgarytower.com
🕐 Daily 9am–10pm, hours adjusted seasonally
💲 Expensive 🍴 Revolving restaurant and grill restaurant atop the tower ($$–$$$) 🚉 C-Train to Centre Street 🚌 433 inner city loop

The Calgary Tower is a major feature of the city's skyline

❷ Glenbow Museum

Pass Calgary by in a headlong rush to reach the Rockies and you'll miss one of western Canada's finest museums – the Glenbow – where outstanding art, historical displays and a First Nations section, second only to the Royal British Columbia Museum in Victoria (▶ 90), provide the perfect introduction to the region.

The Glenbow is one of the new breed of museums – bright, modern and well-designed, which makes it easy to negotiate. Built in 1976, it takes its name from the ranch of the oil tycoon who donated large portions of the museum's collection, and it is his largesse and taste that are responsible for the somewhat eclectic nature of several of the exhibits on the upper floors. The museum presents material using different media.

Asian Art
The museum's second floor houses Many Faces, Many Paths: Art of Asia, an exhibition of sacred objects from the Buddhist

Left: Displays in the museum

and Hindu cultures of Asia. Sculpture in stone, wood, metals, reliefs, masks and paintings from the early centuries AD to the 18th century are on display. The second floor is also used for temporary exhibitions, which usually rotate every three or four months.

Albertan History

The museum's third floor has been redeveloped with the dynamic Mavericks: An Incorrigible History of Alberta gallery, an exciting portrayal of the history of the region. Based on a 2001 book of the same name, by Aritha van Herk, it tells the stories of 48 remarkable characters who sum up the province's psyche. You will learn not just about the political activists, ranchers, railway builders and oil-men, but also

The exterior of the museum

about people like Charlotte Small, who in the early years of the 19th century dragged many of her 13 children an incredible 40,200km (25,000 miles) in the wake of her surveyor/fur trader husband; Emily Murphy, Nellie McClung, Irene Parlby, Louise McKinney and Henrietta Muir Edwards, known as the "Famous Five," who campaigned "for women to be recognized as persons" (in 1929!); Fred Bagley, who joined the Mounties at age 15; and Tom Three Persons, who tamed the wildest bucking bronc at the 1912 Calgary Stampede. It's a compelling story, well told.

The Mavericks exhibition (above and right)

First Nations Art

Equal weight on the third floor is given to the First Nations Gallery, whose collection focuses on the artistic and cultural background of the Blackfoot, Sarcee and Stoney peoples, partly nomadic tribes from North America's plains and interior, as opposed to the coastal peoples – notably the Haida – whose sedentary, fishing-based culture is celebrated in Victoria.

Certain themes are common to both groups, however, most notably the exquisite nature and immense diversity of the crafts, costumes and jewelry displayed, as well as the equivocal language and manifest unfairness of the treaty documents signed by tribal chiefs and white politicians. Other areas of the First Nations section deal briefly with the Inuit and Métis, the latter the mixed-race descendants of European and First Nations parents, a heritage that for years made them some of the most marginalized of all Canadian inhabitants.

Upper Floor

The fourth floor of the museum has an outstanding collection of gems, stones and minerals, many of them from the mines of western Canada. it also hosts one of the world's most extensive displays of arms and armor, and the associated Warriors section, an exploration of combat across a range of cultures. A third exhibition is 'Where Symbols Meet', a celebration of African achievement. The sculpture that rises up through the floors represents the northern lights.

TAKING A BREAK

Manny's Café just inside the entrance to the museum is a good refreshment stop.

✚ 202 D1 ✉ 130–9th Avenue SE ☎ 403/268-4100; www.glenbow.org
🕐 Daily 9–5 (also Thu 5–9) 💲 Expensive 🚆 C-Train to Centre Street or Olympic Plaza

GLENBOW MUSEUM: INSIDE INFO

Top tips Various guided tours are available, not just within the museum, but also throughout downtown.
- The hard-to-find entrance is a little way east down the street by the Marriott Hotel. There's another entrance from the Stephen Avenue Mall.
- If you have children in tow, visit the ARC Discovery Room on the second floor for art-based activities.

At Your Leisure

🔒 Eau Claire Market

The Eau Claire Market is a vibrant mixture of food stalls, cafés, specialty shops and restaurants that gives much-needed heart and soul to downtown Calgary. Better still, it lies close to Prince's Island, the city's nicest area of green open space, and the ice-clear Bow River.

The oil boom since the 1970s has been good to Calgary, providing the finances to rebuild or refurbish large areas of the city center with marble, glass and concrete. While few people have lamented the transformation, there's no doubt the glittering new downtown plazas and skyscrapers rather lacked the human touch.

The opening of the Eau Claire Market changed all that, its bold, converted warehouse look deliberately designed to bring life, color and a sense of focus to the city. The multi-level complex consists of bars, cafés, arts-and-crafts shops, food concessions, cinemas and a lively communal eating area where you can sit and people-watch while digging into food and drink bought from the

The colorful stands of indoor Eau Claire Market

surrounding concession stands.

Alternatively, take your food to Prince's Island a couple of minutes' walk to the north, a lovely park area with quiet, shady corners. The Bow River here has a fine **waterside walkway**, part of over 200km (124 miles) of bicycle and walking routes around the city. For a longer walk, maps of the system are available from the visitor center.

➕ 202 C2 ✉ Corner of 2nd Avenue and 2nd Street SW ☎ 403/264-6450 or 403/264-6460; www.eauclairemarket.com 🕐 Stores Mon–Sat 10–6 (also Thu–Fri 6–8), Sun 11–5 💲 Free 🍴 Many cafés and food stands ($) 🚆 C-Train to 3rd Street SW 🚌 403 inner city loop

🔒 Fort Calgary Historic Park

Fort Calgary was Calgary's birthplace, a wooden stockade built in six weeks by the North West Mounted Police in 1875 to help curb the lawlessness created by illegal whiskey traders spilling over the border into the United States.

Today the original fort is long gone. The first stockade was pulled down as early as 1882, and the entire fort was rebuilt from scratch following a fire in 1887. It remained a police post until 1914, when the area was sold and redeveloped by the Canadian Pacific Railway. By the 1970s the site was all but derelict, buried under rail tracks and semi-industrial wasteland. Calgary reclaimed the area in 1975 as part of the city's centennial celebrations, producing a broad swathe of parkland but revealing only a few stumps of the earlier forts.

Now a replica of the first **stockade** has been constructed, complemented by a museum filled with evocative photographs and exhibits that recall the fort's origins and the first half-century of Calgary's existence. The surrounding park is pleasant to wander around, nestled in a bend of the Bow and Elbow rivers, the "clear running water" that helped inspire the fort's name. Close by lie two other historic properties, **Hunt House** (not open to the public), built in 1876, and **Deane House**, built in 1906 by Superintendent Deane, local head of the Mounties.

202 E1 750-9th Avenue SE 403/290-1875; www.fortcalgary.com Daily 9–5 Site free; museum expensive C-Train to City Hall 1, 14

5 Calgary Zoo

Canada's second largest zoo has made strenuous efforts to create "natural" habitats for its 1,200 or so creatures and has won conservation awards for its breeding and reintroduction programs. There are special aspen woodlands, rocky mountains and northern plains habitats, among others, together with the flora and fauna appropriate to each.

There are also underwater viewing areas for fish and marine mammals, including polar bears, as well as tropical, arid and butterfly gardens, an Australian section, a prehistoric park (with life-size dinosaurs), botanical gardens, and perennial zoo favorites such as gorillas, elephants, giraffes and tigers.

202 off E2 1300 Zoo Road NE C403/232-9300 or 1-800/588-9993; www.calgaryzoo.org Daily 9–6 (last ticket 5) Expensive Fast-food concessions ($) Whitehorn branch C-Train to Zoo Station

A red panda in Calgary Zoo

FOR KIDS

The Creative Kids Museum (701 11th Street SW, tel: 403/268-8300) offers art-based, mind-expanding fun.

Farther Afield

❻ Royal Tyrrell Museum of Palaeontology

It takes a lot to make visitors think twice about heading west from Calgary to the Rockies, but the Royal Tyrrell Museum – 140km (87 miles) east of the city – is more than equal to the task. One of western Canada's most popular museums, the Tyrrell is devoted to dinosaurs, but also appeals by virtue of its position in the so-called Alberta Badlands, an otherworldly moonscape of barren, sun-drilled hills, mud gullies and soaring mesas at the heart of the Prairies.

The Alberta Badlands were created by meltwater during the last ice age and, but for the fact that the region is one of the world's most abundant sources of dinosaur fossils, might have remained merely a diverting geological anomaly. Instead they have spawned three of Alberta's most popular sights: The Royal Tyrrell Museum of Palaeontology, a superb modern museum devoted mainly to dinosaurs; the Dinosaur Provincial Park, a UNESCO World Heritage Site and source of many of the museum's dinosaur fossils; and the Dinosaur

Top right: A giant T-rex at Drumheller
Below: Dinosaur diorama at the museum

Trail, a 51.5km (32-mile) circular drive from Drumheller embracing some of the most interesting parts of the Badlands.

Foremost of the three is the Tyrrell Museum, located in sparse, somber countryside 6.5km (4 miles) northwest of Drumheller. It takes its name from Joseph Tyrrell, who in 1884 discovered an Albertosaurus, the first of the hundreds of complete dinosaur skeletons since removed from the Badlands.

Today the museum has some 35 complete skeletons, more than any other museum in the world. All are strikingly presented, forming the centerpiece of many thousands of exhibits that relate to the dinosaurs' evolution and eventual disappearance. Among the skeletons are the original Albertosaurus and predictable crowd pleasers such as Tyrannosaurus rex, as well as more unusual creatures such as the Xiphactinus, striking for the delicate beauty of its skeleton, and the Quetzalcoatlus, believed to be the largest flying creature ever to have existed.

There's far more to the Tyrrell than old bones, however, for the museum plots a chronological course through evolutionary history, making its

points with the help of computer stations, audiovisual aids, hands-on displays – or hands-in displays in the case of some simulated dinosaur dung. You can also watch scientists working on fossils in on-site labs, learn more about Yoho's Burgess Shales (► 146), or browse around the remarkable paleoconservatory, a collection of living prehistoric plants, many of which, fossil research suggests, would have been growing at the time of the dinosaurs some 60 million years ago.

🔳 197 off F3 ⊠ 6.5km (4 miles) northwest of Drumheller ☎ 403/823-7707 or 1-888-440-4240; www.tyrrellmuseum.com ⊘ Mid-May to early Sep daily 9–9; early Sep to mid-Oct 10–5; mid-Oct to mid-May Tue–Sun 10–5 💷 Moderate 🍴 Museum café ($) 🚌 Greyhound bus service to Drumheller

The Hoodoos, part of the Badlands scenery near the Royal Tyrrell Museum

ROYAL TYRRELL MUSEUM OF PALAEONTOLOGY: INSIDE INFO

In more depth About 48km (30 miles) from the town of Brooks and some 100km (60 miles) southeast of Drumheller is the **Dinosaur Provincial Park**. Its focus is the Field Station, a base for scientific research, but also home to dinosaur remains and other exhibits. Most people come for guided walks and the Badlands bus tours, which take you to parts of the park otherwise out of bounds to visitors. For latest schedules and to reserve a place call 403/378-4344.

Top tip It's possible to reach Drumheller by Greyhound bus and then take a taxi to the museum, but it pays to **rent a car for the day** in Calgary so that you can explore the rest of the Alberta Badlands.

Where to... Stay

Prices
Expect to pay per double room:
$ under CDN$100 $$ CDN$101–$200 $$$ CDN$201–$300
$$$$ over CDN$300

Calgary has a preponderance of business-oriented hotels, but there are mid- and lower-priced options. B&Bs are available but may be some distance from the center. Reserve in advance if you plan to visit for the Stampede.

✦✦✦ Days Inn-Calgary Airport $$–$$$

Most downtown hotels are high price and for better deals you need to look on the edge of the city. The surroundings of this modern small hotel are hardly scenic but the hotel has very comfortable and good-size business-class rooms and light complimentary breakfast. There's an airport shuttle, but to get to downtown, other than by a taxi, it's a ten-minute walk to the C-train light rail system.
✚ 202 off E3 ⊠ 2799 Sunridge Way
☎ 403/250-3297

✦✦✦✦ Fairmont Palliser $$–$$$$

The Palliser is Calgary's most prestigious hotel, thanks to its pedigree – it's part of the Canadian Pacific hotel chain (bought by Fairmont) that include Banff Springs and Chateau Lake Louise. Built in 1914, it has long been the choice of VIPs and visiting royalty, and yet its rates are generally only a touch higher than the city's other upscale hotels. Rooms are spacious, air-conditioned and decorated in traditional style, and there are steam room, health club and exercise facilities. There's no charge for under 18s sharing their parents' room. From the Palliser you can reach the Calgary Tower and the Glenbow Museum by taking the Skywalk covered walkway.
✚ 202 D1 ⊠ 133 9th Avenue SW, T2P 2M3
☎ 403/262-1234; toll free in North America 1-800-441-1414; www.fairmont.com/palliser

✦✦✦ 5 Calgary Downtown Suites $$$–$$$$

This 28-story highrise might not be oozing old-world character, but it does offer an excellent value in view of its all-suite accommodations, its range of amenities and its central downtown location. All the suites have a kitchen, a good-size TV and internet access, and all but the studio suites have a separate living area. Buffet breakfasts are included in the room rate. The restaurant also serves lunch and dinner, and there's a fitness center and a spa.
✚ 202 C2 ⊠ 618-5th Avenue SW, T2P 0M7
☎ 403/451-5551, reservations 1-888/561-7666; www.5calgary.com

✦✦✦ Westin Calgary $$$–$$$$

Beautifully appointed rooms with modern decor and furnishings distinguish this high-rise hotel in a good downtown location. There are luxury suites available also and facilities include an indoor swimming pool, rooftop sauna and whirlpool, a gym, restaurant and gift shop. There is no charge for under 18s sharing parents' rooms.
✚ 202 C2 ⊠ 320-4th Avenue SW, T2P 2S6
☎ 403/266-1611; toll free in North America 1-888/625-5144; www.westincalgary.com

Where to...
Eat and Drink

Prices

Expect to pay for a three-course meal for two without wine:
$ under CDN$50 $$ CDN$50–$100 $$$ over CDN$100

For years Calgary restaurants are renowned for some of the best beef in North America. Steaks here are still superlative, but the city has also seen an explosion of restaurants offering ethnic and more varied cuisines.

〰〰 Earl's on Fourth $$

Earl's is part of a mid-market chain and rarely lets you down. There are six locations in Calgary. Menus are long and varied, and often include surprisingly sophisticated dishes from around the world.

➕ **202 off C1** 🗺 **2401-4th Street SW**
☎ 403/228-4141 🕓 Breakfast, lunch and dinner daily

〰〰 Joeys $–$$

As part of the popular Joeys chain, you can expect a buzzing vibe and an eclectic menu of New World cuisine. New twists and bold flavors add a real zing to the long menu of appetizers, salads, steaks, chicken and ribs, fish dishes and stir-fries. Great sandwiches, too. This branch is on the edge of Eau Claire Market.

➕ **202 C2** 🗺 **200 Barclay Parade SW**
☎ 403/263-6336; www.joeysmedgrill.com

〰〰 River Café $$–$$$

This relaxed restaurant should be your first choice if you want a treat in Calgary. True to its name, the River Café stands in a park by the Bow River just a minute or so from the Eau Claire Market. From the first mouthful you know you're in the presence of superlative chefs. Menus change regularly and feature dishes inspired by the ingredients of the Pacific Northwest (including game). Reservations essential.

➕ **202 C1** 🗺 **Prince's Island Park**
☎ 403/261-7670; www.river-cafe.com
🕓 Mon–Fri 11–11, Sat–Sun 10am–11pm (brunch is served at weekends); closed Jan

〰〰 Teatro $$$

It's a close-run thing between Teatro and the River Café for the title of Calgary's best restaurant – the two have part-owners in common – and if Teatro tends to attract a touch more praise it's only because both the neoclassical setting and food are rather more formal and showy. The restaurant's housed in a grandiose former bank building – suits and cocktail dresses won't be out of place here. The inspiration for the food comes from northern Italy, and includes dishes such as lobster ravioli and rigatoni, but the cooking also embraces Far Eastern and West Coast (fish and seafood) influences.

➕ **202 D1** 🗺 **200-8th Avenue SE**
☎ 403/290-1012; www.teatro-rest.com
🕓 Dinner daily, lunch Mon–Fri from 11:30am

BARS

〰〰 Brewster's Brewpub $–$$

Part of a Saskatchewan brewpub chain, Brewster's serves up a dozen of their own excellent beers plus imported beers, not to mention great food. This is one of four in Calgary. It has a patio for summer days, and happy hour is from 4–7pm.

➕ **202 off B1** 🗺 **834 11th Avenue**
☎ 403/265-2739; www.brewstersbrewingco.com 🕓 Daily 11am–midnight (to 1am Fri, 2am Sat)

Where to... Be Entertained

Calgary boasts plenty of outstanding theaters, movie houses and classical music ensembles, as well as good bars, pubs and clubs for dancing and live music. Much of the city's cultural life revolves around the **Epcor Centre for Performing Arts** and its five performance spaces (205-8th Avenue SE, tel: 403/294-7455; www.epcorcentre.org). Inquire at the visitor center (▶ 162) for information on cultural events, in particular for details of concerts by the acclaimed Calgary Philharmonic Orchestra (www.cpo-live.com).

Contact Ticketmaster (tel: 403/299-8888; www.ticketmaster.ca) for details of **sports events** – notably games from the Calgary Flames ice hockey team – and tickets for a range of cultural and sports events.

To hear live **jazz**, visit Beat Niq (811 1st Street SW, tel: 403/263-1650) and for rock head down the McLeod Trail to the Back Alley (4630 McLeod Trail S, tel: 403/287-2500).

Calgary's cowboy links mean **country music is popular** and Ranchman's (9615 Macleod Trail, tel: 403/253-1100) has won the Canadian Country Music Association's award for best club for the last five years running.

Bars such as the Castle Pub (1217 1st Street SW, tel: 403/264-5759) often have **live music, as do numerous places** on 17th Avenue, also known as "Electric Avenue" because of its concentration of bars and clubs – though many are big, bland, raucous affairs that you might prefer to avoid.

Where to... Shop

Calgary's ferocious winters mean that most shops are in malls and shopping centers. The main **downtown malls** are between 5th Street SW and 1st Street SE along 8th Avenue. Among them are the **Bay** (8th Avenue SW, tel: 403/262-0345); **Toronto Dominion Square** (7th Avenue and 2nd Street SW, tel: 403/206-6490); the **Calgary Centre** (8th Avenue and 4th Street SW); and the outdoor **Stephen Avenue** mall. Specialty stores can be found in the **Eau Claire Market** (▶ 168) and in the **Kensington** neighborhood (10th Street NW at Kensington Road).

For a list of stores pick up the monthly **Where Calgary magazine**, which is available free from hotels and the visitor center.

TOP TIP
For a huge range of inexpensive places for lunch, don't forget the food halls of the Eau Claire Market and downtown shopping malls.

🍺 The Joyce on 4th $$
The popular James Joyce pub in the Mission district is a cut above most mock-Irish bars, not least because of its mix of fittings, many of which are sourced from the old country. The entrance alone sports a tin roof embellished with Victorian light fittings. Inside is an impressive long mahogany bar. Draught Guinness keeps the atmosphere going and there's good food such as Irish stew and fish and chips. There's usually live Irish music and dancing on Friday and Saturday evening.

✚ 202 D1 🖂 114 8th Avenue SW
☎ 403/262-0708; www.jamesjoycepub.com
🕐 Sun–Mon 11:30am–midnight, Tue–Thu 11:30am–1am, Fri–Sat 11:30–2am

Walks

1 VANCOUVER

Walk

This walk takes you across Vancouver's downtown peninsula from north to south, starting on the waterfront at Canada Place and exploring the city's two key streets – Burrard and Robson. It then touches on Library Square, home to some of the city's most impressive modern architecture, before traversing the hip Yaletown district and crossing False Creek by ferry to Granville Island.

DISTANCE 3km (2 miles) **TIME** 2 hours Allow extra time for window-shopping, refreshment stops and visiting museums **START POINT** Canada Place ✚ 199 F4 **END POINT** Granville Island ✚ 198 C2

Page 175: Canada Place, Vancouver

Below: Vancouver's Marine Building

1–2

Walk around the perimeter of **Canada Place** (▲ 50) if you haven't already done so. Then, with your back to the water, cross the plaza area and main road in front of you and bear right a few steps before turning left onto Burrard Street. Almost immediately on your right as you walk up Burrard Street is the 1930 **Marine Building** (No 355), designed to suggest a rocky headland. Note the to the fascinating **Bill Reid Gallery of Northwest Coast Art**. Return to the junction with Georgia Street, cross over and visit the **HSBC Bank**'s Atrium Gallery reception area with its massive pendulum and art displays. Cross Georgia, and continue on Hornby to the **Vancouver Art Gallery** (➤ 53), whose classical outlines – this was once the city's main courthouse – are straight ahead. The Gallery Café is a good place for refreshments, especially in good weather, when you can sit outside.

Christ Church Cathedral

and sell the site to developers in 1935. Developers did grab the site behind the cathedral, however, obliterating an art deco building here to build the present postmodern Cathedral Place in 1991.

2–3

Across the road from Cathedral Place, where it meets West Georgia Street, is the grand Canadian Pacific **Hotel Vancouver**, another fine period building (completed in 1929) topped with a distinctive green copper roof. Turn left along Georgia Street to its junction with Hornby Street. Divert left down Hornby Street

bas-relief motifs on its facade, which portray Zeppelins, old planes and a variety of marine environments, then admire the amazing door and walk into the lobby to see the inlaid zodiac in the paving, vaulted ceiling and old lift doors. Two blocks further along Burrard Street on the left, just beyond a pretty garden and waterfalls, is **Christ Church Cathedral**, a 19th-century neo-Gothic building that survived plans by the church authorities to demolish it

Granville Island

BC Place Stadium

SMITHE STREET (4)

NELSON STREET (5) Chintz & Company

SEYMOUR ST

Granville Street

Helmcken Street

Homer Street

Hamilton Street

Mainland St

Yaletown Brewing Company (6)

YALETOWN

PACIFIC BOULEVARD

HOWE

Davie Street

Drake Street

BURRARD

GRANVILLE BRIDGE

False Creek

(7)

0   300 m
0   300 yds

3–4

The gallery's main entrance opens onto Robson Street by way of **Robson Square**, a partly sunken city plaza. Turn left on Robson Street and continue through the busy pedestrian flow. Cross Granville Mall, Seymour Street, Richards Street and Homer Street, where the imposing outlines of **Library Square** come into view. This magnificent development contains Vancouver's main public library – the striking visual parallels to Rome's Colosseum, say the building's architects, are completely unintentional.

Visiting a library would not normally feature on a sightseeing wish list, but here you should make an exception: The views and interior architecture of the seven-story structure are magnificent. If you need a break, the postmodern arcade on the building's flanks is full of little cafés.

Inside Vancouver Art Gallery

4–5

Looking down Robson Street to the east from The Centre in Vancouver for Performing Arts you'll see part of **BC Place Stadium**, a great-domed building in the distance. A survivor of the '86 Expo, it's used as a sports and trade show area: It features one of the world's largest air-inflated domes, its Teflon-fiberglass roof supported by 16 jet-engine fans. Locals refer to it as the "mushroom" or "marshmallow in bondage" – after its shape – but it's not really worth a diversion. Instead you should turn south and follow Homer Street, passing Chintz & Company on the left, an Aladdin's cave of a shop (▶78).

5–6

There's little of note on Homer Street, but just as you start to get bored, turn left into Helmcken Street and suddenly you enter **Yaletown**, once a semiderelict district but now one of Vancouver's trendiest quarters. You won't be able to miss the area,

as the signs of transformation are everywhere: Old warehouses and shops have been converted into hip loft apartments and every street is lined with art galleries, bookstores, bars and restaurants.

This is a great place to window-shop or browse, or to sit with a coffee at a sidewalk café and watch the world go by (old warehouse loading bays now make ideal patio areas). One of the area's key buildings is the large **Yaletown Brewing Company** at 1111 Mainland, a combination of bar, pub, restaurant and working brewery.

6–7

From Yaletown you need to head west through a mainly residential area, turning right off Hamilton Street onto Davie or Drake Street. Cross Granville Street and Howe Street. When you come to Hornby Street, turn left and you eventually come to the waterfront at False Creek. Here there is a small landing stage where you can catch one of the small ferries that run across to **Granville Island** (▶56), a good place to finish your walk.

From the island you can catch a bus back to the center of downtown or catch another ferry onward to Vanier Park and its museums (▶58).

VICTORIA
Walk
2

This walk takes you through the lovely old-fashioned heart of old Victoria, touching on the pretty harbor area and most of the sights and colorful flower-decked main streets. It also delves into some of the smaller streets en route, and explores Market Square and Chinatown, two appealing enclaves of specialty stores.

DISTANCE 2.5km (1.5 miles) **TIME** 1 hour 30 minutes Allow extra time for window-shopping, refreshment stops and visiting museums. **START/END POINT** Inner Harbour Visitor Centre ✚ 201 B3

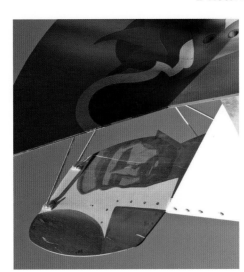

Old Town 1880, a sculpture by Luis Merino in Market Square

1-2
With your back to the Visitor Centre entrance turn right and walk down the steps and along the waterfront. Walk up the steps at the far end and cross Belleville Street to look at the Parliament Buildings (▶ 86). Then walk east along Belleville Street (away from the water and Parliament Buildings), cross Government Street and turn right at the alley by the totems beyond the **Royal British Columbia Museum** (▶ 90). On your left stands **Helmcken House** (▶ 96) with St Anne's Schoolhouse just beyond. Exit onto Douglas Street between Helmcken House and the Schoolhouse. Turn

left and then turn left along Belleville Street. Cross right and go through the gardens of the **Empress Hotel** (▶ 100). Exit on Government Street and turn right to the Visitor Centre.

2-3
From here you're going to head north along Government Street, Victoria's main thoroughfare, and duck into the smaller streets that run across it from east to west. The first of these smaller streets is Courtney Street, but first walk a few steps beyond the intersection to see (and smell) **Roger's** chocolate shop on the right (▶ 104). Then backtrack and turn left (east) on Courtney Street. Cross Gordon Street to reach the **Victoria Bug Zoo** at No 631, a menagerie of live insects and other tiny creatures – the scorpions and tarantulas are favorites.

the wall mark the site of the original walls, but the fort complex extended beyond Fort and Broughton streets, and reached as far as Bastion Square in the west (▶ 181).

Continue north along Government Street, past View Street on your right. Turn right at the next junction, Trounce Alley, a tempting retreat filled with old gaslights, heraldic crests and colorful hanging baskets. The alley's bars and brothels have been replaced by a medley of specialty shops and boutiques – **All in Bloom**, a garden store at No 616 (tel: 250/383-1883) midway down on the left, is particularly worth a look.

Turn left at Broad Street, cross Yates Street and turn left at the top of Broad Street into Johnson Street. Cross Government Street and a short way down the westerly continuation of Johnson Street on the right is one entrance to the shops, restaurants and bars of **Market Square** (▶ 88).

5–6
Explore Market Square's medley of specialist stores (arranged over two levels) and then return to Johnson Street and turn right (west). Turn right on Store Street and then take the

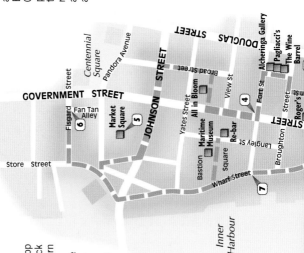

3–4
Return to Gordon Street and turn right. At the junction with Broughton Street, turn right. Drop into **The Wine Barrel** at No 644 (tel: 250/388-0606) just past Broad Street, for top British Columbian and other vintages. Go back and turn right into Broad Street, and then turn left on Fort Street to return to Government Street. Both Broad Street and Fort Street are full of appealing shops and restaurants. One of Victoria's liveliest restaurants, **Pagliacci's** (▶ 102), is at 1011 Broad Street, while the city's premier native arts gallery, **Alcheringa Gallery**, is at 665 Fort Street (tel: 250/383-8224). On the right hand side of Fort Street is a side entrance to The Bay department store (tel: 250/385-1311). A short distance further on is the absorbing **Artevo Gallery** (tel: 250/389-1699) which exhibits fine art works from all over the world.

4–5
At the junction of Fort Street with Government Street, note the building, No.1022 ,on the opposite west corner of the junction. This was once the heart of Fort Victoria, built in 1843 by the Hudson's Bay Company. Light-colored bricks on the sidewalk and a plaque on

second right turn into the unmarked Fisgard Street, focus of Victoria's small **Chinatown** (▲89). Halfway down Fisgard Street on the right is **Fan Tan Alley**, named after a Chinese gambling game and reputedly the world's narrowest street. Formerly it was a hotbed of brothels, bars and opium dens; today it's a rather pale shadow of its former self but is given some color by several Chinese shops, galleries, boutiques and New Age stores.

or take time out in one of several cafés and pubs. Walk straight on a short distance, to the corner of Langley Street, and you can indulge in one of the healthy concoctions served up at the Re-Bar at 50 Bastion Square (▲103). Retrace your steps and turn left on Wharf Street, which will take you back to the Inner Harbour past all sorts of funky stores, cafés, galleries and tattoo parlors. Acclaimed as the city's most picturesque street, it's also a departure point for whale-watching trips.

Empress Hotel

GOVERNM

Belleville Street

Royal British Columbia Museum

BC Legislative Buildings

Government St

Helmcken House

Cridge Park

0 — 200 m
0 — 200 yds

6–7
Return to Store Street and turn left. At Johnson Street, keep ahead onto Store Street's continuation, Wharf Street. After about 175m (190 yds) detour left into **Bastion Square** (▲88), a picturesque square where you can visit the **Maritime Museum** (▲88)

Bastion Square in Old Town

PLACES TO VISIT

Alcheringa Gallery
⊠ 665 Fort Street ☎ 250/383-8224 ◷ Mon–Sat 9:30–5:30, Sun noon–5 ▣ Free

Victoria Bug Zoo
⊠ 631 Courtney Street ☎ 250/384-2847 ◷ Daily 10–5:30 ▣ Moderate

3 MORAINE LAKE
Walks

Sublime and accessible scenery makes Moraine Lake one of the best places in the Rockies to experience a variety of walks and hikes in a short time. Those after an easy stroll can walk along the lakeshore or clamber over the rockfall that created the lake. If you want a slightly more demanding path, walk through the forest to Consolation Lakes, pretty lakes in an impressive mountain setting.

For the longest, toughest and most varied walk, hike all the way to Sentinel Pass. A shorter version of this walk, excluding the (not hugely rewarding) climb to the pass, ends in Larch Valley. This route shares much of the trail to the pass, and can also be combined with the walk to Eiffel Lake.

Ideally, you would spend two days here, but stronger walkers could accomplish the area's two principal walks – to Consolation Lakes and

DISTANCE Round trips to Lake Shore 1.6km (1 mile). Moraine Lake–Consolation Lakes 4km (2.5 miles). Moraine Lake–Eiffel Lake 5.5km (7 miles), 352m (1,155-foot) ascent. Moraine Lake–Larch Valley–Sentinel Pass 9km (5.6 miles), 755m (2,475-foot) ascent. **TIME** Lake Shore 20 minutes. Consolation Lakes 1–2 hours. Eiffel Lake 3–4 hours. Larch Valley 3 hours. Sentinel Valley 4–6 hours.
START/END POINT Moraine Lake Lodge 🕮 197 D3

Eiffel Lake or Larch Valley – in just one day. Note that bear activity may restrict access to some hikes above the lake.

1–2
The starting point for all walks is the unmissable Moraine Lake Lodge, a hotel on the lake's northern tip with a café and restaurant open to nonresidents. All the paths are well worn and clearly marked. There's no camping and no other accommodations at the lake. The next nearest center is Lake Louise (13km/8 miles). The walk along the lakeshore is obvious and straightforward, as is the lattice of paths and interpretive boards on the landslip ("moraine") by the lodge. The obvious path to Consolation Lakes starts to your left as you face the lake, and requires no route-finding – the only junction is the Panorama Trail to the left (which you ignore) signed to

Walks around Moraine Lake provide magnificent views

"Taylor Lake." The path is mostly through trees until the last few minutes. Once you've admired the lakes you have no choice but to retrace your steps.

2-3

All three of the longer walks start from the same point just around the lake to the right from the lodge, and all three share the same trail for the first 2.5km (1.5 miles) and 302m (990 feet) of ascent. This trail winds in a long series of hairpin bends through the forested slopes above the lake – take it steady – with incredible views of the lake way below. At the 2.5km (1.5-mile) mark the trail levels off and you come to a major trail junction.

3-4

The best and least-tramped trail runs left at this point to Eiffel Lake, toward the grandiose mountain scenery at the head of the valley. You've now done most of the climbing, and the path is all but level, and scores more highly than the Sentinel Pass trail (▶ 4–5) for its prettier and less desolate scenery. Views

of the mighty Wenckchemna Valley across the lake, however, are spellbinding whichever route you follow. At Eiffel Lake you see the trail continuing onward and upward toward Wenckchemna Pass (2,078m/6,814 feet), the joint highest point reached by a trail in the Rockies. For the extra 8km (5-mile) round trip and 340m (1,115 feet) of climbing, however,

you don't get much more in the way of views or other scenic rewards. From Eiffel Lake you retrace your steps to the 2.5km (1.5-mile) junction.

4-5

Your second option at the 1.5-mile junction is to turn right, a trail which leads into Larch Valley, a more pastoral stretch of trail that is particularly beautiful in fall. Views are breathtaking. Beyond the trees the scenery becomes far rockier, and it's a moot point whether the extra effort involved in climbing Sentinel Pass (2,622m/8,596 feet) is necessary, other than for the satisfaction of an objective gained. You can see the pass and path ahead clearly, however, and thus what is involved, allowing you to make the decision for yourself. In either case, your only return option is to retrace your steps – there is no convenient loop back to Moraine Lake.

Map showing Moraine Lake area with trails: Taylor Lake, Panorama Trail, Lake Louise, Moraine Lake Road, Moraine Lake Lodge, Moraine Lake, Consolation Lakes, 2605m Sentinel Pass, Larch Valley, 3085m Eiffel Peak, Eiffel Lake, Wenckchemna Peak, Valley of the Ten Peaks, 2065m Wenckchemna Pass. Scale: 0–2 km / 0–1 mile.

4 LAKE LOUISE
Walks

DISTANCE Chateau Lake Louise–Lake Agnes 3km (2 miles) one way, 403m (1,320-foot) ascent. Plain of the Six Glaciers–Chateau Lake Louise 5.3km (3.3 miles) one way, 367m (1,204-foot) ascent.
TIME 3–5 hours depending on fitness and additional loops
START/END POINT Chateau Lake Louise ⊞ 197 D3

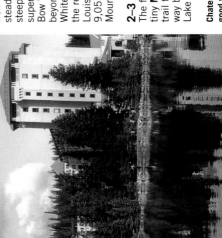

Forests, lakeside views, sweeping valleys, immense mountains, magnificent panoramas and vast glaciers: Walks in the sensational scenery around Lake Louise have everything – even a cup of tea at the end. Well-worn paths from the Chateau Lake Louise hotel wind to picture-perfect Lake Agnes, where a wooden "teahouse" offers refreshments, and then continue to a choice of magnificent viewpoints and two straightforward onward options that eventually loop back to the hotel along the shores of Lake Louise. The routes are popular – you won't be on your own here – but the beauty of the scenery easily outweighs the company of others.

1–2

Start on the promenade in front of Chateau Lake Louise. Facing the lake, and with your back to the hotel, follow the path that leads off to your right. Then take the path signed to Lake Agnes which strikes off to the right almost immediately. The trail – which is so

well worn it's impossible to lose – climbs steadily through pine forest, with occasional steep zigzags and plenty of breaks to allow superb views across the broad sweep of the Bow Valley. On the valley's eastern flank, beyond Lake Louise village, rises Mount Whitehorn (2,686m/8,808 feet), focus of the region's skiing. To the south, above Lake Louise, rise Fairview Mountain (2,762m/9,055 feet) and, to its right, the redoubtable Mount Aberdeen (3,173m/10,402 feet).

2–3

The first major division in the trail comes at tiny **Mirror Lake**, where you should take the trail to the right signed to Lake Agnes. A short way beyond, the trail steepens and reaches Lake Agnes (2,149m/7,045 feet), a lovely

Chateau Lake Louise is the starting point for several good walks

upland lake whose abrupt appearance comes as a pleasant surprise – a pleasure surpassed only by the Lake Agnes Tea House (open: Jun to mid-Oct daily 9-6). The Tea House serves sandwiches, soup, cakes and, of course, tea. You may have to wait a while during frequent busy periods. The original tea house was built in 1901 as a mountaineering refuge. It was replaced with the present picture-postcard building in 1981.

Many people, having drunk their tea, turn tail for home, but at least two worthwhile onward routes are possible. One is simply to follow the marked trail northeast from the Tea House to Little Beehive, a beehive-shaped outcrop and viewpoint. Another is to push on around the lake and complete the longer return route to Lake Louise.

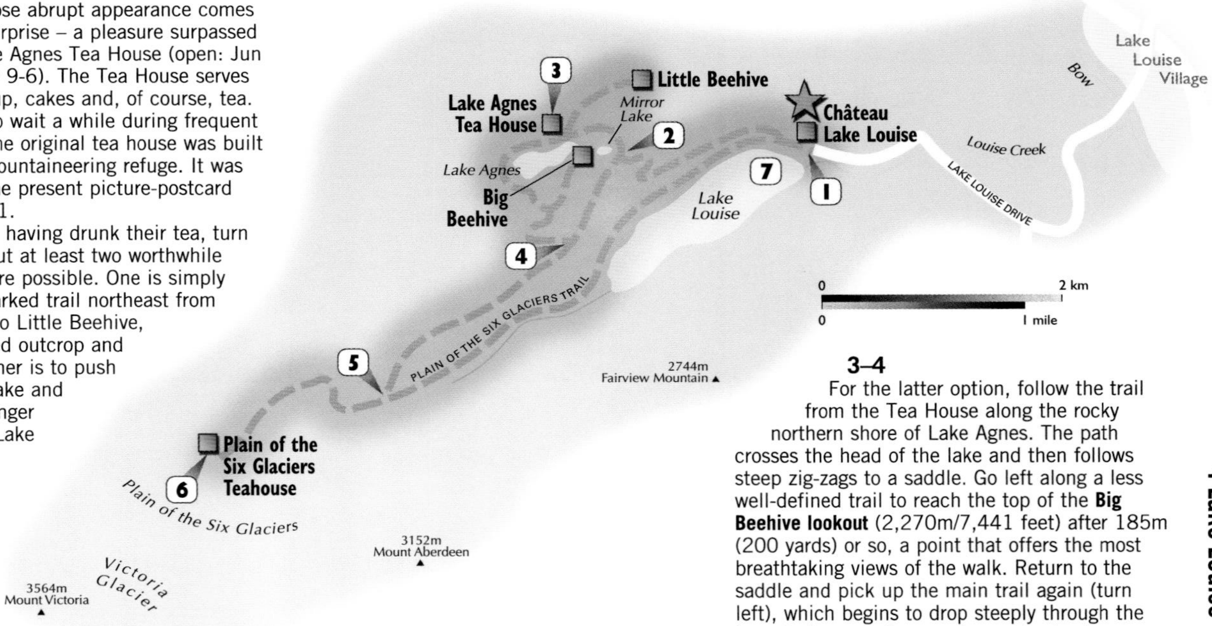

3–4

For the latter option, follow the trail from the Tea House along the rocky northern shore of Lake Agnes. The path crosses the head of the lake and then follows steep zig-zags to a saddle. Go left along a less well-defined trail to reach the top of the **Big Beehive lookout** (2,270m/7,441 feet) after 185m (200 yards) or so, a point that offers the most breathtaking views of the walk. Return to the saddle and pick up the main trail again (turn left), which begins to drop steeply through the trees before meeting another major track.

Lake Louise Village

Bow

Louise Creek

LAKE LOUISE DRIVE

Château Lake Louise

Little Beehive

Mirror Lake

Lake Louise

Lake Agnes Tea House

Lake Agnes

Big Beehive

2744m Fairview Mountain

PLAIN OF THE SIX GLACIERS TRAIL

3152m Mount Aberdeen

Plain of the Six Glaciers Teahouse

Plain of the Six Glaciers

Victoria Glacier

3564m Mount Victoria

2 km

1 mile

4–5

Turn left here and you come to Mirror Lake (▶184), where you could retrace the earliest part of the walk in reverse and return to Lake Louise (1–2). For variety, and a longer and more rewarding walk, however, turn right. This takes you along a path that eventually meets the main Plain of the Six Glaciers Trail, a trail which to this point has followed the shore of Lake Louise and traversed the increasingly wilder scenery above it. Following this trail

all the way from Chateau Lake Louise is relatively dull, but using it as a route to return to the hotel is far more rewarding. Simply turn left when you meet the Plain of the Six Glaciers Trail and walk back down to the lake and hotel.

5–6

For a still longer walk, however, and one that's well worth the extra effort, turn right at the junction and follow the Six Glaciers Trail

as far as it goes – to another teahouse – at the Plain of the Six Glaciers. This gives you a chance to enjoy a far closer look at the stupendous Victoria Glacier, as well as at the vast peaks of Mount Victoria (3,482m/ 11,415 feet) and its neighbors that close the valley. The glacier once reached the lip of Lake Louise, but has retreated over a kilometer (0.6 mile) in the last 150 years alone. Evidence of this retreat lies in the glacial moraines and stark, rocky scenery in this part of the valley, another good reason for adding this final leg to your walk.

6–7

Take a break at the tea house (open: Jun to mid-Oct daily 9–6) or leave it until later while you continue for another 1.6km (mile) to reach a narrow stony ridge, known as The Lookout, directly above the glacier. Go carefully here as you want to go – a high cliff eventually blocks the way. The views are stupendous. Retrace your steps to the tea house and then head all the way back downhill for the long haul along the shores of Lake Louise to the Chateau

Lake Louise, with the surrounding scenery reflected in the water

Practicalities

BEFORE YOU GO

WHAT YOU NEED

		UK	Germany	USA	Canada	Australia	Ireland	Netherlands	Spain
● Required	Some countries require a passport to remain valid for a minimum period (usually at least six months) beyond the date of entry – check before you travel.								
○ Suggested									
▲ Not required									
△ Not applicable									
Passport/National Identity Card		●	●	●	○	●	●	●	●
Visa (regulations can change – check before you travel)		▲	▲	▲	▲	▲	▲	▲	▲
Onward or Return Ticket		●	●	▲	▲	●	●	●	●
Health Inoculations (tetanus and polio)		▲	▲	▲	▲	▲	▲	▲	▲
Health Documentation (▶ 192, Health)		▲	▲	▲	▲	▲	▲	▲	▲
Travel Insurance		●	●	▲	▲	●	●	●	●
Driver's License (national)		●	●	●	●	●	●	●	●
Car Insurance Certificate		△	△	●	●	△	△	△	△
Car Registration Document		△	△	●	●	△	△	△	△

WHEN TO GO

Vancouver

Peak season   Low season

JAN	FEB	MAR	APR	MAY	JUN	JUL	AUG	SEP	OCT	NOV	DEC
43°F	45°F	52°F	57°F	63°F	70°F	73°F	72°F	66°F	57°F	48°F	43°F
6°C	7°C	11°C	14°C	17°C	21°C	23°C	22°C	19°C	14°C	9°C	6°C

☀ Sun   ☁ Cloud   🌧 Wet   🌦 Sun/Showers

Weather in western Canada is best in July and August, when temperatures can rise to over 26.5°C (80°F), but this is also the busiest time of year to travel. Summer is the best time to see the Rockies, though many mountain areas are also busy during the winter skiing season (Dec to Mar). Whistler will normally accumulate some 3m (10 feet) of snow over the winter, and Sunshine Village near Banff is another resort with reliable amounts of good snow. Winter temperatures can be extremely low up in the mountains. Early fall and late spring offer the chance to avoid the rains (up to 254cm/100 inches annually in some areas) and the worst of the crowds in British Columbia, but many sights and smaller museums are only open between Victoria Day (Monday before May 25) and Labour Day (first Mon in Sep).

GETTING ADVANCE INFORMATION

Websites
- Travel Alberta: www.discoveralberta.com
- Tourism British Columbia: www.hellobc.com

In Canada
- Travel Alberta
  PO Box 2500,
  Edmonton, Alberta
  T5J 2Z4
  ☎ 1-800/252-3782

- Tourism British Columbia, Plaza Level, 200 Burrard Street , Vancouver V6C 3L6
  ☎ 604/683-2000

GETTING THERE

By Air Both Vancouver and Calgary have busy international airports: Vancouver (tel: 604/207-7077; www.yvr.ca) handles the most flights, but Calgary (tel: 403/735-1200 or 1-877/254-7427; www.calgaryairport.com) is more convenient for the Rockies. Victoria's airport has few direct international flights, but lots of connections to Vancouver and airports in the western United States.

From the US Many airlines fly direct to Vancouver and Calgary from major US airports. From parts of the western United States – notably Seattle – you can travel to Vancouver by bus or train, although the savings over air travel are often minimal.

From the UK British Airways and Air Canada fly directly to Vancouver and Calgary. From the rest of Europe The national carriers of most European countries plus Air Canada have direct flights to western Canada, but you may have more choice – and pay less – if you book a flight routed through London Heathrow.

From Australia and New Zealand Qantas and Air New Zealand have daily flights to Vancouver. **Ticket prices** for flights to western Canada are highest from July to mid-September. Easter and Christmas are also usually expensive, and seats to Calgary may be more difficult to come by during the skiing season. To save money look out for charter deals or special promotions and reserve your tickets as far ahead as possible. Package tours and fly-drive deals arranged before you travel should also offer good value.

TIME

Western Canada is divided between Mountain Standard Time (MST) and Pacific Standard Time (PST). MST is seven hours behind Greenwich Mean Time (GMT) and two hours behind Eastern Standard Time (EST); PST is eight hours behind GMT and three hours behind EST.

Daylight-Saving Time (Canadian Summer Time). Since 2007, for daylight-saving time, clocks go forward one hour on the second Sun in March and back on the first Sun in November.

CURRENCY AND FOREIGN EXCHANGE

Currency The units of Canadian currency are the cent (¢) and the dollar: $1 = 100 cents. **Notes** are printed in English and French in the following dollar denominations: 5, 10, 20, 50, 100. **Coins** are issued in denominations of 1¢, 5¢ (nickel), 10¢ (dime) 25¢ (quarter), 50¢, 1$ and 2$. The dollar coin is known as a "loonie" after the bird on one face. Not surprisingly, the two dollar coin is the "toonie." US dollars are often accepted on a "one-for-one" basis, but as the US dollar is usually worth a little more than the Canadian dollar it makes sense to exchange US currency. **Traveler's checks** made out in Canadian dollars. These are widely accepted as cash, and change is given in cash.

Exchange Exchange rates are best in banks, and there is no limit to the amount of Canadian or foreign currency that can be exchanged or brought in or out of the country. You can withdraw money from most Canadian ATMs with a credit or debit card. It is wise to let your credit card company and bank know that you will be traveling in Canada and will be using your credit card. Companies have been known to block cash withdrawals if they are unaware that you are in the country.

In the UK
- Use the website www.BritishColumbia. Travel for all inquiries.

In the US
- Use the website www.hellobc.com or phone for inquiries.
☎ 1-800/435-5622

In Australia
- Canadian Tourism, Suite 105, Jones Bay Wharf, 26–32 Pirrama Road, Pyrmont, NSW 2009
☎ 1300 300 576

WHEN YOU ARE THERE

CLOTHING SIZES

UK	Rest of Europe	USA		
36	46	36		
38	48	38		
40	50	40		
42	52	42		Suits
44	54	44		
46	56	46		
7	41	8		
7.5	42	8.5		
8.5	43	9.5		
9.5	44	10.5		Shoes
10.5	45	11.5		
11	46	12		
14.5	37	14.5		
15	38	15		
15.5	39/40	15.5		
16	41	16		Shirts
16.5	42	16.5		
17	43	17		
8	34	6		
10	36	8		
12	38	10		
14	40	12		Dresses
16	42	14		
18	44	16		
4.5	38	6		
5	38	6.5		
5.5	39	7		
6	39	7.5		Shoes
6.5	40	8		
7	41	8.5		

NATIONAL HOLIDAYS

Jan 1	New Year's Day
Mar/Apr	Easter: Good Friday and Easter Monday
Mon before May 25	Victoria Day
Jul 1	Canada Day
First Mon in Sep	Labour Day
Second Mon in Oct	Thanksgiving Day
Nov 11	Remembrance Day
Dec 25	Christmas Day
Dec 26	Boxing Day

In addition, provincial holidays are observed in Alberta on Heritage Day and also in British Columbia on British Columbia Day. Both holidays take place during the first week in August.

OPENING HOURS

○ Stores   ● Post Offices
● Offices   ● Museums/Monuments
● Banks   ● Pharmacies

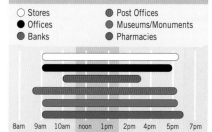

8am 9am 10am noon 1pm 2pm 4pm 5pm 7pm

□ Day   ▨ Midday   □ Evening

Stores Most open Mon–Sat 9–5.30, though some stay open later, especially on Thu and Fri.
Banks Open weekdays 10–4; extended hours on Thu and Fri. Some banks open on Sat.
Post Offices Usually open 8:30–5:30 on weekdays, and occcasionally Sat 9–noon.
Museums Tend to follow store hours, though some may have limited Sun, seasonal and public holiday opening. City museums may open late one evening a week.

TIME DIFFERENCES

GMT	Canada	USA New York	Germany	Spain	Australia
12 noon	(Vancouver) 5am	7am	1pm	1pm	(Sydney) 10pm

PERSONAL SAFETY

Western Canada is relatively crime-free, but you should take the usual precautions, particularly at night in the larger cities.

- Avoid parks, train stations and other non-commercial parts of towns after dark.
- Don't carry around large quantities of cash, and keep passports and credit cards in a pouch or belt.
- Leave jewelry and other valuables in the hotel safe.
- Try not to leave luggage or valuables in cars.
- Report any crime to the police and note the crime reference number.

Police assistance:
☎ 911 from any phone

TELEPHONES

Local calls from public pay phones cost 25¢. For longer distance or calls outside an area, you may need to prefix your number with 1. This connects to an operator who will tell you how much your call will cost. Some pay phones also accept credit cards. For international calls dial the country code, the area code minus the first zero if appropriate and the number. Reverse charge or "collect" calls can be made by dialing 0 for the operator.

International Dialing Codes
Dial 011 followed by

USA	No country code required
UK	44
Ireland:	353
Australia:	61
Spain:	34

MAIL

Vancouver's main post office is at 349 West Georgia Street, open Mon–Fri 8–5:30. Opening times vary in larger city branches. Look out for Canada Post signs inside stores, department stores or train stations. Poste restante service is available at main post offices.

ELECTRICITY

The power supply is 110 volts AC (60 Hz), the same as the US. Sockets take two-prong, flat-pin plugs. An adaptor is needed for appliances with two-round-pin and three-pin plugs.
European appliances also need a voltage transformer.

TIPS/GRATUITIES

Tipping is expected for all services. As a general guide:

Restaurants (service not included)	15–20%
Bar service	15%
Tour guides	optional
Hairdressers	15%
Taxis	15%
Chambermaids	optional
Porters	optional

POLICE 911

FIRE 911

AMBULANCE 911

HEALTH

 Insurance Foreigners requiring treatment on vacation must pay to use Canada's health service. It is therefore essential to take out travel insurance before your visit. If you become ill you will be treated and charged later.

 Dental Services As with all medical services in Canada, dental services are excellent, but you should make sure your travel insurance will cover the cost. If you need dental treatment, your hotel should be able to give you a recommendation; otherwise, consult the Yellow Pages.

 Weather The topography of British Columbia means that weather variations between areas, even within quite short distances, can be quite extreme. Vancouver has a temperate climate.

 Drugs Medicines can be bought at drugstores. Most towns and cities have at least one 24-hour pharmacy for prescription drugs and other goods. It is advisable to bring supplies of any regular medications, but bring your prescription in case you need to renew your medication, to help the pharmacist and avoid problems at customs.

Safe Water Tap water is safe, except in some campgrounds; spring water in the back country should be boiled for 10 minutes.

CONCESSIONS

Students/children Many hotels offer reductions or free accommodations for children sharing their parents' room, and restaurants offer children's menus. Via Rail offers free travel for under-2s, half-price fares for children 2–11, and student rail passes with discounts of 10–50 percent. There are also discounts on entrance charges to museums and other attractions.
Senior Citizens Many museums and attractions offer reductions to senior citizens. There are also concessionary fares on all public transportation, but they may vary depending on the type of ticket bought. Some offer discounts for over-60s, others for over-65s, and you may need to carry proof of age.

TRAVELING WITH A DISABILITY

In western Canada all public buildings must have wheelchair access and provide special toilets and most curbs are dropped. For details on public transportation contact: Via Rail (tel: 1-888-VIARAIL; www.viarail.ca); BC Transit (tel: 250/385-2551; www.bctransit.com); Translink (tel: 604/953-3333; www.translink.bc.ca); Calgary Transit (tel: 403/537-7770; www.accesscalgary.ca). The BC Coalition of People with Disabilities (tel: 604/875-0188; TTY 604/875-8835; www.bccpd.bc.ca) can also advise.

CHILDREN

Hotels and restaurants are generally child-friendly, although baby-changing facilities are far from universal.

RESTROOMS

Restrooms can be found in public buildings, museums, shopping centers and transportation terminals.

LOST PROPERTY

Local visitor centers have details of lost property offices. Contact the nearest police station to report a loss, and if possible obtain a copy of reports to back up claims on your travel insurance.

CONSULATES

UK
604/683-4421

USA
604/685-4311

Ireland
604/683-9233

Australia
604/684-1177

New Zealand
604/684-7388

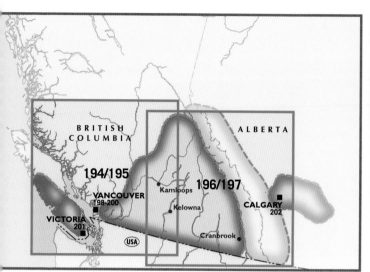

To identify the regions, see the map on the inside of the front cover

Regional Maps

194-197

0	30 km
0	20 miles

════════ Highway
──────── Major road
──────── Minor road
──────── Railway
─·─·─·─ International border
─··─··─ Province/state border

National/Provincial park
Built-up area
Glacier
▲ Height in metres
□ Town/village
✈ Airport
▣ Featured place of interest

Streetplans

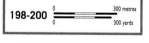

198-200

0	300 metres
0	300 yards

════════ Highway
──────── Major road
──────── Secondary road
──────── Minor road
──────── Railway
●━━━● Skytrain line & station
◐ Canada Line (under construction)
─⛴─ Ferry route

201

0	400 metres
0	400 yards

202

0	400 metres
0	400 yards

Park/garden/cemetery
✝ Church
ℹ Tourist information
✉ Post Office
● Monument/statue
▣ Featured place of interest

Atlas

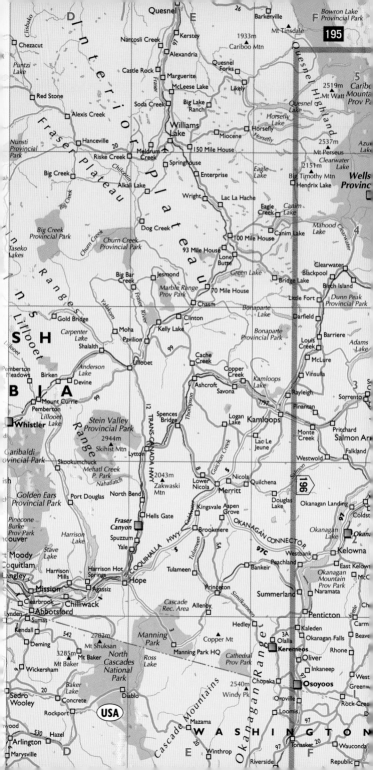

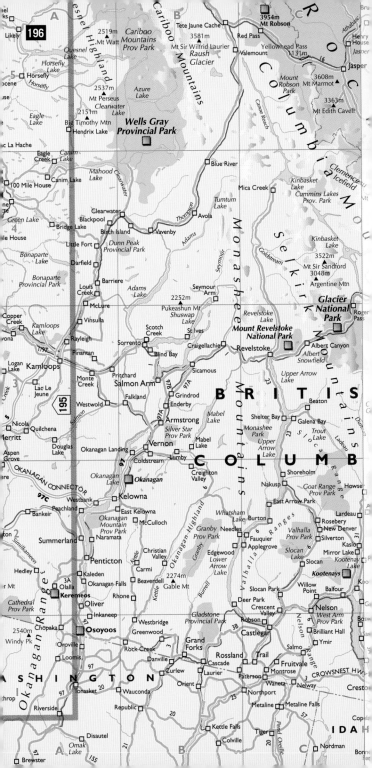

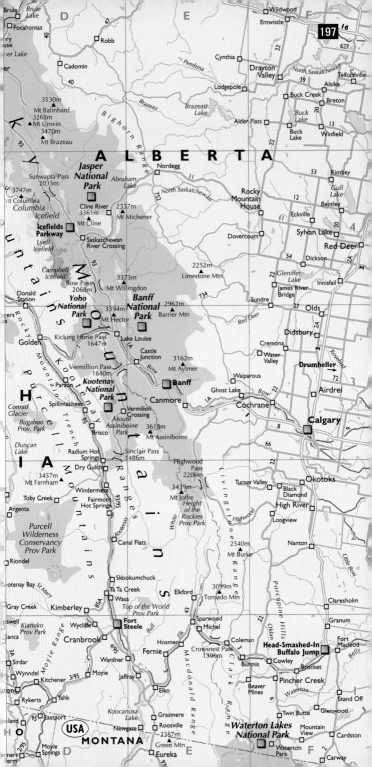

ALBERTA

Jasper
National
Park

Banff
National
Park

Yoho
National
Park

Kootenay
National
Park

Icefields
Parkway

Banff

Drumheller

Calgary

Red Deer

Golden

Cranbrook

**Fort
Steele**

Kimberley

**Head-Smashed-In
Buffalo Jump**

**Waterton Lakes
National Park**

USA
MONTANA

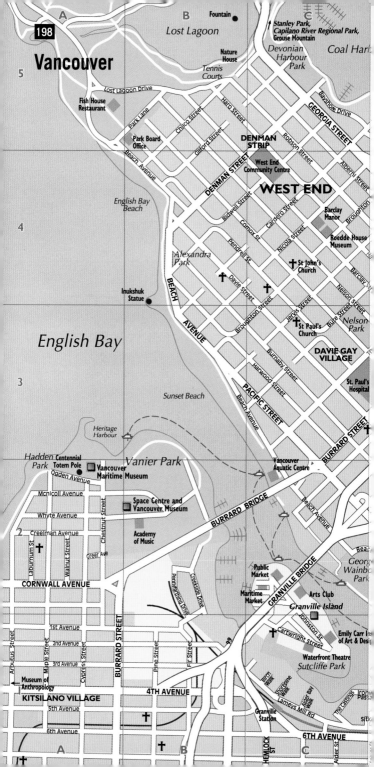

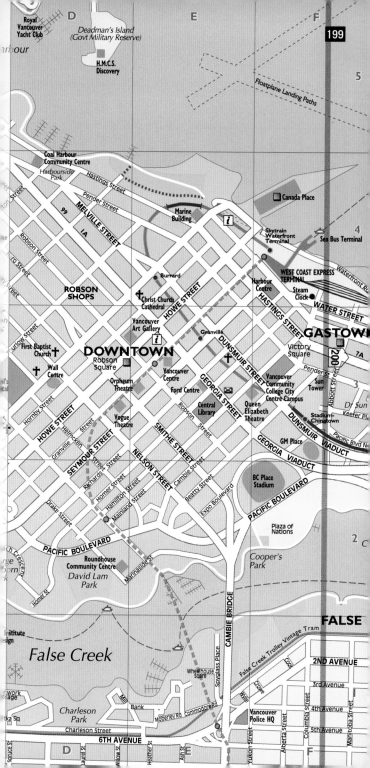

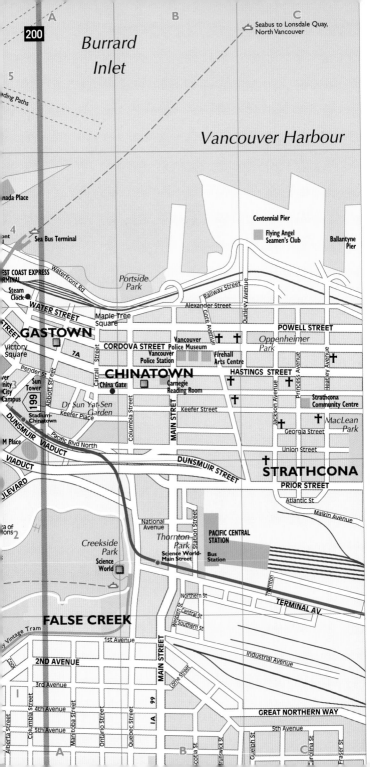

A   B   C

Burrard Inlet

Seabus to Lonsdale Quay,
North Vancouver

5

ding Paths

Vancouver Harbour

nada Place

Centennial Pier

Flying Angel
Seamen's Club

Ballantyne
Pier

4

ront

Sea Bus Terminal

EST COAST EXPRESS
RMINAL

Waterfront Rd

Portside Park

Railway Street

Alexander Street

Cordova Avenue

Dunlevy Avenue

POWELL STREET

Steam
Clock

WATER STREET

GASTOWN

Maple Tree
Square

Oppenheimer Park

 victory
Square

7A

CORDOVA STREET   Vancouver
Police Museum

Vancouver
Police Station

Firehall
Arts Centre

Heatley Avenue

Pender St

er
unity
City
Campus

Sun
Tower

199

Carrall Street

Abbott Street

China Gate

CHINATOWN

Carnegie
Reading Room

HASTINGS STREET

Princess Avenue

Jackson Avenue

Strathcona
Community Centre

Dr Sun Yat-Sen
Garden

Keefer Place

Columbia Street

Main Street

Keefer Street

MacLean
Park

Stadium-
Chinatown

Pacific Blvd North

Georgia Street

M Place

DUNSMUIR VIADUCT

VIADUCT

DUNSMUIR STREET

Union Street

STRATHCONA

LEVARD

PRIOR STREET

Atlantic St

Malkin Avenue

a of
ions

2

Creekside Park

Science
World

National
Avenue

Thornton Park

Science World-
Main Street

Station Street

PACIFIC CENTRAL
STATION

Bus
Station

Thornton

TERMINAL AV.

FALSE CREEK

Northern St

Western St

Central St

Southern St

1st Avenue

y Vintage Tram

2ND AVENUE

3rd Avenue

Main Street

Industrial Avenue

Alberta Street

Columbia Street

4th Avenue

5th Avenue

Manitoba Street

Ontario Street

Quebec Street

1A

99

Lorne Street

GREAT NORTHERN WAY

5th Avenue

cotia St

Brunswick St

Guelph St

arolina St

Fraser St

A   B

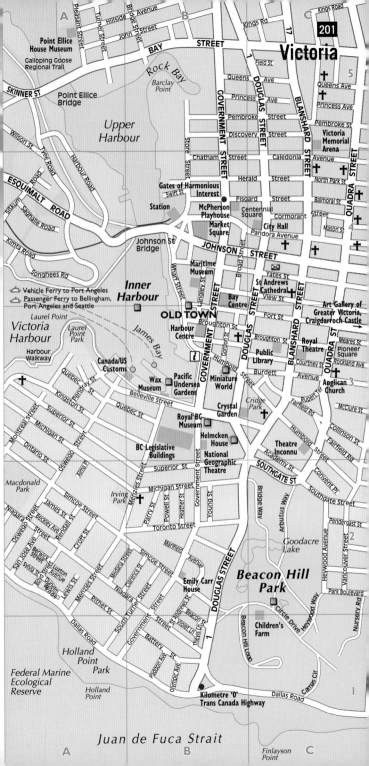

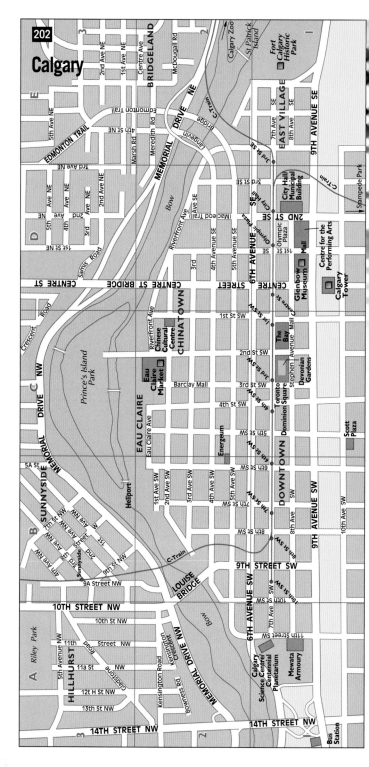

202

Calgary

Picture Credits/Acknowledgements

The Automobile Association would like to thank the following photographers, companies and picture libraries for their assistance in the preparation of this book.

Abbreviations for the picture credits are as follows: (t) top; (b) bottom; (l) left; (r) right; (c) centre; (AA) AA World Travel Library.

2(i) AA/J Tims; **2(ii)** AA/J Tims; **2(iii)** AA/P Timmermans; **2(iv)** AA/P Bennett; **3(i)** AA/J Tims; **3(ii)** AA/J Tims; **3(iii)** Photolibrary Group; **3(iv)** AA/C Sawyer; **5l** AA/J Tims; **5c** AA/C Sawyer; **5r** AA/N Sumner; **6/7** AA/C Sawyer; **8** AA/M Dent; **8/9** AA/J Tims; **9** AA/C Coe; **11l** © Simone Joyner/Getty Images; **11r** © JEWEL SAMAD/AFP/Getty Images; **12** Mary Evans Picture Library; **13t** AA/C Coe; **13c** AA/J Tims; **14c** Getty Images/Photodisc; **14b** AA/P Bennett; **15** AA/J Tims; **16t** AA/P Bennett; **16b** Getty Images/Photodisc; **17** AA/C Coe; **18** AA/P Bennett; **18/19** AA/C Coe; **20/21** Photolibrary Group; **22** AA/P Bennett; **23** AA/J Tims; **24** AA/C Sawyer; **25** AA/C Coe; **26l** Photodisc; **26r** AA/P Bennett; **27l** AA/P Bennett; **27r** AA/P Bennett; **28/29** AA/N Sumner; **30t** © Robert Harding Picture Library Ltd/Alamy; **30b** © Lindsay Hebberd/CORBIS; **31l** AA/J Tims; **31c** AA/C Coe; **31r** AA/J Tims; **45l** AA/P Timmermans; **45c** AA/C Coe; **45r** AA/J Tims; **47** AA/J Tims; **48c** AA/C Sawyer; **48b** AA/J Tims; **49t** AA/P Timmermans; **49b** AA/J Tims; **50** AA/J Tims; **51** AA/C Sawyer; **52** AA/C Sawyer; **53** AA/J Tims; **54** AA/J Tims; **54/55** AA/J Tims; **56** AA/J Tims; **57** AA/J Tims; **58** AA/J Tims; **59t** AA/J Tims; **59c** AA/J Tims; **60** AA/C Sawyer; **61t** AA/J Tims; **61c** AA/J Tims; **62** AA/P Bennett; **63** AA/J Tims; **64** AA/J Tims; **65** AA/J Tims; **66** AA/J Tims; **67** AA/J Tims; **68** AA/J Tims; **69** AA/J Tims; **70** AA/P Timmermans; **70/71** AA/J Tims; **71** AA/J Tims; **81l** AA/P Bennett; **81c** AA/J Tims; **81r** AA/C Sawyer; **84** AA/C Sawyer; **85t** AA/J Tims; **85c** AA/C Sawyer; **85b** AA/P Bennett; **86/87** AA/P Bennett; **87** AA/J Tims; **88** AA/J Tims; **89t** AA/J Tims; **89c** AA/J Tims; **90** AA/J Tims; **90/91** AA/J Tims; **91** AA/M Dent; **92t** AA/J Tims; **92c** AA/J Tims; **93** AA/J Tims; **94** AA/C Sawyer; **95t** Photodisc; **95b** AA/C Sawyer; **96** AA/J Tims; **97** AA/J Tims; **98** AA/P Bennett; **98/99** AA/P Bennett; **105l** AA/J Tims; **105c** AA/J Tims; **105r** AA/J Tims; **106** AA/J Tims; **108c** AA/C Sawyer; **108b** AA/J Tims; **109** AA/C Sawyer; **110** AA/C Sawyer; **111** AA/J Tims; **112/113** AA/C Sawyer; **114** AA/C Sawyer; **115** AA/C Sawyer; **116** AA/C Sawyer; **117** AA/C Coe; **118** AA/J Tims; **119** AA/C Sawyer; **120** AA/J Tims; **121** AA/C Sawyer; **125l** AA/J Tims; **125c** AA/J Tims; **125r** AA/J Tims; **126** AA/J Tims; **127** AA/J Tims; **128c** AA/J Tims; **128b** AA/J Tims; **129c** AA/J Tims; **129b** AA/J Tims; **130** AA/J Tims; **131** AA/J Tims; **132** AA/J Tims; **133** AA/J Tims; **134/135** AA/J Tims; **136** AA/J Tims; **136/137** AA/J Tims; **138** AA/J Tims; **139** AA/J Tims; **140** AA/J Tims; **141** AA/J Tims; **142t** AA/J Tims; **142b** AA/J Tims; **143** AA/J Tims; **144** AA/J Tims; **145l** AA/J Tims; **145r** AA/J Tims; **147** AA/J Tims; **148** AA/J Tims; **149** AA/J Tims; **150** AA/J Tims; **151** AA/J Tims; **152** AA/P Bennett; **159l** Photolibrary Group; **159c** © Wolfgang Kaehler/Alamy; **159r** © nagelestock.com/Alamy; **160** Photolibrary Group; **162** AA/P Bennett; **163** AA/P Bennett; **164** Images courtesy of Glenbow Museum; **165** AA/P Bennett; **166** Images courtesy of Glenbow Museum; **167** Images courtesy of Glenbow Museum ; **168** AA/C Sawyer; **169** AA/P Bennett; **170** AA/P Bennett; **171t** AA/P Bennett; **171c** AA/P Bennett; **175l** AA/C Sawyer; **175c** AA/J Tims; **175r** AA/J Tims; **176** AA/J Tims; **177** AA/J Tims; **178** AA/J Tims; **179** AA/J Tims; **181** AA/J Tims; **182** AA/C Sawyer; **184** AA/P Bennett; **186** AA/J Tims; **187l** AA/J Tims; **187c** AA/J Tims; **187r** AA/J Tims; **191t** AA/J Tims; **191cl** AA/C Sawyer; **191cr** AA/J Tims;

Every effort has been made to trace the copyright holders, and we apologise in advance for any accidental errors. We would be happy to apply any corrections in the following edition of this publication.

The author would like to thank the following individuals and organizations for their help during the research of this book: James and Vicky Ballantyne, Canadian Airlines, Fairmont Hotels and Charlotte Fraser.
The verifier would also like to thank Emily Armstrong of Vancouver Tourism, Zoom Airlines, Westjet Airlines and the Westin Grand, Vancouver for their help during the research of the updated 2008 edition.

SPIRALGUIDE
Questionnaire

Dear Traveller

Your comments, opinions and recommendations are very important to us. Please help us to improve our travel guides by taking a few minutes to complete this simple questionnaire.

You do not need a stamp (unless posted outside the UK). If you do not want to remove this page from your guide, then photocopy it or write your answers on a plain sheet of paper.

Send to: The Editor, Spiral Guides, AA World Travel Guides, FREEPOST SCE 4598, Basingstoke RG21 4GY.

Your recommendations...

We always encourage readers' recommendations for restaurants, night-life or shopping – if your recommendation is used in the next edition of the guide, we will send you a FREE AA Spiral Guide of your choice. Please state below the establishment name, location and your reasons for recommending it.

_____

_____

_____

_____

_____

Please send me AA Spiral _____

(see list of titles inside the back cover)

About this guide...

Which title did you buy?

_____ **AA Spiral**

Where did you buy it? _____

When? m m / y y

Why did you choose an AA Spiral Guide? _____

_____

_____

_____

Did this guide meet your expectations?

Exceeded ☐   Met all ☐   Met most ☐   Fell below ☐

Please give your reasons _____

_____

_____

_____

_____

continued on next page...

Were there any aspects of this guide that you particularly liked?

_____
_____
_____
_____
_____

Is there anything we could have done better?

_____
_____
_____
_____

About you...

Name (Mr/Mrs/Ms) _____

Address _____

_____ **Postcode** _____

Daytime tel no _____ **email** _____

Please _only_ give us your email address and mobile phone number if you wish to hear from us about other products and services from the AA and partners by email or text or mms.

Which age group are you in?

Under 25 ☐   25–34 ☐   35–44 ☐   45–54 ☐   55–64 ☐   65+ ☐

How many trips do you make a year?

Less than one ☐   One ☐   Two ☐   Three or more ☐

Are you an AA member? Yes ☐   **No** ☐

About your trip...

When did you book? m m / y y   **When did you travel?** m m / y y

How long did you stay? _____

Was it for business or leisure? _____

Did you buy any other travel guides for your trip? ☐ Yes ☐ No

If yes, which ones? _____

_____

Thank you for taking the time to complete this questionnaire. Please send it to us as soon as possible, and remember, you do not need a stamp (unless posted outside the UK).